SENSING
CHICAGO

SENSING
CHICAGO

Noisemakers, Strikebreakers, and Muckrakers

ADAM MACK

UNIVERSITY OF ILLINOIS PRESS

Urbana, Chicago, and Springfield

Library of Congress Cataloging-in-Publication Data
Mack, Adam, 1973–
Sensing Chicago : noisemakers, strikebreakers,
and muckrakers / Adam Mack.
pages cm. — (Studies in sensory history)
Includes bibliographical references and index.
ISBN 978-0-252-03918-8 (hardcover : alk. paper) —
ISBN 978-0-252-08075-3 (pbk. : alk. paper) —
ISBN 978-0-252-09722-5 (e-book)
1. Chicago (Ill.)—History—19th century.
2. Chicago (Ill.)—History—20th century. 3. Senses
and sensation—Illinois—Chicago—History—19th
century. 4. Senses and sensation—Illinois—
Chicago—History—20th century. 5. Chicago
(Ill.)—Social conditions—19th century. 6. Chicago
(Ill.)—Social conditions—20th century. I. Title.
F548.3.M19   2015
977.3'1103–dc23   2014042404

To my mom and dad

Chicago. Name from an Indian word variously translated as "garlic," "skunk," or "wild onion."

—from *Illinois Place Names* (1989)

CONTENTS

Illustrations follow page 50

ACKNOWLEDGMENTS

It's a pleasure to thank the many people who helped me prepare this book. I owe an enormous debt to the School of the Art Institute of Chicago (SAIC), a vibrant artistic and intellectual community that serves as my institutional home in the Windy City. At SAIC I have benefited from the guidance and generosity of two department chairs, Paul Ashley and Raja Halwani. The administration has been equally supportive and helpful. I thank the dean of faculty, Lisa Wainwright, for her enthusiastic response to my work and for the Faculty Enrichment Grant that made finishing it much easier than it would have been otherwise. The extraordinary administrative staff at the Liberal Arts department, especially Shay DeGrandis and Teena McClelland, have helped me with just about everything related to the management of my research and teaching. SAIC's Computer Resources and Information Technologies service kept my data secure and saved me—more than once—from terrifying computer malfunctions of my own making.

The students in my classes have provided encouragement and advice, reminding me of the value of broadly accessible scholarship. A coincidence of my arrival at SAIC is that my predecessor, the late George H. Roeder Jr., issued one of the original calls for a sensorial history of American life. My hope is that *Sensing Chicago* speaks to the growing scholarship on sensory history in productive ways and that my colleagues and students at SAIC will find it an intriguing approach to Chicago's past and present.

Mark M. Smith, the editor of the Studies in Sensory History series, has been helpful, patient, and encouraging. My intellectual debt to Mark extends back to graduate school at the University of South Carolina, where he, along with Larry Glickman, delivered formative lessons in research, writing, and teaching. The two readers for the University of Illinois Press, James R. Barrett and Daniel Bender, furnished truly useful critiques of my initial draft. One of the pleasures of finishing the book has been to benefit from the critiques of two scholars whose work speaks so directly to the issues that interest me. My copyeditor, Jill R. Hughes, provided expert advice, much to my delight. The director of the University of Illinois Press, Willis Regier, responded to my queries with the type of prompt and efficient communication that made getting the book into print a clear and exciting process.

Like all historians, I would never have finished my research and writing without the support of librarians and archivists. The librarians and interlibrary loan staff at SAIC's Flaxman Library have been first-rate in helping me collect materials from Chicago and far afield. The archivists at the Chicago History Museum assisted me with the type of efficient and generous support reflective of their world-class holdings. I thank the museum's Rights and Reproductions department for their professionalism and courtesy as well. The librarians at the Chicago Public Libraries, particularly the staff in the Government Information section of the Harold Washington branch, accommodated my multiple requests with courtesy and care. It was a pleasure to profile my research at local forums, including SAIC, the Chicago History Museum, the Newberry Library, as well as other national meetings.

Of course, my family and friends are what really made it possible for me to complete the book. My dad, an award-winning history teacher in Virginia's public schools, is responsible for first nurturing my interest in the past. Both he and my mom, a superb editor, provided the kind of encouragement—and example—that helped me enjoy good times and weather bad ones. I send a buoyant *mahalo nui loa* to my family in Hawaii—especially my in-laws, Steve and Sharon McKee and the entire Brewbaker clan—a group of great people who have welcomed me and tutored me on island life. My friends Matt Badger, Pete Hanks, Ben Lilienthal, Steve Proctor, Steve Balut, and Chad Lucien have been shaping my attitudes about work and play for decades now—all to the good, I'm sure. My old friend Larry Grubbs generously critiqued the entire manuscript. His input and his original work on sensory history have been invaluable.

My stepchildren, Nainoa and Mahea, have been hearing about this book for a long time. Their continued good cheer, youthful vision, and open arms have meant the world to me. My wife, Michelle, knows more than anyone the debts I have accumulated over the course of this work, none more substantial than those I owe to her. One of my goals has been to write a book that she would enjoy reading, no matter the author. Her intelligence, generosity, and unrivaled cool make her a great audience and, as always, an incredible partner.

SENSING
CHICAGO

INTRODUCTION

In 1909 the *Tribune* summoned John Callan O'Laughlin to Chicago to write a series of articles on the "physical, civic, and political" condition of the city. The Chicago-born journalist boasted a wealth of urban experience, having seen most of the major cities in the United States and Western Europe. He seemed the perfect choice to help his hometown readers understand how "others look upon their city." Yet much to his readers' chagrin, if not surprise, O'Laughlin found vast sections of Chicago unsightly. Air pollution from locomotives dashed the journalist's hopes for a view of Lake Michigan from his hotel room. He found the central business district, clouded by the same smoke and crisscrossed with grimy streets, "a vast ugliness." O'Laughlin approved of the city's park system, but observed that it, too, suffered from pollution. Many of the parks seemed "desert-like" in their lack of healthy trees. The paucity of green "to relieve the eye" from the oppressive grayness of the downtown, the assessment implied, rendered Chicago's official motto, *Urbs in Horto* ("City in a Garden") cruelly ironic.[1]

O'Laughlin understood that assessing Chicago's physical and civic condition demanded that he listen, smell, feel, and taste, as well as look. The clang and puffing of the trains reminded him so during his first night's sleep, ringing in his ears and waking him at 2:00 A.M. The railroad yards, to say nothing of the Union Stockyards, also exuded foul odors that choked and disturbed his stomach when he left the confines of his hotel. During one of his strolls downtown, O'Laughlin unwisely passed under a structure being cleaned. The result was a deluge of black dirt, "falling like a cloud" on his head and face, an ignominious shower that no doubt made its way onto his tongue. His conclusion was unsparing: "Noisy, dirty, ill-smelling, Chicago stands preeminent among the big cities of the western world."[2]

The journalist warned of the consequences, insisting that squalor and dirt bred social pathology and cultural vulgarity. In publically articulating such concerns, O'Laughlin joined a long tradition of connecting Chicago's sensory environment—the sights, sounds, smells, tastes, and haptic sensations people associated with the city—to its civic health. *Sensing Chicago* is an effort to elucidate that tradition by exploring how members of the urban middle classes used their five senses as barometers of civic health and social distinction.[3] The book's most basic goal is to demonstrate that Chicago's sensory landscape constituted more than mere "background" to urban life.[4] As O'Laughlin's readers well knew, the sensations they encountered on city streets, workplaces, and leisure spots helped people think through the perils and prospects of Chicago's growth and the metropolitan age more generally.

It is worth noting that the relationship between the industrial city and the human sensorium was a familiar one to a range of turn-of-the-century analysts, including social scientists. Some dealt with how urban life seemed to radically multiply visual information, something evident in the density of city crowds.[5] As the historian Alan Trachtenberg explains, the faceless crowd emerged as one expression of "a new unintelligibility in human relations" that students of the city pondered. The rise of metropolises like Chicago expanded the sense of mystery long associated with urban centers so that "daily performances . . . now seemed to more and more commentators to be parades of obscurity, of enigma, of silent sphinxes challenging the puzzled citizen."[6] Trachtenberg's comment alludes to the innumerable sights that confused city dwellers, but it also indicates that their eyes often fell short as perceptual instruments, raising questions about the importance of the nonvisual senses as sentinels and guides.

The evidence for a multisensory history of Chicago is, surprisingly enough, often hidden in plain sight. As O'Laughlin's reporting exemplifies, references to potent smells, dirty sights, and other sensate phenomenon animate a wide range of historical documents. They are difficult to miss in manuscript sources, contemporary fiction, photographs and other visual art, as well as newspapers. Yet only in recent years have students of

Chicago benefited from a literature in sensory studies, a growing corpus of works that has provided conceptual frameworks and case studies.[7] One goal of these works has been to remedy a heavy emphasis on vision and seeing in academic writing, including that on the city.[8] Sensory scholars point out that the emphasis on vision mirrors a set of modern cultural values that valorize the eye as the barometer of truth and reason and tend to devalue the proximate, "lower" senses as crude and less rational. The growing power of the eye may well be one of the markers of modern life, but sensory scholars extend understandings of perception by recovering how people employed their ears, noses, tongues, and skin to render meaningful judgments about their worlds.[9]

Consider the Chicago River (see fig. 1). In his magisterial book *Nature's Metropolis* (1991), the environmental historian William Cronon notes that the river occupied a rather limited place in visions of the Windy City. "So hemmed in was the river that it did not figure very prominently in people's mental image of the city," he writes. The power of Lake Michigan as a "visual icon," Cronon explains, meant the Chicago River shaped perceptions of the city far less than the Mississippi River did for St. Louis.[10] While the comparison with Chicago's Midwest rival may be accurate in terms of contemporary "images," a survey of local newspapers will reveal that the offensive smell of the river expanded its presence well beyond its actual banks. The stench registered far and wide, generating a great deal of public complaint, which pushed city leaders to approve a major engineering project to "reverse" the river's flow after the Civil War. The point here, as the anthropologist David Howes has suggested, is the value of research strategies that seek not simply to "read" or "visualize" the city, but instead to "delve into the significance of 'sensing' the city through multiple sensory modalities."[11]

This is not to license a research methodology in which historians attempt to recreate the impermanent, often fleeting sensations of the past in order to investigate with their own five senses. Although such an approach might instructively evoke material culture, it risks divorcing evidence and context if taken to extremes, as debates in the profession's main journals have indicated.[12] Rather, historicizing Chicago's sensory past is possible because people recorded their sense impressions in print. Historians, in short, can "sense" the city through textual and pictorial evidence. It tests common sense to say that textual evidence captured the whole range of sensations that historical actors experienced. Yet the selective nature of their perceptions—often recorded in ways that strained the limits of vocabulary, if not the written word—is what makes them so useful in re-constructing their efforts to reckon with Chicago's astounding growth.

Sensory historians are thus heedful of the dual meaning of the term "sensing"—that is, an act both physical and cultural. "Sensing involves a fusion of sensation *and* signification," Howes writes, "of stimulus *and* meaning."[13] *Sensing Chicago* explores the meaning that people attached to sensory experience and how they expressed those meanings as a form of representation. As the labor historian Daniel Bender points out, sensory studies provide a way to link experience and cultural representation to clarify notions of social differentiation, in this case social class.[14] Through research in textual sources, historians study the point where experience meets description to elucidate social class as "a set of cultural representations, cultural differences, and physical perceptions that are experienced in multisensory ways."[15] This concept of class includes not only material resources and associational life but also what the historian Alain Corbin has referred to as a "regime of sensory values," in which sensory refinement signals social standing. "What was decisive," Corbin argues, "was the degree of delicacy of the hand, the greater or lesser aptitude to silence and detachment, the level of thresholds of tolerance, the unequal vulnerability to disgust and enthusiasm suggested by refinement."[16] Refined senses indicated freedom from manual labor to verify membership in the respectable classes, a form of sensory politics.

Corbin's notion of social distinction as sensory politics can be applied to metropolitan Chicago, a place where the familiarities of small-town life no longer applied. Sensory distinction provided a strategy for the middle classes to stake claim to an impersonal urban environment. It allowed them to transcend the social and physical world of what the historian Robert Wiebe described as the intimate "island communities" that dotted antebellum America and that characterized its social life.[17] Acclimating one's senses, for instance, helped people avoid some embarrassing pitfalls of urban life, such as the humiliations of the confidence man. Difficult to identify by appearances alone, the con man, as the cultural historian Karen Halttunen wrote, raised the fear that the people one met on the street might be merely "passing" as members of the respectable classes when in fact they had more sinister motives, such as seduction or even robbery.[18] Chicago proved an especially fertile ground for con men, as thousands of strangers moved through the city every day by rail.[19] It was a fluid and dangerous situation, captured by Theodore Dreiser in the opening scene of his novel *Sister Carrie* (1900), in which small-town girl Carrie Meeber negotiates a fraught train ride into Chicago.[20]

Much as visual appearances marked social status in preindustrial contexts, nonvisual behavior constituted a performance of social distinction that resonated in the impersonal metropolis.[21] As the popular etiquette manuals of the nineteenth century explained to middle-class readers, the suppression of bodily sounds, smells, and unwelcome touching constituted proper manners.[22] Affecting a deportment of neutral or positive sensory markers such as the absence of body odor, quietude in speech, and subtlety in gesture connoted the cultivation and self-discipline that indicated middle-class status. Bodily cleanliness—after year-round bathing became widespread beginning in the mid-nineteenth century—set apart those who were clean as morally sound, further evidence of membership in the respectable classes.[23] An unsullied body evidenced non-manual employment and the spiritual refinement reflected in the cultural link between the clean and the godly.[24]

The flip side of the sensorial refinement of the middle and upper classes was the supposed coarse senses of workers and poor people. Growing apace with Chicago's rapid economic expansion after the Civil War, the city's working class remained largely of foreign parentage in the nineteenth century, intertwining ethnicity with class as a basis for sensory stereotypes.[25] Echoing Southern discourses on race that defined blacks as rough sensory beings, urban elites cast working-class immigrants as loud, dirty, and malodorous.[26] Manual labor hardened workers' senses, the argument went, rendering the stench and filth of the slum acceptable to them. The imbalance in sensory refinement indicated moral as well as material poverty to signal and justify hierarchies of social class.

Yet in drawing class distinctions in sensory terms, elite actors revealed as much about themselves as about their subjects. Sensory description provided a language for the respectable classes to distance themselves from the material poverty and vulgarity that they believed marked poor people and the city's industrial neighborhoods. The accounts of journalists often reveal what Corbin terms a "desire to distinguish" the sensory refinement of the author and, implicitly, the readers from the subject of the description.[27] Even sympathetic accounts reflected what the historian Mark Pittenger calls a "dialectic of attraction and repulsion" that is common in narratives of slum tourism.[28] Here champions of the poor expressed horror at the squalid conditions of the slum even as they conveyed disgust to underscore their own middle-class standards of taste.

Descriptions of class distinctions in terms of repulsion and disgust appear in a surprisingly wide range of sources—newspapers, reform tracts, municipal publications—because the senses informed an elite effort to promote Chicago's civic health in a period of growth. A principle of sensory studies is that sounds, smells, and tactile sensations tend to breach the boundaries that people create to order urban experience.[29] In this fashion Chicago's sensory landscape challenged elite attempts to categorize urban space for political purposes. The art historian Dell Upton, for example, has described how civic leaders in antebellum Philadelphia sought to reorder their crowded and polluted city through architectural grids. The grid—visually evident in street layouts as well as important centers of consumption such as shopping arcades—promised to create the rational, harmonious, and inclusive spatial order necessary for a "republican city of hierarchically organized but essentially similar citizens."[30] The ordering of Philadelphia continued in the decades after the Civil War. The urban historian John Henry Hepp argues that the continuing urge to classify the city made it an exemplar of middle-class notions of order in the Progressive Era. Inspired by scientific principles of taxonomy, the middle classes worked to make Philadelphia "logical and rational and well catalogued."[31] A history of the senses clarifies the ordering impulse of the middle classes by exploring how unwelcome sensations transgressed the cultural categories they valorized. As everyday urban nuisances signaled social ills, sensory regulation and reform became an important strategy in building a healthy urban order.

The urban nuisance that has provided the most fertile terrain for sensory historians is noise.[32] Peter Payer's study of nineteenth-century Vienna exemplifies how scholars have used social class and notions of refinement as analytical categories to understand noise abatement campaigns. Payer explains that Vienna's middle classes found the aural expressions of the working classes vexing. Middle-class complaints were based on aesthetic contrasts between "sounds" that were judged pleasing (church bells, for example) and objectionable "noises" like shouting in the street, barking dogs, and street musicians. Middle-class actors tended to associate "noise" with the working classes, because it represented "expressions of a rough and unrestrained nature that had to be resisted." Payer's larger point is that the conflict over noise "camouflaged a class struggle" in which elites distanced themselves from what they heard as the crude manners of the working classes.[33] In Vienna, home to high cultural traditions that Chicago's boosters admired, elite intellectuals blasted noise as an enemy of civilization itself. Their critique of noise as a threat to Vienna's culture was summed up in the motto of the city's Anti-Noise Society, "Silence is Noble."

Studies of noise abatement campaigns in the United States have extended the set of issues at stake to include the smooth functioning of the city itself. As the historian Emily Thompson has suggested on noise control in turn-of-the-century New York City, few complaints targeted sounds that were synonymous with material progress—the literal and figurative "hum" of industrial production. Instead, New York's noise suppression society focused on the "unnecessary" noises of the older methods of trade and transportation that violated middle-class reformers' emphasis on efficiency. "The city itself was characterized as a social machine," Thompson writes; as such, it "required some redesign in order to maximize its productive capacity."[34]

Yet the scientific engineering of the Progressives singled out noisemakers who offended class-bound notions of order. Street vendors, for one, attracted a great deal of complaint and official sanction. The historian Derek Vaillant has argued that Chicago's immigrant street vendors raised the ire of the city's middle classes because their foreign tongues bespoke a lack of cultural assimilation. Even more, the vendor's cry signaled the persistence of sales techniques that were incongruent with modern merchandising, as embodied by the categorized, well-ordered department store.[35]

The response to such nuisances—sensory regulation and reform—reflected middle-class notions of progress. Proponents cast sensory reform as cultural uplift, an unapologetic attempt to enhance the civility and moral character of its targets. Sensory reform, by definition, indicated that its advocates believed the unrefined senses of workers and the poor were not immune to change, however difficult effecting that change might be. Yet change was pressing, because an unruly sensorium portended one of the middle classes' long-running anxieties: social chaos and riot. As the historian Lilian Radovac has noted on noise control in New York City, regulators often understood noisemaking as both a sign and a cause of urban disorder, a connection that informed Mayor Fiorello La Guardia's "War on Noise" in the Great Depression. La Guardia heard potential riot in the notes of political and labor protest, using "noise as a[n] aural barometer of the chaos of New York City."[36] In nineteenth-century Chicago, another metropolis where economic stress and urban disorder threatened, reformers advocated sensory discipline to foster the habits of a productive working class—industry, sobriety, and efficiency—all much needed for Chicago's whirlwind growth.

Sensing Chicago adopts the themes of social distinction and urban regulation that inform the scholarship on noise control but also extends the scale of the investigation to the sensory apparatus as a whole, and the scope to a wider cross-section of urban space. The issues under scrutiny are broader than the fears of "urban disorder," which many historians identify as the main theme in middle-class thinking about the metropolitan age.[37] "Civic health" is my preferred term, because it encompasses the anxieties about violent disorders as well as other perils like pollution, filth, disease, accidents, and disasters. "Civic health" also works because it incorporates how the middle and upper classes linked notions of social problems, regulation, and reform to the sensing body in both literal and metaphorical ways. Finally, "civic health" is a useful category for the analysis of positive sensory experiences—for instance, a day at Chicago's White City amusement park. As we will see in the book's concluding chapter, entrepreneurs argued that rejuvenating the senses promised to enhance the city's civic health as much as regulation.

Chicago is an ideal site for such a sensory history because the city embodied the economic and demographic growth that characterized the United States in decades following the Civil War. Chicago's population growth, economic expansion, and rapid change were common characteristics of the industrial city. Even so, the Windy City represented something unique. One of the city's remarkable features is that it grew so rapidly, effectively compressing the economic and demographic expansion of Eastern cities like New York in time and space.[38] From its roots as a small trading post in the 1830s, Chicago emerged as the second largest U.S. city and a leading manufacturing center in mere decades. Its population nearly tripled between 1860 and 1870; it *more* than tripled between 1870 and 1890, exceeding one million persons.[39] Chicago, as the literary critic and historian Carl Smith put it, stood for "the power of all the new historical, social, and economic forces in an expanding and interconnected commercial and industrializing nation."[40] It should come as little surprise, then, that novelists like Dreiser turned to the city to capture the national journey from countryside to metropolis.[41]

In his classic urban history, *Victorian Cities*, Asa Briggs coined the term "shock city" to refer to late nineteenth-century Chicago. The city, he pointed out, attracted visitors who wished to see the historical changes of the industrial age. Their reactions—or "shock"—ranged from fascination with the new technology to horror at the poverty and filth. For visitors from around the world, Chicago presented a concentration of the social and economic challenges of modernity, "forcing to the surface what seemed to be intractable problems of society and government."[42] Historians have since adopted Briggs's moniker to frame studies of Chicago as well as cities around the world.[43] A recent example is Harold Platt's study of Chicago and Manchester, England, as a series of ecological shocks. With heavily polluted environments, both cities stood as "paradoxical portents of the technological future and throwbacks to social barbarism."[44] *Sensing Chicago* continues the tradition started by Briggs but explores a broader notion of Chicago's environment as a multilayered sensory landscape. It focuses on how that landscape—with ecological, mechanical, and human sensory features—quite literally shocked the senses to raise questions about the future in terms of civic health and social distinction.

CHAPTER 1

SMELLING CIVIC PERIL

The Chicago Styx

By 1869 a journey down the Chicago River tested the hardiest of noses. In August an official "smelling committee" set about an inspection tour, a civic ritual that forced them to brave the waters at the hottest time of the year, when the combined stench of the riverside slaughterhouses, rendering concerns, and distilleries reached its noisome zenith. The committee included the acting mayor, the city's sanitary superintendent, the health officer and other medical officials, as well as an observer, Mr. Stewart Kingsbury from Centralia, who the *Tribune* reported "had heard a great deal of the fame of Chicago as a watering place, and wished to test the properties of its waters," although for exactly what purpose it did not say.

The trip started out on a pleasant enough note, with moderate winds and temperature, as the committee departed on a tug waiting in the main branch to journey southward to the Chicago neighborhood of Bridgeport. When they passed under the Madison Street bridge, the group saw "patches of oily scum" floating on the top of the water near the city's gasworks but noted only a moderate stench. The same held true when the party chugged past a number of sewer outlets that emptied directly into the river. Here the *Tribune* reporter noted that the water carried sewage of "admirable stenches," evidence of the city's antebellum decision to use the river as a receptacle for Chicago's household waste.

When the inspectors reached Van Buren Street, farther south, the situation grew worse. The *Tribune* commented on an unknown odor, one that "baffled the efforts made by the noses of the gentlemen to analyze it." Off the port bow the committee watched a group of boys swimming in the ambiguously smelling water, having left their clothing behind. Another group of boys dressed themselves on the bank, their skins "tinged by the black water." While the young bathers might have found relief from the summer heat, the newspaper reporter reminded readers that the boys found no cleanliness.

The men next encountered "the supreme odor known as the Twelfth Street smell," a fetor "thick enough to cut." The sanitary superintendent, perhaps mindful of Mr. Kingsbury's untested nose, passed around cigars. The tobacco smoke probably helped to disguise the "Sixteenth street smell" that followed ("a big one"), although it could not have shielded the party from the sights that accompanied the next olfactory assault, the consistently termed "Eighteenth street smell." The water stood calm, darkly colored and filled with garbage as well as discarded timber from a rail yard. A dead pig floated past. Here debate ensued when some members of the inspection committee argued that the bloated carcass was actually a cat that had been seen in the North Branch two weeks past. "The smell was somewhat similar," they observed, and the cloud of insects that hovered over the expired animal looked familiar.

Reaching the mouth of a South Branch slough, the tug turned its screws to unleash the stink as fully as possible: "The water came up thick and black. The surface was covered with a filthy froth and bubbles of gas, while a terrible stench rose over the inky water. . . . It was positively sickening. There was a strength and substance in it." Two women standing near the bank covered their noses with their shawls, but still the tug stirred the dark mixture. "Again and again the screw was put in motion," the reporter wrote, "and the black froth ran in small waves along the side of the slough, while the stench rose higher and higher and stronger and stronger." The party remained only a few minutes, but already Mr. Kingsbury had developed a headache and, the *Tribune* remarked, "began to lose confidence in the healing powers of Chicago waters."

The tug retraced its route to finish the journey in the North Branch, but Mr. Kingsbury found only meager relief. Even before it passed the riverside glue factories, the party smelled their foul signatures. They soon came upon a defunct slaughterhouse, one whose malodor lingered: "The smell originated from heaps of old hams that have lain in the river for

years and are in a state of decomposition." Next came the stench of distilleries—Hallihan and Hulls in this case. It included "two acres of decaying swill," a by-product of the distillation process fed to cows in nearby
sheds that then polluted the water with their own noxious evacuations.
The smelling committee could report some progress, however. Since their
last inspection, the distillery had treated the swill with lime and heavy oil,
giving it a "somewhat thinner" stench. In addition, the "creeping things
that looked so disgusting on the last visit" seemed disbursed by the lime,
although "hordes of flies hovered over the foul spot." The optimistic notes
continued at the end of the voyage. After four hours on the river—the
"Chicago Styx" according to the newspaper—the party landed back at La
Salle Street. Here the *Tribune*, no doubt in keeping with its regular prod-
ding of city officials to clean up the waters, noted that the "river is greatly
improved since the last inspection."[1]

The *Tribune*'s campaign to prod municipal officials to clean up the
Chicago River reflected a fear among the city's elite that the foul conditions that had brought on Mr. Kingsbury's headache threatened the civic
health of the metropolis. As the newspaper's reform-minded readers well
knew, the river acted in concert with other receptacles of industrial and
household waste to befoul Chicago's physical environment. The grimy
streets and alleys, the clamor of wagons and streetcars, the smoke that
perpetually hung over the city, and the putrid smell of the offal left to
decompose in the river registered on the senses to foretell disease, moral
chaos, and even economic ruin.

Recent scholarship has clarified the attitudes of turn-of-the-century actors toward pollution by bridging the fields of urban and environmental
history.[2] Air pollution has caught the attention of many historians, much
as it did the hometown reporter John Callan O'Laughlin, the critic quoted
in the introduction to this book. Urbanites, even the business leaders who
presided over the dirtiest industries, cared about abating pollution, albeit
in a self-serving fashion.[3] The urban historian David Stradling's study of
Cincinnati's railroads and their smoke problem evinces how calls for abatement often served the politically influential and economically powerful.
Middle-class reformers in Cincinnati endeavored to control air quality to
keep "dirty work and dirty workers" out of sight in order to promote a
shared idea of the "civilized, residential city."[4] The most aggressive abatement measures occurred when pollution breached the residential districts
of the city to sully affluent households. What remains unclear, however,
is how middle-class actors interpreted smoke and other forms of pollu-

tion as sensory phenomenon to make decisions about the benefits and drawbacks of metropolitan life.

This chapter seeks answers by exploring the public debate on the pollution of the Chicago River between the Civil War and the 1871 effort to "reverse" its flow. The Chicago River is an important case because the waterway served as the fountainhead of the city's commercial expansion in the second half of the nineteenth century. The river also constituted a potent sensory nuisance. It is not too much to say that the awful smell of the polluted stream punched Chicagoans in the nose; the loathsome odors forced a raw confrontation with pollution that sometimes left residents feeling physically ill, much like Mr. Kingsbury. The river offended the eyes and tongue too, but the stenches generated the most complaint because they ranged so widely and powerfully across urban space.

Urban-environmental historians have largely neglected olfaction as a barometer of pollution. An important exception is studies of stench nuisance litigation.[5] The advantage of these studies is that they identify who actually brought suit against violators of the olfactory status quo and, by implication, who did not. Historians such as Christine Meisner Rosen and Andrew Hurley have shown that poor people in the industrial city faced the worst stinks, because they lived closest to the working parts of the city and because they lacked the resources to sue. Hurley, focusing on municipal efforts to abate the noisome emissions from St. Louis's rendering establishments, found that influential figures in business and politics regulated stench by effectively quarantining the stink industries to neighborhoods with the lowest property values and income levels.[6]

Still, the broad range of reasons why the malodors offended the senses of the affluent classes remains unexplored. Material concerns such as fears of disease and declining property values clearly mattered, as we will see in the case of the Chicago River. Yet concerns related to cultural sensibilities are often minimized in existing writing, explained away as "simply matters of aesthetics or inconvenience."[7] Sensory historians have more to say about seemingly minor matters of aesthetics and inconvenience. Showing how elites used their noses to draw lines of social differentiation, scholars such as Alain Corbin have suggested that the study of olfaction can expand understandings of the creation of class distinctions in the modern urban world.[8]

The control of odors also figured in broader efforts to create a healthy urban order. The historian David Inglis's study of the "bourgeois faecal experience" in nineteenth-century Western Europe demonstrates how hiding human waste by shifting it to underground sewers became an essential function of urban government, a test of civic health.[9] As a form of sensory regulation, sewer construction not only reduced waterborne diseases but also eased the minds of elites about the social disorder implied by the freely roaming reek of feces. The implications for civic health in Chicago relate to the attempt to "hide" the human and industrial wastes that found their way into the city's river. The reversal of the river's flow (to change the ultimate destination of the waste from Lake Michigan to regions west of the city limits) underlines how urban elites used their noses to index civic health and modernization. Ultimately the decision to build two of Chicago's most substantial public works projects—a water tunnel under Lake Michigan for drinking water and the deepening of the Illinois and Michigan (I & M) Canal to change the flow of the river—cannot be understood without historicizing the stench of the Chicago Styx.

Sewer Chicago

Presuming that the dead pig spotted by Mr. Kingsbury did not find its own way into the river, its presence there violated long-standing municipal law. In 1833 the first regulation promulgated by the town trustees banned the dumping of dead animals in the river, mandating a penalty of three dollars for each offense. The next year, in a pattern that would continue for several decades, local leaders faced a cholera epidemic that compelled them to tighten the regulations. The new regulation expanded the dumping ban to include putrid meat, decaying vegetables, as well as "any other offensive substance whatever," and increased the fine to five dollars for each offense.[10] The incorporation of the city in 1837 brought further regulations, including one in 1849 (also following a cholera outbreak) that would have limited the number of floating pig carcasses in the river by banning the construction of new slaughterhouses within the city limits. The original town ordinances provided for the appointment of a health board to monitor sanitary conditions in the streets and alleys. The subsequent city charter (1837) provided for the creation of a new board of health and the appointment of a health officer to keep tabs on people with infectious diseases and to investigate the city's hygienic environment more generally.[11]

Yet the river continued to serve as a dumping site for dead pigs—and all other matter of filth—because municipal authorities neglected to enforce the ordinances. The board of health existed chiefly on paper until the 1850s and seems to have been mostly inert until at least the outbreak of the Civil War, acting only in times of major epidemics. Even during the war the overall neglect continued despite the commercial expansion that accelerated the transformation of the river into the noisome mess that was the "Chicago Styx."[12] "Although ordinances had been passed with regard to the river," the sanitary superintendent of the city, John H. Rauch, lamented in 1871, "there had been no one to see that they were enforced, and, as a necessary consequence, the cupidity and selfishness of individuals was allowed to run riot in this respect, at the expense of the public."[13] Here Rauch articulated the fear that business had gone too far in creating an environment that taxed the senses. He joined in the chorus of elite voices that identified the stench of the river as a barometer through which to judge the proper balance between individual gain and civic well-being.

In many ways Rauch's fears about the river reflected the consequences of the antebellum transportation revolution and the economic growth it stimulated.[14] In Chicago the year 1848 marked a key turning point because it saw the completion of the I & M Canal and track laid for the city's first railroad, the Galena and Chicago Union. Further railroad construction linked the city with Eastern markets to help the city emerge by the end of the Civil War as a commercial gateway between the East and the West.[15] The expansion of local business and the population growth that followed multiplied the scale of the industries most responsible for polluting the river—meatpacking, rendering, and distillery plants—so by the outbreak of the war the condition of the river had become a regular topic in the city's newspapers. During the 1860s, public meetings, often chaired by influential citizens in business and the professions, amplified the complaints in the newspapers with such frequency and venom that municipal leaders found the issue difficult to ignore.

Before the city determined the best way to clean up the river, however, it approved the construction of a sewer system that only compounded the problem. Following an especially hot summer in 1854, in which Chicago again faced a cholera outbreak, the state legislature created a special tax district with independent governance to develop a modern sewer system apart from the political squabbling of the common council. The board of sewerage commissioners, incorporated the next year, hired engineer Ellis Sylvester Chesbrough to develop the overall plan. The self-trained Chesbrough, who at the time was serving as chief engineer for the city of Baltimore, promptly traveled to Europe to study urban waste disposal systems.

The plan he recommended called for the large bulk of the city's sewage to be emptied directly into the river.[16] The risk of pollution problems from the river's flow into Lake Michigan, where the city drew its water supply, seemed small compared to the health risks of a system that emptied the sewage directly into the lake, one of the alternatives he considered.

Chesbrough's European tour convinced him that depositing waste directly into Lake Michigan threatened to create the type of offensive odors that had rendered the small English town of Worthing, which emptied its sewage directly into the English Channel, unattractive to its traditional core of tourists. The Worthing case, he argued, "shows that the mere discharge of filth into the sea gives no security against its being cast back in a more offensive state than ever" with the prevailing winds.[17] Chesbrough warned that the foul odors of decomposing sewage threatened to stain the city with a reputation for stinky living conditions, a consideration that involved concerns about public health, civic pride, and economic prosperity. To check the potentially offensive smells created by his system, he proposed periodically flushing the river with water from Lake Michigan. In 1856 construction on the sewer system, which required the campaign to raise the grade of Chicago's streets by as much as eight feet to facilitate drainage, commenced.[18] By 1861 the new sewer system, the first of its kind in the nation, carried the city's household waste and the drainage from its streets through fifty-four miles of sewers to mix with the carrion of the riverside industries and from there to Lake Michigan.[19]

The commercial and demographic expansion of the war years worsened the condition of the river. Demand for the livestock and wheat processed in Chicago—stimulated in large measure by the trade interruptions suffered by cities near the front lines like Cincinnati and St. Louis—kept pace with the city's population boom.[20] The pork industry illustrates the rapid growth. In the last winter before hostilities commenced, the city's slaughterhouses processed nearly 275,000 hogs, a figure eight times greater than that of 1848. By the winter of 1862–1863, when demand from the Union Army peaked wartime production, almost one million hogs let out their final squeals in Chicago's slaughterhouses. Yet city officials still failed to enforce the ordinances against dumping. In 1860 they reduced municipal expenditures by refusing to appoint an official to enforce the local codes. City leaders appointed a policeman as acting health officer two years later, but Chicagoans waited until 1867 for a permanent board of health with its full complement of sanitary inspectors to keep tabs on river pollution.[21]

As the condition of the river worsened, the press, local government, and citizens placed blame. The city insisted that illegal dumping by riverside industries, not its new sewer system, accounted for the bulk of the smell problem.[22] The various investigations—multiple trips by smelling committees, exposés by the local press, and the accounts of individual citizens—came to no real consensus about which individual actors bore the bulk of the responsibility for befouling the city's waterway. In 1863 the *Tribune* lamented how the various investigations all seemed to reach the same, sensorially obvious conclusion. "Learned reports from smelling committees, technical chemical analysis, . . . [all] the conceptions of fertile brains," the paper read, "have accomplished but little more than to announce the grand discovery that the Chicago River is a bed of filth—a fact which was patent without investigation, to every one's nose."[23]

The investigations nevertheless clarified the contours of the river's smellscape in broad terms. The 1869 "smelling committee" traced the general outlines. On the North Branch a range of industries polluted the river, but distilleries emerged as the main culprits, especially after meat processing began to concentrate on the South Branch, around the Union Stockyards.[24] The distillation process produced a swill composed of corn malt and water, which the distillers fed to the cows they kept in nearby sheds to produce milk and beef. In 1864 the *Tribune* reported that four distilleries on the North Branch kept as many as nine thousand head of cattle, a number that generated nearly "nine thousand bushels of abomination" each day. Some of the abomination—a warm stew of cow manure, excess swill, mulch from the animal's hay, and the decomposed material from the sheds themselves—found its way directly into the river, by both accident and design.

The bulk of the swill, however, ended up in nearby bogs, where it lay to attract all manner of insects before seeping into the river. As the 1869 smelling committee observed, the mess constituted an eyesore of the worst kind. "Look at it," the *Tribune* cried, "as it lies there rotting in the sun, boiling and bubbling like the lake of brimstone, and emitting the most villainous fumes." Thick swarms of flies circled, yet the reporter found the "countless billions of maggots . . . squirming and wriggling" in the cesspool even more grating to the eye. "Watch them, if you can, for a few minutes," he challenged readers, "as they deport themselves in [a] playful mood, and as you drink in with your nostrils the fullness of the aromatic grandeur which rises so plentifully there."[25]

The fullness of the aromatic grandeur on the South Branch, by contrast, could be attributed to the meat industry. The rapid expansion of that industry could be observed at the Union Stockyards itself, a massive complex opened in 1865 that contained five hundred animal pens, stretched over sixty acres. After three years of operation, it had expanded even further to twenty-three hundred pens on one hundred acres, a yard capable of holding seventy-five thousand hogs and more than twenty thousand each of cattle and sheep at one time.[26] The slaughterhouses that surrounded the stockyards also acted as a magnet for rendering outfits, businesses that used the discarded animal matter to manufacture products like lard, glue, and soap. The conglomeration of livestock in various stages of life and death along with the noxious fumes of the rendering generated smells of the foulest kind, often shocking the noses of visitors.

Despite the heavy pollution, fingering individual offenders could be tricky, because plant owners were known to encourage inspections during the off-season and to dump blood and offal into the river after dark. In 1864 the *Tribune* told its readers to spy on the slaughterhouses late at night, charging that they dumped their refuse into the river only at 1:00 AM as the local police changed shifts. Even those readers whose eyes could not see through the darkness at the riverbank could gather evidence against the offenders by dipping a bucket into the water. "Take up a bucket full of the slush called water and you shall see and smell the blood," the newspaper suggested. The bucket-wielding investigators could also sample the substance that lay at the river bottom, often mistaken for "mud." "You find it," warned the *Tribune*, "to be more pregnant with animal matter than the adder full of venom; it is all one conglomeration of blood and brains and mulch, mingled and decomposed by the action of the fluid above."[27]

Twelve years later, in 1876, the *Tribune* was still complaining about the nocturnal timing of the South Branch malodors—in this case the fetid gasses produced by the rendering plants. In an editorial titled "The Stench Nuisance," an unidentified author employed the lurid adjectives typically used to condemn the river stinks—and the people forced by geography and economics to reside in their shadows—in a clear demonstration of how languages of disgust worked in the service of social distinction.[28] The author insisted that the odors of Bubbly Creek (see fig. 2), a slough on the Chicago River that the meatpackers used as a sewer, raised few objections in Bridgeport, a working-class Chicago neighborhood settled by Irish canal workers and frequently identified in the *Tribune* as a vicious slum.[29] Such "local smells" mattered little to the author because they were "confined to the neighborhood which tolerates them, and rarely trouble anybody." The real problem was when the "insufferable stink" reached the "desirable residence portion" of the South Side after dark, where his own home sat.

At night, when the rendering plants illegally vented their boilers to avoid censure by city inspectors, the vile smells arrived "suddenly, in a mass like a cloud." The stench assaulted the editorialist's discriminating nose with a fetor "almost thick enough to cut with a knife." In his view the only solution was for municipal authorities to closely monitor the rendering plants and file legal charges when warranted. Workers, he reasoned, could not be counted on to demand abatements of the malodor, as their own noses had become desensitized to foulness. "The men who work in this business become indurated with the stinks in which they live," the author argued. "Their mental and moral natures," he continued, "seem to grow as hard and dead as their olfactory nerves."[30] The connection between a dull sense of smell, manual labor, and moral poverty condemned workers as cultural inferiors; at the same time, it highlighted the refinement of the author's own senses. In denouncing the hardened nose of labor, the author disassociated himself from the industrial workplace. His reasoning recalls Corbin's observation made about nineteenth-century France that claims to middle-class status often expressed themselves as "ignorance of the sweat of hard labor."[31] In this case the author asserted social distinction by expressing something stronger—disgust—at the material conditions of the stockyards district and the sensibilities of the people who worked and lived there.

The Drinking Water Problem

Since the pollution of the municipal water supply via Lake Michigan threatened the entire city, it constituted the most pressing matter for the civic elite. The Chicago City Hydraulic Company, a public enterprise created in 1851 by the state legislature, operated the main pumping works. Its wooden intake pipe, located one-half mile north of the mouth of the Chicago River, extended only a few hundred feet into the lake, meaning the water Chicagoans drew for their homes mixed with river pollution. The problem worsened with seasonal change. Throughout the winter months, as the slaughterhouses and distilleries dumped carrion, offal, and manure into the river, the refuse compounded and froze. While the river ice held the bulk of the waste in check, in a kinetic and olfactory sense, the spring freshet drove the whole mess into the lake, unleashing the pent-up stench and driving the polluted water into the city's intake system.

In 1862, for example, the freshet combined with a southwesterly wind and low lake levels to render the drinking water "exceedingly disagreeable" to the tongue, as Chesbrough put it.[32] Even persons merely passing by the lakeshore, he explained in a report to the board of public works (BPW), the municipal body that oversaw the water supply, perceived the "well-known disagreeable effect upon the taste and smell" of the foul matter.[33] The BPW insisted that the complaints of the public reflected only an occasional flaw in the system. The more worrisome issues concerned the eye: the wind and wave action of the lake kicked up clay that often gave the water a turbid appearance. The turbidity, although harmless, often drove residents to wrongly conclude that the city provided unhealthful water.[34] The notion that the "daily drink of our citizens is the discharge of the sewers, the refuse of the slaughtering establishments, . . . [is] wholly untrue and cannot fail to do harm," the BPW blustered in its 1863 annual report.[35]

Even as it assured Chicagoans that they did not drink from an open sewer, however, the BPW faced growing complaints in the press. The 1862 floods, according to the *Tribune*, brought water that was repellant to all the physical senses into people's homes: "a brackish, fishy, glutinous, dirty, odoriferous fluid, fit only for the purposes of cleaning the dirtiest of Augean stables." The "fishy" aspect of the water offended Chicagoans' sight as much as their senses of taste and smell.[36] In March 1862 a citizen named N. C. Burnham complained to the newspaper that his kitchen hydrant had recently yielded water filled with "half a pint or more of rotten fish from 2½ to 3½ inches in length." Burnham's domestic servant informed him that she, too, had drawn kitchen water of a piscatorial flavor, although she believed her sample included even greater amounts of fish matter. "There have been enough fish come through my . . . kitchen during the last five days," he huffed, "to taint more water than runs [though it] in a week," making the fluid impossible to stomach.[37]

The *Tribune* amplified Burnham's complaint, pointing out that the sizeable fish often showed up in water pitchers in all conditions of life, "some alive and wriggling, others with backs broken, and others still dead and in [the] process of decomposition."[38] While the 1862 "fish nuisance" led some Chicagoans (including Burnham) to argue that the real problem of river pollution derived from a failure of screens at the intake point, subsequent repairs and the reduction of fish in the city water exposed the nuisance as more reflective of the limited interruption that the BPW described in its 1863 report.[39]

Still, the less "fishy"—but brackish, glutinous, dirty, and odoriferous—fluid that Chicagoans drew from household hydrants continued to offend the senses in fearful ways. Anxieties about disease drove much of the concern. Here it is crucial to keep in mind that despite advancements in medical knowledge in the 1840s linking disease transmission with germs, many doctors still understood infection as the product of the foul-smelling vapors (miasmas) that surrounded crowded, dirty urban areas. Miasmatic theory, based on the notion that miasmas carried dangerous, invisible matter through the environment and into the body, continued to haunt the public mind well into the second half of the nineteenth century.[40] As the *Chicago Times* reminded its readers, in a poor choice of metaphor, the nose was the "vigilant watchman" that protected them against disease.[41] A "practical civil engineer" wrote to the *Tribune* in 1862 about how he sniffed out such dangers. His household water reeked with "an odor and taste from the decomposition of slaughter-houses, distilleries, and sewer substances," the stench of which he feared would breed pestilence. The engineer recommended that the city use pumps to permanently turn the flow of the river backward so that it emptied in the Illinois River (west of the city), a solution that municipal leaders already used as an occasional remedy.[42]

Other citizens argued that the odoriferous water that found its way into households endangered Chicagoans' souls. Temperance advocates feared that the unpalatable water undermined public morality by driving people to refresh themselves with stronger drink. Tea, coffee, and milk produced by cows watered from the lake all "smell abominably and are thrown aside in disgust," the *Tribune* lamented. Boiling did not help at all, for it only added to the "peculiarly fishy, gasy [*sic*], odor." The newspaper predicted that soon women would cook only with beer.[43] Their concerns were not unfounded. As a historian of Chicago's saloons has observed, water in slum neighborhoods was often rejected as foul. With milk untrustworthy and easily spoiled, poor Chicagoans turned to beer as a nutritive, pasteurized, and cold refreshment.[44] The *Tribune* charged that the city water company encouraged the habit, since the product it provided was unfit for human consumption. Only the "iron stomachs of the steam fire engines" could handle the "mingled concentration of all offensiveness" that was the city's drinking water, a fluid fit only "for fires and common laundry work, and to sprinkle the streets with, and for bath purposes."[45]

Much to the dismay of the *Tribune*, however, the city's dirty water seemed to discourage bathing altogether. This concern reflected the long-standing cultural ideal, common among members of the Protestant middle class, that spiritual health necessitated physical cleanliness. With cleanliness next to godliness, a penchant for filth suggested a predilection to sin. As a Cincinnati newspaper put it in 1849, "All testimonies agree in affirming that there is scarcely anything more distinctive of paganism than its love of dirt." Catholicism, according to the author, represented the best example of paganism's "disgusting character." Catholics, "whether [they] sun themselves in the streets of Naples, or crouch on the mud floor of an Irish cabin," decoupled physical and spiritual purity to threaten public morality.[46]

Chicago's advocates of personal cleanliness feared that social chaos and violence represented the ultimate consequence of Irish paganism. One reporter for the *Tribune* indicated as much when he celebrated the 1859 displacement of an Irish settlement from the banks of the North Branch of the Chicago River. Before the city evicted the residents, the settlement housed the "vilest and lowest population" of Chicago. Mobs of drunken, cursing Irish women accosted visitors. Facing a range of threats to their personal safety, visitors might be drowned in mud, suffocated by the fetor of the filthy shanties, or, worse, "bludgeoned in wild Celtic freakishness."[47] The connections between filth, Irish-ness, and moral decay demonstrate how nativists employed languages of sensory disgust in ways that joined ethnic and class-based stereotypes. In this article the Irish immigrants—people sometimes "confused with dirt itself," as the historian Suellen Hoy put it—are so indurated by the material conditions of poverty and so debased by their alien religious practices that they are rendered animalistic.[48]

The fear that Chicago's dirty water undermined the moral health of the city applied to non-Catholics as well. The secular version of the cleanliness ideal held that avoiding dirt nurtured civic virtue. By the end of the Civil War—a conflict in which the United States Sanitary Commission demonstrated the benefits of preventive hygiene—municipal reformers began urging residents to keep clean in order to check epidemics and to bolster an orderly democracy.[49] Cleanliness encouraged industriousness, sobriety, and thrift; a polluted water supply and lack of bathing furthered the type of squalor that gave rise to mob rule. "Bathing the hands and face," the *Tribune* complained, "has become obsolete in Chicago, and our inhabitants are becoming literally entitled to the appellation, 'the great unwashed.'"[50] The anxiety about bathing linked clean faces and hands with the enterprising middle class, even before marketers bombarded American consumers with advertisements for personal care products in the early twentieth century.[51] The unwashed contrast—mobs of immigrants, like the Irish, whose daily habits seemed so different to many in the native middle class—threatened the civic health of the city and, when taken to its logical conclusion, the progress of American civilization as a whole.[52]

A permanent solution to Chicago's water problem required municipal sponsorship. The BPW debated solutions as early as 1862, rejecting continued pumping to reverse the flow of the Chicago River as an impractical long-term remedy and an outright ban on riverside industries as politically impossible. Eventually the BPW approved a massive public works project to improve the city's water supply by moving the intake farther from the mouth of the river. Chesbrough reported that the river flow polluted Lake Michigan for several miles along the shoreline but only about one mile straight into the deeper water. In 1863, acting on Chesbrough's recommendation, the city approved the construction of a water tunnel, to be five feet in diameter, running under the lakebed and with an intake crib located two miles into the lake.[53]

The city held a formal ground-breaking ceremony for the tunnel early the next year. Workers first tunneled from the shore under the lake, an exhausting exercise in manual labor that nonetheless progressed an average of about twelve feet per day. Another set of workers soon dug from a lake shaft toward the shore at about the same rate. The two digging parties met in late November 1866; the BPW reported that the two ends of tunnel lined up remarkably well, falling only 7½ inches short of a perfect match. Construction ended early the next month when the mayor placed a commemorative stone near the meeting point. Triumphant local leaders walked the length of the tunnel and then took a tugboat from the intake crib back to the city.[54]

The city opened the tunnel for its intended use in late March 1867, an occasion during which local leaders enjoyed general congratulations. Chesbrough noted that the water quality far exceeded that which the city provided through the old intake pipe, although it sometimes varied in "clearness, taste or temperature" due to wind conditions or a large spring freshet.[55] The *Tribune* offered a far headier celebration of "that magic archway of brick and cement," ranking it as the eighth wonder of the world and invoking biblical language to characterize the improvement in the municipal water supply. "We have long since bid farewell," it announced that summer, "to the muddy excrements which washed down the river from the ends of sewers . . . and made a compound scarcely less villainous than the waters of the river Egypt in the days when Moses plagued Pharaoh and his people because they would not let the children of Israel go."[56] The lake tunnel delivered such clear water that consumption skyrocketed, forcing the BPW to recommend increasing the pumping capacity of the city waterworks. Yet even a major increase in pumping capacity could not keep pace with population growth. Chesbrough estimated that demand for water would exceed the tunnel's capacity by 1875. The city awarded the contract for the construction of a second tunnel only months before the Great Chicago Fire of October 1871.[57]

The Continuing River Problem

Less noted in the celebration of Chicago's successful campaign to improve its water supply was the fact that new lake tunnel sidestepped the underlying problem of river pollution. As the water tunnel bore its way through the lakebed, pollution of the Chicago River continued unabated. As noted earlier, the city failed to police the riverside industries in a consistent and effective fashion through the war years; distillers and packers largely ignored municipal sanitary regulations that prohibited dumping. Positive local measures to cleanse the river, chiefly pumping through the I & M Canal, failed to keep pace with the volume of pollution generated by the leaps in economic and demographic growth. Even as the city designed and built the lake tunnel—a grand pubic works project that promised to make Chicagoans healthier and cleaner—a parallel debate took shape about the dangers that the sights and smells of the Chicago Styx itself posed to the civic health of the city.

The spread of infectious disease remained a major concern. In some ways the emphasis on miasmas as the source of diseases meant the stench of the river posed an even wider threat than the polluted drinking water, because it spread throughout the city to mix with the foul vapors of privies and alleyways to endanger the public health. In 1863, the same year the city approved the water tunnel project, a local physician reported an outbreak of erysipelas (a disease characterized by large patches of raised, red skin on the face and legs) to the board of health. Noting that the cases hugged the South Branch, he condemned the meatpacking houses for dumping offal and other filth into the nearby sloughs, blocking them up with a "semi-fluid mass of putrefaction," the odor of which he deemed indescribably offensive. The stench wafted for miles, mixing with other putrid airs to put residents of the South Side at risk of diseases, including typhoid, typhus fever, and malignant dysentery. "No city can be bathed in putrid air with impunity," he told municipal authorities. "If Chicago shall neglect to make a thorough removal of its filth," the doctor went on, "it will be infallibly scourged with these pestilences which through all time have smitten cities which commit sins against cleanliness and pure air."[58]

Cleanup efforts also promised to abate the concerns about the moral health of the city. Unlike the debate over the condition of household water, the concerns about the river focused less on a lack of bathing (although worries remained, as demonstrated by the case of the bathers observed by Mr. Kingsbury) than on the general fear that the river stinks mingled with other offensive odors to promote a general sense of spiritual decay. Here, too, the concern echoed age-old ideals that held cleanliness next to godliness, filth to sin. The garbage in the streets and the filth in the alleyways, one local reporter bemoaned, combined with the stinks of the South Branch sloughs to reveal, "in tomes not to be mistaken, the physical ungodliness of Chicago, and the pressing need for improvement."[59]

In a refrain on the debate about drinking water, the concerns about public morality and the condition of the river related to calls for temperance. The author of the article on Chicago's ungodliness noted that a recent drop in the price of whiskey had discouraged production by the North Branch distilleries, which naturally reduced the amount of swill and cow manure that found its way into the river, all to the good for the city's civic health. Nevertheless, greater city oversight to prevent illegal dumping in the river remained essential if Chicago were to earn the reputation for "all the essentials of a complete community," by which he meant a modern one—that is, one committed to public health, technological advancement, and expanding enterprise.[60]

If protection against disease and the promotion of moral purity constituted refrains from the debate about how the pollution of Lake Michigan harmed the city's supply of household water, the concern about Chicago's identity as a fully "modern" urban community emerged as the key theme in debates about the condition of the Chicago River itself. Of course, clean water for household use constituted a key ingredient in the city's claims to modernity; after 1867 its boosters held out the tunnel as evidence for those claims. Yet the stink of the river continued to embarrass boosters and regular citizens who were concerned about Chicago's standing in the national mind; they feared the stinks might even undermine their city's commercial future.

Residents concerned about Chicago's reputation deplored how the river stinks gave outsiders the impression that it was impossible to enjoy vigorous, healthy lives in the city. Writing in late June 1862, an editorialist conceded as much when he bashed the municipal celebration of the Fourth of July within the city limits. Far better to go ahead with the existing plans for an official celebration to be held in the countryside, as the city's smell would dampen the whole affair. "Is the noble Chicago river, fit emblem of Styx, so odorous in [the city leaders'] noses, so unapproachably fragrant in their paternal nostrils, that they are unwilling to entrust their beloved constituents to the smell of green woods and the sight of water-colored water?"[61] Invoking the sensorial vigor of the countryside, he suggested that the river stinks could forever damage what one writer termed Chicago's "reputation for healthfulness."[62] The stench would discourage healthy and productive people from moving to the city, thus reducing the population to those of the lowest social status and threatening future growth.

The debate about the stench of the river forced Chicagoans to consider how much of their physical environment they were willing to sacrifice in the name of commercial growth. A minority of voices called for the city to use any possible means to stop the pollution, arguing that commercial gain never trumped the public's right to clean air and water. In December 1864, for example, a citizen, "E.C.L.," wrote to the *Tribune* to assert that the river constituted common property and that its clean condition could not be sacrificed for any reason. No "increase of business or wealth [is] desirable which must be purchased at such a sacrifice," the writer argued.[63] The same month, the *Tribune* published a letter that echoed E.C.L.'s view by using the debate over the river to question the city's well-known ethos of commercial striving altogether: "Are our citizens so absorbed in the one over-mastering passion of money making as to have become insensible to all that makes life attractive and agreeable?"[64] The river clearly endangered the public health but, even more, gave visitors the impression that Chicagoans did not care to maintain a clean, respectable urban order.

At the same time, a minority of voices insisted that sensory discomfort constituted the unavoidable yet bearable consequences of industries that provided the far greater payoff of jobs and income. One meatpacker challenged the criticism of his industry by arguing that it derived from unreliable visual assessments of the river, particularly from the sight of blood in the water. "The fact that the water is *colored* with blood is no evidence that a large quantity of blood is run into the river," he wrote in a letter to the *Tribune*. Challenging the commonsense view that blood-colored water indicated that pollution had reached an unhealthy level, he explained that small quantities of blood often changed the color of large swaths of the river. The bulk of the blood ended up not in the river but in the carts that packers used to carry the waste to the prairie for dumping. The blood that did find its way into the water, he insisted, remained harmless as long as the temperature of the river stayed cold enough to prevent its decomposition, as was the case in December, when he wrote. The real cause of the loathsome stenches could be found on the North Branch. Its distilleries and cow sheds, combined with the sewage that emptied into the river, created a stench whose power to offend far outweighed the visual discomfort created by bloody water. "It passes comprehension," he cried, "that a community that will tolerate such a state of things [on the North Branch], should be so intolerant of the *color* of blood in the water."[65]

The argument that many packers carted their waste material to the prairie for dumping—and so should not be blamed for the river's foul smell—ignored the fact that the heaps of material that decomposed outside the city limits generated their own stinks. It also reflected the frustration of the smaller packers, for whom the dumping on the prairie proved more costly than dumping into the river, putting them at a competitive disadvantage with the larger packers. Much of the defense of the packing industry, in fact, appears to have been presented by the smaller packinghouses.[66]

The smaller houses nonetheless cast themselves as representatives of an industry that employed vast numbers of Chicagoans. Responding directly to E.C.L., another packer wrote a letter to the *Tribune* that blasted the idea of poverty as an acceptable alternative to stinky prosperity as an olfactory conceit of the well-heeled: "Such articles . . . cannot fail to call forth, among a class of people who know nothing [about] what the packers are doing with their blood, lungs and livers, and tank refuse, a deep and intense hatred toward that great branch of industry to which Chicago owes half its population." The sewers created the real problem, the packer insisted. Any action to reduce pollution that harmed the packers threatened to undermine Chicago's claim as the wonder of the hog-butchering world. The indictment of the packing industry unjustly placed the responsibility for "your own filth to a body of men whose enterprise on the shores of our slough elicits the wonder of the world, and of whom we ourselves can be justly proud."[67]

The majority of the voices in the public debate tried to find a middle ground, both acknowledging the downsides of the stinks as well as the benefits that the riverside industries brought to the city. The *Tribune* gave voice to such an approach when it assured readers that it did not share the views of those who wished to see the industries driven from the city or even completely forbidden from using the river itself as a sewer. Those industries, it maintained, "are the life blood of our trade; but for them the Chicago of to-day might still be a trading post, and the Indian's wigwam be not an infrequent object within the present city limits."[68] Yet the stenches produced by the rampant pollution of the river created problems that ultimately threatened the very commercial growth that transformed the city from an Indian trading post to the booming city of the war years.

For one, it drove down property values. "We, as the denizens of this loyal burgh," the *Tribune* announced as early as 1862, "cannot afford to incur the risk of damage to the reputation of the city, consequently to the value of the property therein, and the risk of pestilence which the condition of the river invites, by saying that the evil will correct itself and nothing need to be done."[69] The same year, the Chicago Board of Trade— hardly the voice of commercial restraint—petitioned the mayor and the common council to abate the river stenches because the foul odors made conducting business near the river intolerable. "Without such relief," the board petitioned, "business of all kinds will be driven from [the river], and sickness and death surround us on every hand throughout the city."[70] A resolution followed, demanding that the BPW take immediate steps to clean the river—"the great highway of [Chicago's] prosperity"—to avoid the trade interruptions that could hamstring the city's commerce.[71]

The concern that the offensive state of the river might drive commerce from its banks also brought up worries about how the stinks acted on the noses of workers. The concern related to the board of trade's argument that conducting business near the river had become nearly intolerable to the senses. In June 1862 the *Tribune* worried that the river stinks could hamper work by spreading disease, asking, "What is to become of our vast shipping interest—the men who navigate our tugs and attend to the bridges, and virtually are forced to live during the season amid the intolerable pestilence-breeding stench of the river?"[72] The newspaper predicted that a week of hot weather would drive the workers from the banks, bringing river commerce to a halt. The board's concern was self-serving, focusing on the dangers of stink as a material, disease-inducing matter. Unmentioned was the notion that the workers might be averse to the river's fetid water because they objected to unpleasant smells on aesthetic grounds, a refinement deemed far more likely from the sensitive noses of the board of trade.

This is not to say that discussions about the reek of the river as offensive to the sensibilities of riverside workers were never raised in the public debate. E.C.L.'s letter expressed those concerns, another way the author's opinions represented a minority view. "Is it possible that the mechanics and laboring men of this city, who number thousands and tens of thousands," he wrote in prose that evoked fears of the unwashed masses, "are going to sit tamely down and permit a few wealthy men to corrupt the air and water, . . . in order that they may pile up additional wealth on their already overladen coffers?"[73] As the fear that colors E.C.L.'s language suggests, the concern had little to do with the idea that riverside workers deserved the same olfactory considerations as the residents of finer residential districts. Instead, E.C.L. used the river stinks to invoke the specter of the howling, working-class mob, a fear that haunted the elite sensorium, as we will soon see.

By the closing year of the Civil War, the combined perils of the river stinks had convinced Chicago's civic elite to begin a serious abatement effort. In 1864 a joint committee of city officials and the board of trade studied the problem, issuing a report to a public meeting at the Metropolitan Hall early the next year. The meeting's chair, the attorney Edward Channing Larned, opened the discussion by remarking that the "subject under discussion required no explanation," as "language was inadequate to convey a truthful description of the condition of the river."[74]

The verbal daggers proceeded to fly nonetheless. During the discussion period, Wirt Dexter, an attorney and real estate developer, offered what one reporter generously termed "spirited remarks" about the origins of the stinks of the previous summer. Louis Wahl, the owner of a glue and fertilizer factory on the South Branch that had suspiciously burned to the ground the previous summer, took offense, responding with "an animated discourse" that spiced up what might have been a fairly somber consideration of water pollution. "His remarks being somewhat personal," the *Tribune* noted, Larned called him to order.[75] Wahl's outburst appeared to complicate, though not necessarily to undermine, the meeting's formal resolution that it was "the unanimous will of Chicago that the public waters of the lake and river shall be made pure and healthful," even if that required raising money for the effort with new taxes.[76] The resolution issued two specific recommendations: to reduce future pollution it called for the city to set new licensing procedures for riverside industries; to clean up the river it called for the deepening of the I & M Canal. The so-called deep-cut plan would reverse the Chicago River's flow so that it emptied not into Lake Michigan but into the Illinois River, via the canal.[77]

The idea of reversing the river by deepening the canal had been on engineers' minds for more than two decades. The original plan for the I & M Canal called for the deep-cut approach, but financial difficulties associated with the economic panic of 1837 had forced engineers to dig the canal on the less expensive shallow cut. After the opening of the canal, the city used pumps on the South Branch to reverse the river as a pollution abatement measure, but that approach was expensive. A permanent reversal promised to forever carry the accumulated filth of the river out of the city without expensive pumping; in addition, a deeper canal could handle heavier shipping between Lake Michigan and the Mississippi River (via the Illinois) and thus bolster Chicago's commercial standing. During the 1850s the *Tribune* advocated the deep-cut plan as a clear sanitary and commercial win for the city. The advocacy continued during the war years, taking on a nationalistic tinge as the newspaper argued that creating a connection for heavy shipping between Lake Michigan and the Mississippi River would benefit the Federal Army militarily and forge stronger bonds of the Union more generally.[78]

By the time of the Metropolitan Hall meeting, the suggestion that the city abate the river pollution by deepening the I & M Canal would have surprised few informed observers. The common council wanted to study the matter just the same, so a few days after Dexter and Wahl insulted each other, it appointed a committee of three engineers to do so. The engineers' report rejected an alternative system of intercepting sewers to carry the filth directly into Lake Michigan, because it was untested and expensive. A self-acting system—that is, the deep-cut approach—seemed the best option. The committee further recommended that the city crack down on illegal dumping and continue to use the pumps at Bridgeport to cleanse the river during the construction period, expected to take three years.[79]

The common council approved the deep-cut plan and negotiated an agreement with the trustees of the canal on the construction procedures in the fall of 1865. Construction delays ensued, however. The city fired the initial contractors because they made little discernible progress during the first year of construction, partly due to a dispute over remuneration. The BPW was forced to advertise for bids again in the spring of 1867, just months after the grand celebrations that followed the opening of the lake tunnel. The work continued through the close of the decade.

Finally, on July 15, 1871, workers cut the last temporary dam across the canal at Bridgeport, allowing a strong current from the South Branch to carry the noisome fluid "backward" to the Illinois River and beyond the city. As Chicago's courthouse bell tolled to mark the occasion, official observers watched as fresh water pulled from the lake replaced the polluted water from the South and Main branches of the river, although the North Branch saw less change. One official observer estimated that the fresh lake water had completely replaced the polluted fluid of the South Branch within thirty-six hours.[80]

That the deep cut failed to draw off substantial amounts of water from the North Branch constituted only part of the reason that city officials would, over time, have less cause to celebrate. It turned out that the 1871 reversal held only under certain weather conditions. When the lake dropped to low levels—a natural and frequent development—the current through the Chicago River was simply too weak to play its cleansing role. Yet it would be some time before engineers concluded that the city would have to return to pumping water through the canal in order to cleanse the river, and even longer before they set about another attempt to permanently reverse it. Not until 1900, with the completion of the Sanitary and Ship Canal (at the time, the largest public works project in the nation), would the city succeed in permanently reversing the flow of the river.[81]

In the meantime the city celebrated the completion of another massive public works project that promised to improve its reputation for malodorous living. The *Times,* generally less enthusiastic about costly public works projects than the *Tribune,* proclaimed the great expense worthwhile. Another voice in the local press used the occasion to reflect on Chicago's early reputation as the "nastiest mud-hole on the face of the Earth." Dirty streets and grimy alleys competed with the "richest drinking water in the world" to disgust residents and visitors alike. "Each pitcherful of water that we drew from our hydrants," he wrote, "was a complete epitome of the history of the previous day, along the Chicago River and its redolent branches." Yet it was the river itself, now clean with water from Lake Michigan, that truly tested Chicagoans' olfactory endurance: "Whatever nuisances other cities might boast—whatever shocks to the senses or the sensibilities New York, or Cincinnati, or St. Louis might devise, we knew that none of them could match our river." "We knew it," he explained, "by smell."[82]

CHAPTER 2

SENSORY OVERLOAD

The Chicago Fire, 1871

John G. Shorthall had fire on his mind when he returned from church early on Sunday evening, October 8, 1871. Yet for this Chicagoan it was not the fiery torments of hell he was thinking about, but fire as spectacle, as conveyed through an eyewitness, one Mr. Hibbard. "You should have seen the fire last night," Hibbard told Shorthall and his wife as they walked home from services. An "amazing spectacle," the fire produced flames that "rose higher than [he] had ever seen before." The eyewitness's recounting of the previous evening's fire, one that burned a tiny portion of the city as compared to the impending Great Fire of October 8–9, piqued Shorthall's interest. He wrote later that he thoroughly "regretted that he had not seen" the blaze, even though he thought chasing down fires was better suited to younger men.[1]

Shorthall's regret at missing the spectacle faded later that same evening, along with the romantic notion of fire gazing. As he prepared to retire, he observed a fiery reflection in the clouds from a window, far from the site of the previous night's blaze: "I stood there a few moments and presently concluded—doubtless impressed by Mr. Hibbard's description . . . that I would go out and see it." His own appearance—like so many Chicagoans that night—might have been more reflective of an evening stroll had he changed from his house clothes, but time seemed short. Wearing only his velveteen housecoat, he left home to follow the growing crowd of spectators on Michigan Avenue and across the Harrison Street bridge, all the while keeping a safe northeasterly distance from the flames. Even in its early hours, however, the fire cast a dangerous visage. Shorthall saw it as an "awful exhibition of the fury of flame uncontrolled."

Visual perceptions of the fury soon joined with observations from Shorthall's other senses to compound his fears. As the blaze spread toward downtown, the flames sounded an ominous roar: "I retired before [the fire] as it moved from house to house, continually spreading, and a great stillness was upon the crowds who had gathered; nothing was audible but the roar of the flame and the cracking of the timbers and sheathing of the houses." A deliberate witness, he watched the blaze turn some of the city's finest homes to cinders, all the while recording the pace of the flames. Shorthall saw one large Harrison Street home reduced to nothing but ashes in a short eight minutes.

The observer had little time to linger, however, as the slashing wind and the heat singed his skin. Wrote Shorthall: "The wind was high, very high, from the southwest. I went along with the crowd, retreating before the fire, burning clapboards and smaller stuff carried high over our heads, or falling about us, the air being filled with the glowing particles that were carried on the wind, now risen to a heavy gale. The heat was dreadful; the heat of both air and fire." He managed to reach the Van Buren Street bridge, where he watched as embers of all sizes blew even farther to the north and the east, threatening his office on the corner of Washington and Clark Streets, opposite the courthouse and the county records office.

Shorthall hurried to his office building. He arrived around 1:00 AM to find that the roar of the fire and the slash of the wind had given way to an unsettling silence. The building sounded "as quiet as the grave," with no one afoot, including the usual janitor, whom he had hoped (optimistically) would help him remove the flammable window awnings. Shorthall quickly concluded that the awning project—and the building—represented a lost cause, so he turned his attention to saving his business papers. With a "perfect rain of fire" falling outside the office, he loaded the papers onto a truck whose driver he convinced to stand idle, even as the falling cinders scorched the papers.

At this point the conflagration overwhelmed Shorthall's sensory apparatus. He became numb to the heat and later could not find the words to express what happened around him: "No description is adequate, and yet so wrought up was I, that I did not feel [the fire], barely was conscious of it, while I brushed the burning cinders off the books, and occasionally shook myself to keep free." His driver threatened to abandon him after learning that federal troops planned to create a firebreak by downing buildings nearby, but Shorthall managed to carry out one final batch of books as he dodged the flames licking through the floorboards of his office.

Outside, the fire took down Chicago's courthouse. Shorthall and company fled the danger zone, but still the fire overtaxed his senses. Hearing only the roar of the flames and the "hoarse noise of the frightened, panic stricken crowd," he failed to register the felling of the courthouse bell, a widely reported aural feature of the disaster. Finally, as Shorthall stopped to watch a State Street building melt before his eyes, he lost the composure that had served him so well at his office. The surreal sight of melting brick unnerved him, forcing the release of the emotion pent up during his escape: "The distructability [*sic*] of all material, the instability of substance, even the most impervious shocked me—I saw those walls crumble with the heat, they seemed to melt, slowly, steadily. . . . I cried like a child, and it was some time before I recovered myself sufficiently to go home."[2]

Shorthall's account reveals much about the Great Fire as a multisensory experience. The numbing of sensation that he alluded to—Shorthall "did not feel" the fire, even as he danced over the flames licking through the floorboards—evidences the self-protective instinct that the historian Jörg Friedrich found in survivor accounts of a different kind of firestorm: the bombing of German cities during World War II. The Germans who waited out the bombs in shelters often "blacked out" their perceptual apparatus to create an "armor around sensation and feeling" that helped them cope with the horror. The sensory "cocoon" did not render the experience antiseptic, but it dulled the terrible sensations that might have strained their sanity. Shorthall faced nothing like the massive and prolonged bombing of World War II, but his account underscores how the fire—a disaster that has become a celebrated moment in the history of Chicago—left real trauma, as well as three hundred dead people, in its wake.[3]

At the same time, Shorthall alluded to the fire as a multisensory spectacle—an object of curiosity and marvel. The notion of the Great Conflagration as a multisensory spectacle relates to the idea that large-scale disasters temporarily disrupt the "modernity" of modern life to both terrify and thrill.[4] The fire destabilized sensory perception, registering as chaotic, fantastic, and horrible, and threw up an array of strange sensations that mocked the civic elite's attempts to control Chicago's sensory landscape, doing so only months after the "reversal" of the city's river. The type of sensory overload that Chicagoans faced in October 1871 recalls the historian Mark M. Smith's observation that the modern effort to regulate the senses was often "embarrassed by the power of nature's most ferocious storms."[5] The firestorm of 1871 called into question Chicago's future as a site of modern industrial capitalism. In more immediate terms, however, it tossed victims back into an earlier world, one that resembled the city's pioneer days.

The historical reversion was temporary, but it tested the senses of victims to expose the connections that elites (the authors of the vast majority of survivor accounts) drew between sensory refinement and social distinction. This interpretation of the fire follows the urban and social historians who have questioned the idea that the disaster served as a collective experience that ultimately demonstrated civic unity. As the historians Karen Sawislak and Carl Smith have demonstrated, the Great Fire leveled parts of the city in material terms even while it compelled business and civic elites to maintain hierarchies of class to realize their vision of the city's future.[6] In the fire's aftermath, affluent Chicagoans took charge of the recovery effort. They stressed values—self-reliance, private property, scientific charity—that were deemed essential to the reconstruction in material and class terms although they insisted that they worked on behalf of all Chicagoans. Their particular "sense of urban or civic order," writes Sawislak, included the maintenance of what they saw as a responsible working class.[7]

A sensory approach reinforces such interpretations by highlighting the experiential aspects of the disaster.[8] The immediate experiential aspects are sometimes lost in the effort to uncover the story of relief and rebuilding, but they are crucial if we are to try to understand the disaster's impact on survivors and how they represented that impact in terms of social difference. Middle- and upper-class Chicagoans represented their own experiences of the disaster as special. They suggested that the refined senses of the urban elite were uniquely sensitive to being turned out of doors, in the middle of the night, to mix with the city's poorer classes. If the fire mocked the efforts to control Chicago's sensory landscape, it flattered the idea that social class expressed itself through the senses, a notion that elites used to promote their vision of civic order even while the city burned.

The Fire Nobody Saw

The witnesses who recorded their experiences in Chicago on the night of October 8–9, 1871, described intense physical sensations. Carl Smith has pointed out that a deliberate and self-conscious effort to describe what witnesses feared might have been "indescribable" marks many of the accounts.[9] Claims of indescribability are an age-old feature of disaster literature, he explains, often employed by victims as a testimony to the epic nature of the disaster as well as a candid disclaimer on the limits of the written word. In the case of the Great Chicago Fire, the disclaimers conveyed the witnesses' belief that the blaze had simply overwhelmed their senses, much as Shorthall recalled.

Charles Elliot Anthony, age fifteen at the time of the fire, said as much.[10] The son of a judge, Charles's recollections convey a sense of terror, disorientation, and physical pain. He likened the fire to a "blazing hell" and described in great detail how, upon returning to his home from an initial investigation of the fire elsewhere in the city, he was "enveloped in sparks and scorched with heat." His hat caught fire with such suddenness that it burned most of his hair and eyebrows, which, taken with the soot covering his clothing and skin, rendered him unrecognizable to his father, who initially refused to let him back inside their family home. Charles noted that when he participated in the family's effort to save valuables from the house, he inexplicably grabbed only a collection of currant jelly, as well as his other favorite preserves, which he carried in a drawer he had removed from a mahogany table. He remembered his father confronting him on his surprising decision to save mere breakfast foods, but nonetheless noted that he refused to give up the items, which were saved, despite the judge's objections.[11]

Charles's experiences seemed to exceed his senses. "How did we act while the fire was cree[p]ing up on us?" he asked rhetorically. "To tell the truth," he confessed, "without exception each one [of] us except the younger boys was ready to break any minute from the mental strain and physical exhaustion." Charles then conveyed how the fire rendered his own attempts to describe the experience nearly impossible: "This fire cannot be written in the third person nor can it be adequately described. Above us was a phantasmagoria of terrifying fantastic images of red demons now charging upon us and then retreating." Charles then shifted from visual to aural language when he likened the fire to a "cannonade," writing that his senses registered "a crash of falling walls amid a hurricane of dense black smoke, gummed with sparks of fiery darts." The whole evening constituted a "debacle of seventy-five thousand men, women and children trying to escape destruction!" "It was like a dream!" he concluded in a remark that captured how the fire rendered the most familiar aspects of the city strange and unstable.

Similar claims of sensory overload run through the official accounts of the fire, including the Chicago Relief and Aid Society's report on the provision of relief. The report observed that a complete and accurate account of the burning of the city was probably impossible, given the "stifling clouds of dust, smoke, and cinders, and the confusion and utter chaos of the night." The whole experience constituted a "picture of appalling horror, distinct in its outlines, weird in its dark shadings, but utterly incapable of verbal representation."[12] The visual language utilized here—"picture," "outlines," "shadings"—suggests that the fire seemed especially powerful because it undermined the eye's powers of observation. The failure of witnesses to "see" the fire as a whole came through in other published works, including Elias Colbert and Everett Chamberlin's *Chicago and the Great Conflagration* (1872) published only months after the fire. The authors wrote that they, too, believed the fire was incomprehensible as a sensory event. "The sensations conveyed to the spectator of this unparalleled event, either through the eye, the ear, or other senses or sympathies, can not be adequately described, and any attempt to do it but shows the poverty of language," they argued.[13]

Yet the authors seemed particularly struck by how the fire challenged the eye's sense of perspective. Noting that they were unable to provide a detailed account of the fire's progress, they "merely noted the general course of the devouring element." They went on to explain that, "as a spectacle," the fire was "beyond doubt the grandest as well as most appalling ever offered to mortal eyes." Even from "any elevated standpoint, the appearance was that of a vast ocean of flame, sweeping in long billows and breakers over the doomed city."[14] While Colbert and Chamberlin's characterization of the fire's magnitude may have suffered from the type of hyperbole employed in published accounts to catch readers' interest, it nevertheless echoed the nonpublished accounts when it claimed that the fire simply could not have been "seen" adequately by any one observer.

One important observer who failed to see the blaze—in this case as a result of individual incompetence—was the city's central fire watchman. Chicago maintained an extensive alarm system that depended both on sight and sound to function properly. A telegraph alarm network, installed in 1865 and upgraded in the months before the fire, allowed citizens to notify the central alarm office, located in the downtown courthouse, by activating one of the numbered alarm boxes located throughout the city. The city also stationed a central watchman in the cupola of the courthouse. Should the watchman spot a fire before the central office received a telegraph alarm—either because the alarm box was never activated or because the signal failed to reach the courthouse—he estimated the location of the fire visually. The central office's operator then used the estimate to dispatch firefighters by ringing the courthouse bell to identify the nearest signal box and by sending a telegraph signal to the individual fire companies.[15]

The contingency system went into motion on the night of October 8 when the initial efforts to alert the central office from a telegraph alarm box near the site of the initial flare-up failed. According to H. A. Musham, a naval architect who wrote the first carefully documented analysis of the fire, the responsibility then fell to the courthouse watchman, who, shortly after 9:00 PM, spotted a growing fire on the city's South Side. The watchman, Musham explained, "located [the fire] through his spyglass" to coordinate with the operator to sound the alarm. Despite his spot high in the cupola of the courthouse and the use of a spyglass, the watchman misread the location of the blaze, directing firefighters to an alarm box fully one mile south of the site of the actual fire. Making matters worse, the operator who sounded the alarm refused to correct the mistake, because he feared that sounding a different alarm would confuse the firefighters who were, he reasoned, bound to see that they were headed in the wrong direction. Some fire companies did correct course quickly, but they lost precious time. Musham concluded that the watchman's mistake, coupled with the refusal to quickly sound the correct alarm tones, contributed to the firefighters' failure to control the initial flare-up. Had the watchman used his spyglass with greater skill, he wrote, the fire might have been quelled fairly quickly [16]

The civilian witnesses saw the fire in varied ways, depending on their physical location but also their personal relationship to the city. For many who happened to be passing through Chicago the fire represented an exciting, if dangerous, visual spectacle. Nine years after the Great Fire, Mrs. Alfred Hebard recorded her experiences as she stopped at Chicago's Palmer House hotel to rest with her family en route to their home in Iowa. The fire had forced the Hebards from their beds, a frightening experience but one that also generated some exciting sights. Mrs. Hebard acknowledged that her own status as an out-of-town visitor allowed her to follow the fire without any great anxiety for personal property, but she also noted her satisfaction at seeing for herself the grand urban fire. "Since it *was to be,*" she reflected, "I have never regretted that we were allowed to see with our own eyes that burning city."[17]

Another witness, William Gallagher, a student at the Chicago Theological Seminary, shared Mrs. Hebard's notion that the fire constituted a grand, history-making spectacle that he was proud to have seen. Writing to his sister a few days after the fire, Gallagher described how he and his fellow seminarians climbed to the roof of the seminary building to watch a "sight such as I never expect to see again, and which few men have had the privilege of witnessing."[18] He believed that even the most talented writers would probably never capture the full range of the sights, though the seminarian made a try. The main body of flame—more than two miles long and one mile wide—blew through the downtown business district on the strength of gale winds, a sight for which his position on the seminary roof provided an unobstructed view. "We were situated where we could take in the whole at a sight, and such a view! Such a magnificent sight!" he crowed. The felling of the downtown buildings proved both exciting and sobering. "It was a grand sight and yet an awful one," he remarked in a comment that underscored how the massive scope of the fire forced even the most enthusiastic observers to consider its cruel significance.

Gallagher also recorded how the massive blaze disoriented his own sense of sight by almost literally turning night into day. "The whole city was as light as day," he wrote to his sister, noting that he might have easily read a newspaper as he stood on the seminary roof to watch the blaze unfold.[19] Common in many witness accounts, the unnatural daylight effect appeared often in visual depictions of the disaster, including Currier and Ives's widely circulated lithograph "The Burning of Chicago," in which a large swath of the city center appears fully illuminated and an eerie glow extends far into Lake Michigan to make the ships at anchor visible from the shore (see fig. 3). What the lithograph fails to capture is how other features of the fire—the crowded routes out of the city, the showers of cinders falling from the sky, as well as the dust and sand kicked up by the high winds—overwhelmed the visual clarity that may have followed from the daylight effect.

Thomas Harding Ellis, writing almost two months after the conflagration, told his younger brother about the challenges of seeing the fire clearly as well as the great pain inflicted upon his eyes by the blowing sand, smoke, and heat. With eyes inflamed and bleeding from the exposure, Ellis found relief only when his wife bathed them in milk.[20] The whole affair left him feeling and looking much like veterans of the most "protracted and bloody engagement[s]" of the Civil War, a condition his veteran brother knew all too well.[21] Other witnesses echoed Ellis's Civil

War analogy, a literary decision that made sense given the memories of the South's burning cities during the war and the post-fire media narrative about the individual heroism in Chicago. Signaling the lingering place of the Civil War in the national mind, the analogies at once suggested that Chicago would emerge a stronger, unified city after the fire, much as the nation had after 1865. As Carl Smith has argued, however, the Civil War analogies also hinted that a fundamental conflict, namely the growing tensions between labor and capital, loomed over the city.[22]

In the meantime the soot and dust threatened to render Ellis unrecognizable, an example of how the fire confused efforts to visualize social distinction. In the midst of the sensory chaos created by the blaze, people looked for visual markers of social class—the dominant index in the preindustrial city—only to find them unclear.[23] Aurelia R. King, the wife of the president of the Chicago Relief and Aid Society, described such confusion when she wrote about her retreat through the city cemetery, a space that had been recently transformed into Lincoln Park. Although the transformation (including the relocation of the interred) had started long before the fire, many of the newly vacant grave pits remained open. Mrs. King and her children threw down their belongings among the empty pits as others took shelter in them.[24]

She observed that the whole night presented strange and unsettling sights. Friends and neighbors were so blackened with soot that only "some look of the eye or some motion" revealed their identity; even more unsettling for Mrs. King, many of the city's respectable classes had been reduced to half-dressed refugees. Fleeing the city under such desperate circumstances proved so unsettling that she later struggled to strike the scenes from her memory: "It seems to me that I can never resume the even tenor of my way, my nerves are so unstrung," she wrote days after the fire. Sleep was difficult. When Mrs. King began to dream, she found herself "forever running from fires with my children and a bundle," a terrible vision that wrenched her to consciousness.[25]

Other witnesses testified to what the novelist Edward P. Roe termed the fire's "awful democracy" when they expressed shock at seeing the city's wealthiest residents retreating through the streets alongside poor people.[26] The sensory refinement that signaled social distinction for the middle and upper classes implied greater sensitivity to the rigors of the outdoors, to say nothing of a sudden and harried retreat from the city. The coarsened senses of the poor—for instance, their presumed comfort with river stench—rendered them less sympathetic as victims. Social distinction proved challenging to maintain in the hurly-burly of the blaze itself, but the sensorial concepts of social class nonetheless emerged clearly in the accounts of witnesses. Social difference, as much as shared experience, defined the fire to the senses of many survivors.

Some witnesses described the sight of wealthy people turned out of their homes as the most unsettling of the entire affair. Emma Hambelton wrote that the fire leveled social distinctions even as it highlighted them. As she fled from her North Side home, she was shaken by the sight of the streets filled with "families of the richest men in Chicago . . . some lost, and many sitting right on the pavement for a moment's breath, dressed in velvets, silk and jewels they were trying to save."[27] The sight of the rich reduced to refugee status also shook victims who escaped to the northern prairie, large sections of which were illuminated by the flames in the city. Gilbert Merrill, a nineteen-year-old telegraph operator, told his mother that the light from the fire made the sight of "thousands and thousands of human beings of all classes and nationalities" waiting out the fire on the prairie visible for miles in every direction. He took special note of meeting a wealthy family who had been "cast homeless and poor with starvation staring them in the face" as a result of the fire. When a woman in the wealthy family—clad in a "splendid dress and magnificent jewelry"—asked him if he thought the fire might reach as far north as Lincoln Park (where, presumably, she lived), Merrill answered in the affirmative, but then found himself so distressed by his questioner's reaction that he had to leave the scene.[28]

Sawislak observed that the fire proved troubling to middle-class Chicagoans because it interrupted the peace and quiet of their home, the institution that sheltered them from the outside world.[29] The sounds of the fire proved especially powerful in this way, further suggesting how the blaze mocked the larger attempt to organize the sensory environment of the city. Although the courthouse bells tolled the alarm within one hour after the initial outbreak—a pealing that rang in ears throughout the city—the victims who had been enjoying a quiet evening at home heard of the fire in different, though equally disturbing, ways. Samuel Greeley, a surveyor by trade, completely failed to register the clanging of the alarm bells. He was awakened instead by a "slight rattle of falling cinders upon roofs and sidewalks."[30] Rising to see a serious fire from his window but no sense of alarm in the homes nearby, Greeley took it upon himself to wake the neighborhood. "I shouted 'fire, fire,' with all my force," he wrote. Lights illuminated in windows and people began to peek their heads out to investigate the source of the commotion. One groggy neighbor, "more sleepy or more stupid than the rest," expressed with great force "his wrath at the disturber of the city's peace, and enquired explosively what was the matter with the fellow on the roof yelling like a maniac in the middle of the night."[31]

As the conflagration grew, however, Greeley faced a chaotic and terrifying sensory upheaval. The gale-force wind howled, and yet the "roar of the flames and of falling walls was more appalling." Suddenly Greeley heard "a crash like a broadside of artillery" and saw a "vast jet of smoke and sparks shot up to heaven." Then the walls of the courthouse collapsed (other witnesses marked that event at 2:00 AM), sending a ground tremor that he felt even though he stood almost one mile from the site. Greeley noted that he could still see the stars above; the glow struck him as incongruously placid: "All nature seemed pitilessly indifferent to the fury and turmoil." The contrast between the quiet order of the heavens and the fury of the burning city, to his mind, stood as one between "relentless fate" and the writhing of a "mob of terrified and helpless mortals."[32]

Victims heard the contrast between the quietude of the home and the rumble of the city's evacuation as disconcerting or terrifying. Martin Stamm, the new pastor of Chicago's First Evangelical Church, was meditating upon a sermon he heard earlier in the day when the first peals of the alarm reached his ears. A great commotion on the street in front of the parsonage followed. "Walking, running, cries, the rumbling of many wagons, and fire engines and signals from their steam whistles gave me to understand that we were in great danger," Stamm said.[33] Signaling that the fire had indeed grown dire, the courthouse bell stopped tolling the location of the flames; instead, it pealed continuously to sound the general alarm. At that point the pastor concluded that the firefighters had lost control of the blaze and that it threatened the entire city. Venturing out to determine the best evacuation route, Stamm gave strict instructions to his wife to remain indoors until he returned. Though he tried his best to project calm, his family failed to contain their fright. "All began to weep and cry" when he left the house.[34] For Stamm, too, the entire experience proved nerve-shattering. The flight from the city—as well as the sight of the dead victims of the fire the following day—made him fearful to spend time alone for more than one month afterwards. The "cries . . . of the dead" continued to ring in his ears, a problem worsened by the "extraordinary exertions" involved in his own flight from the flames.[35]

Chicagoans fled the burning city by traveling to the West Side, which the flames spared; by moving east to huddle on the shore of Lake Michigan; or by outpacing the fire by escaping north. Many accounts emphasized the exposure of the city's better sorts to the awful democracy of the blaze at the lakeshore. Lavina Clark Perkins, an educator in Chicago's public schools, argued that the suffering was greatest for those who fled to the shore of the lake. Cutting off escape to the north, the fire forced hundreds of victims to the beach, where the smoke and torrid air forced them to wade into the water itself, leaving their personal possessions scattered on the sands. Even worse, the blowing cinders eventually burned the victims' belongings and drove the motley crowd—"rich & poor . . . mothers with young children . . . children with helpless parents"—further into the waves, crowding them together like cattle in a situation that grew more and more perilous.[36]

The author of one of the best-known fictional accounts of the conflagration, Roe, similarly highlighted the scene at the lake as one that brought special dangers to middle-class people. In his 1872 best seller, *Barriers Burned Away*, Roe's protagonist, gentleman Dennis Fleet, fled with his love interest, the aristocratic Christine Ludolph, to the lakeshore, where he found an "unparalleled disaster [in which] all social distinctions were lost, leveled like the beach" on which the victims huddled.[37] Roe did not mean that social class became irrelevant in the midst of the disaster; instead his observation referred to the unwelcome—and dangerous—mixing of the rich and poor as that which "erased" social distinctions.

Refined sensory habits hinted at the class status of the individuals mixing at the lakeshore. While respectable Chicagoans quietly prayed or inquired about loved ones, the poor guzzled whiskey they had stolen from abandoned taverns. The result was an uproarious drunkenness that threatened Christine's sensibilities as well as her physical safety. The unruly poor—the "drunken, howling, fighting wretches"—had been set free to act out their basest instincts and so "committed excesses that cannot be mentioned," including salutes of the most "obscene epithets and words."[38] All this proved too much for Christine, Dennis thought, as her "luxurious past" had "shielded [her] from every rough experience," precisely the kind of sensory refinement that signaled social distinction."[39] Only the strong presence of Dennis (armed with a pistol he had earlier wrestled from a villain intent on raping Christine) allowed her to remain composed. Dennis's heroism underlined how the social mixing wrought by the fire challenged the gendered prerogatives of the urban middle class, here Christine's need to maintain what the historian John Kasson terms "privacy in public"—the need to shield oneself from violations of female modesty, in the form of prying eyes, rough language, and even potential assault.[40]

The survivor accounts focus less on criminal assault on the lakeshore, an aspect of the fire that played out chiefly in rumors and after-the-fact storytelling, than on the less dramatic ways the fire forced victims to navigate a chaotic sensory landscape, rubbing elbows with persons they would have preferred to keep at a distance. West Side resident Charles Monreau Sampson, a former colonel in the Union Army, penned a letter to his aunt only days after the fire that gave voice to such fears. Sampson's wife had roused him from his sleep around midnight to investigate the bizarrely lightened sky. The former officer dressed hastily and started for the downtown to check on his business, quickly becoming enveloped in a crowd that seemed to have a life of its own. "Imagine . . . everybody moving at once and all in one direction as they were on Michigan, Wabash Ave. and State St.," he wrote.[41]

The downtown arteries were clogged with vehicles and the sidewalks were crowded with people carrying household possessions, including furniture, that they hoped to remove to safety. In breathless prose, Sampson then described how the noise of the crowded avenues indicated a frightful lack of direction: "Everybody excited, no one knew which way to go or what to do. Women and children lost and alone, crying, screaming and kicking; . . . horses as wild and frantic as the people." Even worse, some of the men who drove the delivery wagons that might have been used to save victims' property had become drunk, a frightful spectacle that raised fears of mob rule. "Draymen worse than the horses by the addition of liquor," Sampson wrote in a comment that echoed the pious Dennis Fleet's concern for his beloved Christine.[42]

The sights and sounds of the flight from the city reflected the reality of a chaotic and frightful evacuation more than the reality of widespread looting and violence.[43] They nevertheless drove some to create private security patrols to quell the riot, more imagined than real, before it got out of hand. When William Gallagher and his fellow seminarians returned home later Monday evening, they formed a patrol, because they feared that angry roughs might not rest until the city lay in ashes. "You see," he wrote to his sister, "we were much more exposed to danger than ever before, for the fire had 'cleaned out' some of the foulest dens of the city, and all the roughs naturally resorted to our side of the city."[44] Gallagher's roughs were "infuriated with drink, and swore that the west side should be burned too." Since the high winds still raked the city, and since the city's main water supply had failed earlier that day, the seminarians feared that they would be unable to stop the incendiaries. The fear stemmed not from actual incendiary activity, however; it was instead a function of how the people he saw as criminal asserted themselves sensorially—loud, drunk, and dirty—to threaten the peace of Gallagher's neighborhood. His objections to the behavior of the rogues reflected his commitment to maintain reposed and sober, sensory habits that were more akin to his class station.[45]

Even for those victims who escaped to the prairie, the sudden exposure to the elements meant great physical strain. "They say people in every class of life are out of doors," Mary Fales, the wife of a local lawyer, wrote to her mother in a comment that indicated her concern for the refined senses of the affluent.[46] Writing six days after the blaze from a safe distance in Waukegan, Illinois, James W. Milner elaborated on Fales's astonishment when he noted how the affluent women who fled to the prairie were forced to endure a rainy night without shelter or food. "Women who had never before lacked any comfort," he explained, "spent Monday night in the open air, with hours [of] heavy rainfall."[47]

A visitor to Chicago, Thomas D. Foster, described a similar concern for the well-heeled in a letter to his parents composed three weeks after the disaster. The city's North Side had been "swept out clear and clean," leaving seventy-five thousand of its residents without shelter and leveling virtually every house. "Altogether," he reported, "one hundred thousand people were rendered homeless and had to camp out on the prairie without any covering for two days and two nights, having little to eat and scarcely any water to drink." Foster found the scene on the prairie distressing: "Delicate people, young children of all classes, huddled together without any comforts." Foster's sympathy for rich as well as poor extended only to children, however. Nowhere did he note the concrete ways in which the fire turned out worse for less affluent Chicagoans—that is, victims who might have lacked the official connections and financial resources to endure the hardship.[48]

Sensing Ruin

Foster's immediate ideas about the scale of homelessness after the fire proved remarkably accurate. Popular notions, however, assessed the damage wrought by the fire in epic terms, implying that it completely destroyed the city. Such notions understandably gained fuel from the magnitude of the sensory and emotional strain rather than a cold, objective assessment of the loss in lives and property. The loss of life was real, but modest considering the scale of the disaster. As stated above, estimates pegged the number of dead at around three hundred out of a population of roughly three hundred thousand.

Chicagoans came to learn that the burnt district—visual depictions of which circulated widely in the national media—covered nearly 3½ square miles of their city, laying waste to much of downtown and leveling the North Side (see fig. 4). The fire destroyed more than seventeen thousand buildings and almost one hundred thousand homes, generating property losses of nearly $200 million, or fully one-third of the valuation of the city as a whole. The fire turned 28 miles of city streets and 120 miles of sidewalk to cinder. It did comparatively little damage to the Chesbrough's 1855 sewer system, although the city's water works suffered. While the water tower remained standing (to later serve as a symbol of the city's persistence), fifteen thousand water pipes were melted or broken, leading to a merciless water shortage in the aftermath of the blaze.[49] At the same time, the fire spared the large bulk of the West Side as well as critical economic resources such as the Union Stockyards and the network of railroad tracks that made Chicago the trading center of the mid-continent.[50]

For many readers of the national and international media, widely published pictures of Chicago's ruins suggested that the city lay in waste. Survivors may have shared such impressions, although they also faced the more personal consequences of emotional trauma. H.W.S. Cleveland, for one, struggled to shed the sensorial "armor" he had created to cope with the fire. A landscape architect, he visited his office to recover valuables once he heard travel was safe. Yet even then he "could hardly trust his senses" and could not shake the "feeling of a reprieved animal." Most of the members of his family felt the same way. Conceptualizing the disaster in objective terms was simply not possible so soon after their senses had been so strained. "What with the fatigue and suffering of the hours of anxiety we had passed in the face of the blinding storm of wind & dust," he wrote, "we all felt bewildered & I constantly found myself trying to force my mind to grasp the situation and take a logical view of the consequences."[51]

A logical analysis of the situation was all the more difficult because the familiar landmarks that Cleveland had used to find his way around the city had been cleared away by the flames. The absence of visual landmarks also struck Charles Elliot Anthony as disorienting and tragic. As he returned home with his father two days after the fire, he came face-to-face with what he termed a "black Sahara" of ruin. "The fire was of such blow-pipe force that it had burned the pavement in the street and the

47

wooden sidewalks," leaving the iron tracks of the railway "bent, twisted and curved into all kinds of fantastic shapes." Eventually they found their home burned to the ground.[52] On Tuesday afternoon, John G. Shorthall surveyed even broader desolation. As he looked north toward Lincoln Park from Madison Street, he spied "two and a half miles . . . with everything in the intervening space utterly destroyed," an observation that indicates the scale of the loss for residents of the North Side.[53]

Other survivors found their sense of hope drained by the confusing maze of ruins. Lawyer Jonas Hutchinson wrote as much to his mother the day after the fire. "Ghastly obelisks are the only signboards to tell the stroller among the ruins where he is," he explained. "One has to ask where such a street *was* in order to get his bearing." With smoke still rising from the debris, he found it difficult to see clearly at all. "I don't know what I shall do," the lawyer concluded.[54] The felling of the courthouse bell created a similarly lamentable aural disorientation. "The court house bell," James Sheahan and George Upton observed, "which for so many years had given hourly warning of the flight of time, raging forth joyous peals in honor of military and civil victories," lay in waste. It lay a "shapeless mass, surrounded by heaps of brick, mortar and stone," much like the burnt district itself.[55]

Yet other observers of the burnt district chipped at the courthouse bell for souvenirs, a small example of the effort to remember the disaster as a history-making spectacle. The "history" that some observers created in the immediate aftermath of the fire amounted to an inventive effort to aestheticize the destruction. Journalists capitalized on the historical reversion suggested by the fallen buildings in order to boost the city's cultural capital, another example of how the affluent classes sensed the disaster in elite terms. Here, too, the spectacle registered on multiple senses. The urban historian Jeffrey H. Jackson's study of Paris's 1910 flood is a telling example of how historians have studied efforts to aestheticize ruins visually.[56] Photographs of the flood, he explains, conveyed a sense of enduring beauty to help Parisians interpret the meaning of disaster and the importance of recovery. The "visual mythology" of the photographs evoked the city's past to cast the flood as an epic story that was appropriate for one of Europe's cultural capitals.

An epic interpretation of the fire suited Chicago well; quite unlike Paris, the Windy City lacked a majestic historical tradition.[57] Sheahan and Upton made the case in their reflections on a nighttime stroll through the burnt district, "Chicago by Moonlight." When they listened to the ruined business district, they heard an incongruous stillness. "The busy men are gone," they wrote. "Nothing is heard but the steady footfall of the patrolman, or the quicker steps of someone hurrying to reach his home."[58] The absence of the productive sounds of trade did not suggest economic paralysis; rather, it indicated how "the prosaic and the commonplace have disappeared forever." Chicago had become the site of a monumental event, one that paused the "hum of the myriads" and the "many-voiced utterances of men" that typically resounded downtown.[59]

The smell of the ruins brought to mind associations with an older, even biblical, historical tradition. "Here there is no feeling of newness," wrote Sheahan and Upton. The "odor that one perceives" did not resemble charred masonry but evoked "a reminiscence of frankincense and myrrh," swung by "cowled and girdled monks or corpulent friars." The use of the ruins to give the city a long historical pedigree colored many of the literary and journalistic assessments of the fire's meaning; indeed, the two authors could not resist the temptation to point out the overuse of such rhetoric. "If it were not so hackneyed," they wrote, "one would be apt to quote certain lines concerning Melrose Abbey."[60]

Other observers lamented that the ruins lost their sensorial majesty too quickly, an all too sudden return of the vulgar world of trade and striving. One, W. A. Croffut, found the sights of improvised business fronts among the ruins disorienting and ugly. "Mammon's invasion" besotted the ruins as burned-out business owners conducted trade out of their homes. In place of the silence that highlighted historical significance, Croffut's ears rattled with the noises of carpentry, a "clatter of hammers" that sounded "as if the ruins were being knocked down to relic hunters by an enraged auctioneer." The air smelled not of the biblical fragrance referenced by Sheahan and Upton, but of a "resinous odor" that indicated how the ruins had become the "Mecca of sign painters," some of whom offended the eye with crude spelling errors, such as the merchant who advertised "SHOOES." "The carelessness and recklessness with which commerce has dropped down into dwelling houses, . . ." Croffut groaned, "is grotesque." A visual offense to the once "aristocratic thoroughfares," the business fronts combined the residential with the commercial to mar the beauty of the ruins.[61]

Not all observers of the ruins were so pessimistic about Chicago's cultural credentials or its future. J. B. Runnion penned an essay on Chicago's pre-fire art scene to argue that the city would not have to rebuild its high culture from scratch. For now, a quick and earnest rebuilding was best.

He heard the pleasant sounds of progress in the burnt district as the "busy bees in great hives" hummed to get business back on track. When he thought of olfactory metaphors to capture such progress, he wrote of the cleansing scent of Lake Michigan rather than two types of resin mentioned by the reports above, the biting odor of carpenters' material or the portentous whiffs of biblical offerings. Just as settlers had erased the "foot-tracks of the Indian with brick and mortar," Chicago's civic leaders would construct a new skyline where the ruins stood.[62]

The city's booster class echoed Runnion's sentiment, creating the well-known recovery narrative that still rings in Chicago's collective ear.[63] The unbounded optimism of the recovery story—in which Chicago rose, "Phoenix like" from the ashes—anticipated a remarkable reconstruction. Much like Runnion's, the ears of the city's leaders rang when they heard the pleasant sounds of productivity, which Sheahan and Upton termed the "clink of the trowel and the stroke of hammer."[64] The city as a whole enjoyed a post-fire economic boom as land values in the burnt district actually increased in anticipation of future growth. The rebuilding process unfolded at a breakneck pace, literally. A sign of the haste with which city leaders sought to rebuild the city is that, as the historian Kevin Rozario has pointed out, more people died from accidents associated with rebuilding than were killed in the fire itself.[65] The city itself had largely recovered within two years, but as those deaths hinted, Chicago would soon face a new series of upheavals involving the rights of labor.

FIGURE 1. In the nineteenth century, lithographic "bird's-eye" views circulated widely in the consumer marketplace. This one depicts Chicago's downtown business district and its eponymous river. The river's main branch enters the city from Lake Michigan at the right corner of the image, eventually dividing into the North and South branches.

As a feature of nineteenth-century visual culture, bird's-eye views empowered sight by rendering entire cities visible at one glance. The perspective lifted viewers above street level (and often ignored aesthetically objectionable elements such as pollution) to cast urban space as ordered and sanitized so as to encourage investment and civic pride.

For visitors to Chicago, however, low-hanging air pollution made seeing the expanse of the city practically impossible from any perspective. Arriving in 1909, the journalist John Callan O'Laughlin termed the grimy air of the business district an "offense to the eye." He also found downtown loud and malodorous—a "dirty house with a hubbub of noise." Drawing connections between filth, vice and vulgarity, he declared Chicago an unhealthy civic order ("Grime and Noise Mar Chicago Life," *Chicago Tribune*, October 4, 1909, 1).

(Lithographer—Poole Bros., 1898; ICHi-14892, Chicago History Museum.)

FIGURE 2. Upton Sinclair's novel *The Jungle* (1906) made Chicago's "Bubbly Creek" an infamous feature of the city's landscape. A sewer for the surrounding meatpacking houses, the slough literally bubbled from the decomposition of the blood, offal, and other waste. The waste also formed solid cakes. The man in this image strikes an investigatory pose on one, no doubt whiffing stench.

Yet debates about the smell of the Chicago River's polluted sloughs had long resounded in the city's newspapers. Writing in 1876, one author insisted that the awful stinks bothered few people in Bridgeport, a working-class Irish neighborhood that abutted Bubbly Creek. In "The Stench Nuisance," he claimed that Bridgeport was "inhabited by people who have grown accustomed" to stench, arguing that it only annoyed when it wafted into affluent neighborhoods. The people in Bridgeport "would rather endure [stench] than take the trouble to make any other disposition of the garbage and offal," an olfactory vulgarity that offended the noses of the affluent classes and served as a marker of social distinction ("The Stench Nuisance," *Chicago Tribune*, August 20, 1876, 4.)

(DN-0056839, *Chicago Daily News* negatives collection, Chicago History Museum.)

FIGURE 3. This lithograph captured the oft-described "daylight effect" created by the massive blaze. It does not, however, capture how the flying debris and dust inhibited victims' efforts to see their way through the city. In addition, the flames pictured above are blowing in the wrong (south-southwest) direction. The winds blew from the southwest, pushing the flames in a northeasterly direction.

(Lithographer—Currier and Ives, 1871; ICHi-02954, Chicago History Museum.)

FIGURE 4. This map of the "burnt district" shows the fire's point of origin in Chicago's Southwest Side (at the upper left corner). The fire spread in a northeasterly direction before it finally stopped around Lincoln Park, on the far right.

The map shows the fire's destructive impact in the central business district (the innermost circle) as well as its terrible effect on the North Side, all in arresting red ink. Yet the map's perspective is limited because it does not situate the burnt district into the city limits in their entirety. The fact that the Great Conflagration burned less than one-quarter of the city's built-up territory is not clear, because the map, like the fire itself, largely neglected Chicago's South and West Sides, including the crucial economic infrastructure housed there.

(R. P. Studley Company, 1871; ICHi-02870, Chicago History Museum.)

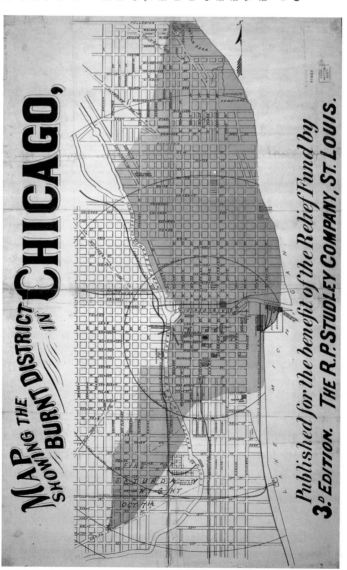

MAP SHOWING THE BURNT DISTRICT IN CHICAGO,

Published for the benefit of the Relief Fund by
3.º EDITION. THE R.P.STUDLEY COMPANY, ST. LOUIS.

FIGURE 5. Industrialist George M. Pullman announced plans to build his "model" company town in the aftermath of the national Railroad Strike of 1877. Repelled by the violent clashes between strikers and federal troops in Chicago, he resolved to tame working-class protest by retraining the senses of his employees. His model town, located fourteen miles south of Chicago, immersed resident-employees in a clean, manicured environment to break what Pullman saw as workers' vulgar sensory habits and the political radicalism those habits nurtured.

In 1885 the economist Richard T. Ely delivered a critical critique of Pullman's town, challenging the serenity and contentment that others saw in its residents as an illusion. In the accompanying image, the Hotel Florence is a fitting focal point, as the inn looks out onto the town's famously clean streets. Pullman urged tourists to see his town—and its model residents—for themselves. Ely listened as well, however, finding a stifling silence that led him to question the experiment in industrial relations. Ely's critique was prescient, as the experiment later exploded in the 1894 Pullman Strike.

(Adapted from Richard T. Ely, "Pullman: A Social Study," *Harper's New Monthly Magazine*, February 1885.)

Palace Car Works.   Hotel.

MAP OF PULLMAN

PULLMAN.

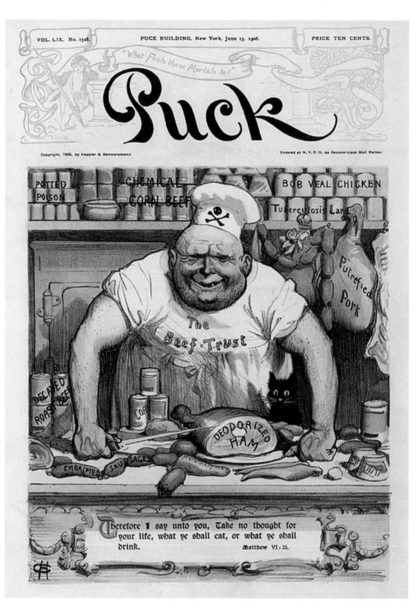

FIGURE 6. *Puck*, a humor magazine, invoked the fear sparked by Upton Sinclair's novelistic exposé of Chicago's meatpacking industry, *The Jungle* (1906). The cover captures an irony of the exposé: it turned readers' stomachs with disgusting descriptions of meatpacking to reveal how mass production scrubbed meat—the "embalmed sausage," "chemical corn beef," and "deodorized ham"—of the unpalatable sights, smells, and tastes that traditionally warned against unsafe food. Chicago's meatpackers had defeated the most basic food safety test—sensory inspection—leaving consumers vulnerable to the machinations of "The Beef Trust."

At the same time, Sinclair, a committed socialist, emphasized how the meatpacking industry robbed workers of their sensory faculties. He argued that the repetitive, gory work of meat processing degraded the senses. The packing plants transformed workers into animalistic creatures not unlike the livestock itself.

(*Puck*, June 13, 1906.)

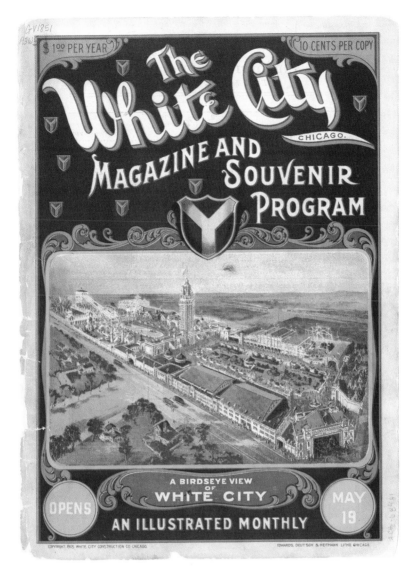

FIGURE 7. Opened in May 1905, the White City amusement park sat at Sixty-third Street and South Park Avenue in Chicago's South Side. The park charged a modest ten-cent admission fee and streetcars stopped nearby, making it accessible to working- and middle-class patrons across the city.

White City appealed to all five senses, featuring a 250-foot tower lighted with electricity to attract the eye, outdoor concerts to delight the ear, mechanical rides for haptic thrills, and restaurants to treat the senses of smell and taste. In advance of opening day, the *Tribune* reported that "almost any sensation" was available at the park ("'White City' Soon," *Chicago Tribune*, May 14, 1905, 7).

White City's developers would have cautioned that respectable sensations were on offer. The pristine bird's-eye view above reflected the promise of propriety and cleanliness. The park's operators promoted their resort as a balm to urban ills, arguing that it enhanced civic health by rejuvenating the senses of its patrons.

(Lithographer—Edwards, Deutsch & Heitmann, 1905; ICHi-68481, Chicago History Museum.)

respectively into the tanks →
and →  . She also
gave an exhibition of fancy
swim ming.

This brings us back to our starting
point – to the exit gate →.
This →  shows the
tower at night. It looks
very beautiful and this → is another
night view. (By the
enclosures you see that  these
little photos may be en- larger
. Referring to the enlarged copy:) The
round object in the sky is the moon.
In the background are the Chutes, the
County Fair, the Devils' Gorge, and at the
extreme left the Shooting gallery. This
photo will give you an idea of the superb
lighting effect at night of the White

FIGURE 8. Letter from John S. Reid Jr. to Hilda M. Sweet, December 25, 1908, page 18. (Manuscript, ICHi-68482; Chicago History Museum.)

TO QUIET THE ROAR OF THE MOB

George M. Pullman's Model Town

In the second half of the 1870s the clink of the trowel gave way to the roar of the mob. On July 29, 1877, as Chicago reeled from a series of violent protests in support of the national railroad strike, the *Tribune* warned that labor politics echoed in new and disturbing ways. The pitched battle between the strikers and federal troops around the Halstead Street viaduct three days earlier suggested that a full-blown working-class insurrection might take hold of the city.

Americans could no longer assume that the truly "dangerous classes" confined themselves to the other side of the Atlantic. The nation's exemption from class conflict was a "pleasing theory," but it no longer held. Increased rates of immigration and the dwindling supply of open lands out west had created the same type of densely populated cities that fostered the radical upheavals in France and Great Britain. Immigration brought "crowds of the worst" European classes to native soil, where they lived in "crowded tenement houses" and spread "their ignorance, their prejudices, their hatred of the rich, and their revolutionary doctrines." Communists could be found in Chicago, where they assaulted the ears of passersby with their "revilings of capital and their exhortations to violence in saloons, on the street corners, and at occasional meetings on the public squares and in dingy halls."[1]

The labor historians John B. Jentz and Richard Schneirov explain that the crisis of 1877 resounded in the minds of Chicago's elite as a "new class phenomenon" in which workers' rage seemed to transcend lines of ethnicity, nationality, and religion.[2] The *Tribune* gave voice to that notion when it suggested that the "crowded tenement houses" and "dingy halls" bred dangerous class politics. The squalor of the slum and the clamor of the meeting hall signaled the moral poverty and lawlessness of a radical-ized working class. Coarse in sensibilities and rabid in political impulses, working-class radicals announced themselves with savage "revilings." The discord evidenced a refusal to listen to reasoned explanations of the na-tional economic crisis and the state of the railroad industry. Even more, it indicated the tendency to foment mob rule.[3]

The dangerous classes "are coarse in tastes and vicious in habits," the *Tribune* charged, "easily maddened by liquor" and thus prone to riot. Dur-ing the railroad strike the previous week, dangerous radicals "swarmed as if from the ground" to infest the civic sphere: "In numbers and omnipres-ence and loathsomeness, they were like the frogs and lice of Egypt." Un-able to control their anger against the capitalist order and naturally given to violence, the dangerous classes stood ready "to join in any outbreak which gives them a sense of power over the decent part of the community, and an opportunity to pillage and destroy," a reflection of their contempt for middle-class order and civility.[4]

"We must act with our eyes open," the *Tribune* counseled. A careful, rational approach to the situation required violence against all threats to the public order. "A little powder, used to teach the dangerous classes a needful lesson, is well burned, provided there are bullets in front of it." Yet the author well knew that bullets and gunpowder would not do as a permanent solution. As he brought the column to a close, he suggested preventive measures to complement the use of deadly force. Along with a strong hand, the respectable classes could encourage religious training and formal education to break the radicals' habits of drunkenness, idle-ness, and mischief. "Whatever tends to industry, sobriety, and economy; whatever destroys the brutal habits and refines coarse tastes and teaches self-restraint" promised to create a productive and responsible working class for Chicago's many industries and to protect the civic health more generally.[5]

The labor historian Eugene E. Leach writes that elite observers fre-quently invoked the term "mob" as a linguistic device to attack labor protest in the late nineteenth century.[6] Fears of mob rule extend back to the Revolutionary period, but they escalated with the rise of a permanent class of wage laborers and the examples of the Civil War draft riots in New York (1863) and the Paris Commune (1871). The examples of 1863 and 1871—riots of a new and greater magnitude—inflamed anxieties about the health of the urban order itself. The chaos generated a "post-Commune consensus on mobs" that conflated violent radicalism with working-class protest.[7] Critics invoked the mob stigma to challenge strikes as normal political discourse and to question the basis of working-class unity in economic concerns.

The *Tribune's* depictions of the crisis of 1877 employed the mob stigma in sensory terms, conveying the distance between the social and political values of the city's middle classes and the striking workers. The newspaper's emphasis on the auditory expressions of labor protest—the actual and metaphorical "roar" of the mob—illustrate the historian Mark M. Smith's findings that the urban elites of the 1870s used their ears to measure civic health. Elites drew distinctions between the "sounds" of industrial production and the "noise" of labor protest. After the severe depression of 1873, argues Smith, elites feared that the "comforting twang of liberal capitalism . . . was beginning to take on the distinct cacophony of class warfare."[8] The aural allusions and metaphors found in contemporary accounts of labor conflict defined it in broad, Manichean terms.[9] For the *Tribune* the railroad strike involved more than a dispute over wage cuts; instead it constituted a broad-based workers' movement against industrial capitalism and private property. The strike threatened to stifle Chicago's continued growth by starving its commerce and unleashing reckless, roaring mobs on its streets.

The newspaper's admonition to act with "eyes open" is a further example of how thinking on the senses dovetailed with its Manichean depictions of social class and labor conflict. The *Tribune* stood with those who used the most rational of sensory faculties to think through the complicated issues of the marketplace: the business elite. Irrational and reckless attacks against capital were immune to reason and so had to be met with force. At the same time, reforming the senses of the working classes promised a peaceful and sustainable solution to the labor problem. The construction of the "model town" of Pullman by the railroad sleeping-car magnate George M. Pullman reflected such an approach.[10] Pullman believed he could tame the sensory values of his workers by promoting the refinement of "coarse tastes" and the "self-restraint" called for by the *Tribune*. Immersing his employees in a community defined by such middle-class sensory standards—and regulated by Pullman—would balm labor's discontent and make him a healthy profit in the bargain.

In the end, however, his effort revealed the limits of paternalistic attempts to regulate workers' sensory lives. The regulation of the town yielded resentment. In the early 1890s, little more than a decade after the founding of the town, Pullman itself became the site of another major railroad strike. This one, like the 1877 affair, was also marked in the public mind by the type of mob violence that the sleeping-car king sought to prevent.[11]

"It Is Here": The Great Railroad Strike of 1877

After the 1871 fire, Chicago's civic elite listened with pleasure to the "clink of the trowel" because it indicated the physical recovery of the burnt district as well as the spirit of economic productivity that they wanted investors to associate with their city. The city made great, some thought miraculous, progress in rebuilding in the two years after the fire, but the national economic collapse of 1873 silenced it.[12] The collapse could not have come at a worse time for Chicago, because the rebuilding effort had attracted thousands of new workers to the city. As unemployment rose and wages dropped, conflicts between labor and capital grew ever more public, leading civic leaders to associate workers' gatherings with the menacing noises of labor protest over the healthy clink of the trowel.

Made up of the nation's newly permanent class of industrial wage laborers, the mob seemed especially menacing, because the economic crisis that fueled it came so soon after Europe's first communist uprising, the Paris Commune. The Chicago papers carried dozens of stories on the violence in Paris, reflecting fears that revolutionary workers' movements might soon emerge in the United States. The city's middle classes spoke in hushed tones about the possibility of a second civil war, a prospect that heightened suspicions that any gathering of labor originated in the machinations of socialists or anarchists.[13]

The Great Railroad Strike of 1877 began in West Virginia in mid-July after the Baltimore and Ohio (B & O) Railroad cut wages by 10 percent. It soon spread westward, engendering violent clashes between police and strikers intent on shutting down rail service. The Chicago papers monitored the riots and interruptions of rail service east of the Mississippi, but their reporters hoped the city would escape the trouble.[14] As late as July 22, the *Times* reported indifference to the eastern strikes among the city's railroad employees, interviewing one "worker" who denounced the violence as the product of criminals and roughs seeking to gratify their own bloodlust. "Honest men, when fighting for a principle, and not simply from a vicious hankering after sensation for blood," the worker purportedly said, "can't afford to form an alliance with disreputable classes."[15] The next day, however, the *Times* reported that railroad officials believed Chicago would not escape the strike. "After a careful and calm review of the matter here," it reported in a passage that highlighted the rational perspective of management, "the oldest and coolest heads in railroading are bound to admit that a strike is inevitable."[16]

In the context of a likely strike, silence itself became menacing for those who feared the dangerous classes. On July 21 the *Tribune* reported that workers on the Chicago Division of the B & O Railroad were "unusually quiet and well behaved," an aural profile that suggested not indifference but an effort to hide their true feelings from probing journalists.[17] Two days later a reporter for the *Times* also registered a disquieting silence, finding the places where the railroad employees congregated deserted. "Scarcely a soul could be found around the usually well-attended haunts in the neighborhood of the round-houses between Fourth Avenue and Sixteenth Street," the correspondent wrote. The silence did not derive from workers' passivity; instead it indicated that they busied themselves in "secret and protracted meetings of the various divisions of their societies" to plan the coming strike. The meetings seemed all the more worrying because they could not be seen. The same reporter suspected that the railroad employees gathered close, probably "not more than a good stone's throw away," although he did not know exactly where.[18]

Clashes between strikers and police on July 25 broke the silence. Under the headline "Terror's Reign," the *Times* reported that "howling mobs of thieves and cut-throats" had taken to the streets to frighten honest laborers into walking off their jobs so as to participate in a general working-class uprising. Tensions rose at the switchyards of the Chicago, Burlington, and Quincy Railroad when police arrived to disperse a crowd of strikers. The instant the crowd spied the police "a wild shout was raised and sticks and clubs were brandished savagely." The crowd responded to the dispersal order with "shouts of anger and derision," forcing the police to draw their revolvers, an act that fueled the mob's fury. "They howled with rage," reported the *Times,* "and showered missiles of every description they could lay upon the officers."[19] The *Tribune,* reporting on the violence under the ominous headline "It Is Here," followed the lead of the *Times* in placing blame at the feet of a howling, irrational mob.[20]

The city's business leaders met the same day to call for the organization of a popular militia to defend property and restore good order. George Pullman, the head of Chicago's Law and Order League, urged aggressive means to respond to the upheaval. The *Tribune* echoed his concerns, calling upon Chicagoans to form a militia twenty thousand strong to help police and military forces quell the unrest. Again, the newspaper described the conflict not as one that involved a series of limited material conflicts between workers and their employers; rather, it called upon Chicagoans to defend the city against a more generalized mob action against private property. "Let every man who has a homestead, who has a store, warehouse, a factory, or an office, which he wishes to protect from abuse," it proclaimed, "enroll himself with his neighbors for his own and the general defense."[21] By the end of the next day, the state and federal governments had answered the call. Units of the Illinois state militia joined with companies of federal troops as well as citizens who had been deputized by the city to quell the mob.[22]

The substantial mobilization against the strikers reflected how the railroad strike raised concerns about a radical mob bent on stifling—even reversing—Chicago's economic modernization. The strike against the railroads threatened to cut off Chicago from the rest of the nation, seizing up the "great system of exchange," as the worried editors at the *Tribune* put it.[23] As trains sat idle in rail yards, Chicago's business leaders were unable to move goods to surrounding markets. Citizens faced rising food prices as farm produce rotted on the outskirts of the city. The situation resembled a wartime siege, but was more terrifying because the enemy roamed the streets. "Chicago is today virtually in a state of siege because her communications with the country are cut off," the *Tribune* warned, "while inside the limits the Commune has risen with the purposes of murder and plunder."[24] The city's newspapers discerned no rational motivation behind the efforts to shut down the railroads, arguing that strikers' passion compelled them to act against their own interests. The strike crippled the industry that provided their paychecks; even worse, it strangled the city's commerce to portend desperation and riot as people struggled to survive. "Had the railroad strikers been guided by any intelligence or reflection whatever, they could have foreseen that they aimed a blow against society itself," the *Tribune* averred.[25]

Chicago's railroad strike reached a bloody climax on July 26 with the fighting at the Halstead Street viaduct. Newspaper reporters caught in the middle of the conflict used words of disgust to highlight their political distance from workers as well as their own social distinction. One reporter for the *Tribune* retreated to a nearby kitchen during the Halstead Street battle, but he found none of the comforts of the home or the women who kept it clean and respectable. "Never before did he realize that there was any disadvantage in wearing a clean shirt," he wrote, "or in displaying a white handkerchief in wiping his wet face."[26] Finding no shelter from the world outside, he argued with threatening characters who locked the door to hold him hostage.

Yet if neighborhood women astonished reporters by refusing them aid, female participation in the fighting truly shocked, because it upended gender norms. In a story picked up by the national media, the Chicago *Inter-Ocean* sounded the alarm about a howling mob of overgrown women—an "Amazonian Army"—that attacked the police with improvised weapons. "As female yells, . . . filled the air," it reported, "brawny, sunburnt arms brandished clubs. . . . Knotty hands held rocks and sticks and wooden blocks." The women opened their shirts and tucked their dresses around their waists to fight, a visual transgression of female modesty that made "open busts [as] common as a barbers' chair." Just as disgusting, they assaulted middle-class ears by cursing the police with the type of language that made even the coarsest men blush. Their crude howlings "brought the blood mantling to the cheek of the worst-hardened men in the crowds of spectators."[27]

The reports of female violence echoed Civil War circumstances in which combat forced men and women to act in ways that were contrary to gender conventions.[28] The wartime analogy suggested the potential for the "second civil war" between labor and capital. As the historian Troy Rondinone argues, the press coverage of the 1877 strikes drew explicitly on Civil War language and themes to suggest the possibility of "national industrial wars" to anxious middle-class readers.[29]

A sensory reading of the reporting suggests anxiety about a return to the unstable gender norms of the war years, as when the *Tribune* noted how "huge, bloated women at the windows [of their homes] yelled encouragement and defiance" during the fighting. Even more, however, the fighting reverberated with the noises of the battles between the blue and the gray. "Pistol balls shrieked" as federal cavalry fought with the mob. "The clash of sabers and the shouts of maddened men made the hot air hideous," a description that evoked not a local episode of labor violence but the type of noise and heat faced by troops at places like Gettysburg, fourteen years earlier. Much like the summer of 1863, "horses were spurred into the mob, and swords rose and fell with cruel significance." The cavalry triumphed, reducing the mob to a collection of broken men, not unlike a defeated army whose wounded "shrieked for rescue" during the fight.[30]

By day's end, governmental forces had defeated the mob and effectively ended the strike in Chicago, with no police officers or soldiers killed. Two days later, trains began to run from the city with military escort. The action at the viaduct left twelve civilians dead and more than twenty wounded, but the newspapers expressed little sympathy.[31] The *Tribune* insisted that the mob threatened the most basic tenets of private property, forcing a most severe lesson upon the rioters. Those killed at the viaduct learned "that the life of a rioter was worthless in the face of lawful and organized force." "Had the mob made any [further] demonstration," it continued, " . . . there would have been streets running with blood."[32]

More surprising than the newspaper's condemnation of the riot, however, was its attitude about the bystanders who lost their lives. "If innocent people are clubbed and shot, and nearly all who have been wounded and killed thus far were mere lookers-on," it announced, "they can blame no one but themselves."[33] Here the newspaper suggested that the fighting at the viaduct represented nothing short of a battle for the survival of the city as a modern center of commerce. Much like curious civilians who wandered too close to the battles of the Civil War—a fight that was necessary for the future of the modern nation—the onlookers at the viaduct took their lives into their own hands when they refused to stay home to let the state put down the rebels.

In the aftermath of the strike, the *Tribune* amplified the view that the state acted with appropriate violence because it stood against an irrational mob. Workers' anger against their employers, fueled by the ravings of dangerous radicals, had rendered them "blind to the logical consequences of their unlawful conduct" and thus fair targets for the bullet.[34] Such justifications related to the descriptions of workers' senses as coarsened and rude. Rough laboring bodies, the historian Constance Classen writes, have often been understood by elites as ones that require the harshest disciplinary measures. In this case lethal force represented the best response to a brutish working class who were unable to listen to reason.[35]

No longer under the spell of the dangerous classes, the *Tribune* predicted that honest railroad men would use their most rational sense to "look at the situation with something like intelligence and reason." As members of the mob, workers had been figuratively blinded, acting not on the basis of a detached look at the conflict but on the radicals' howling exhortations against capital. The normally respectable railroad employees "may not have foreseen—probably did not foresee—that their conduct would precipitate riots, plunder, arson, and murder," but that made them no less responsible for the upheaval.[36] At this point, the newspaper counseled, the railroad employees would be best served to "sit down quietly" in order to cultivate the sensorial equipoise that would save them from acting against their own interest in such destructive fashion in the future.[37]

Sensorial Equipoise: George M. Pullman and the Model Town

George M. Pullman, who first made his mark in Chicago when he directed the antebellum project that raised the city's buildings to make way for the sewer system, watched the clashes between workers and police in horror. The howling mobs threatened his Palace Car Company, the leading producer of luxury rail cars, but even more the violence cast doubt on the future of the city he had helped rebuild after the Great Fire. Three years after the railroad strike, Pullman announced an ambitious plan to build a corporate town south of the city that would retrain workers' senses to ease the conflict between labor and capital without sacrificing the profit motive. The basic concept of the town, a self-contained community where employees worked and lived, rested on the assumptions that served his Palace Car Company so well—namely, the notion that corporations could elevate individuals' sensibilities by surrounding them with luxury. "That which is harmonious and beautiful has been recognized as having an incitive energy of its own," a company pamphlet argued, "capable in its way of being turned to account as a force in the production of results, just as is the force of the steam engine itself."[38] In the self-named town of Pullman, the company planned to provide the modern factories, manicured public spaces, and comfortable homes that would produce the model worker—industrious, healthy, compliant—an actor whose sensorial equipoise redounded to the benefit of all.[39]

The provision of sanitation services, attractive public spaces, and well-maintained residences would set Pullman apart from Chicago's slum districts in visually striking ways. The historian Thomas J. Jablonsky's study of Back of the Yards, the working-class district that housed the city's meatpacking industry, clarifies how the worst slums lacked the kind of amenities proposed by Pullman. In Back of the Yards, residents found few of the public institutions where the affluent classes sought leisure and services.

The slum featured "no department stores, no parks, no libraries—and no bathing facilities." The physical landscape was also distinctive for what it lacked. A "distinct absence of trees, grass, and shrubbery, and few houses [with] sewer connections" characterized Back of the Yards. The houses themselves were of monotonous frame design and often a dirty grayish hue, a residential landscape "devoid of color."[40]

Jablonsky observes that the unappealing visual landscape rivaled the muckraking journalist Jacob Riis's photographic depictions of poverty in New York City. Riis himself visited Chicago in 1900. He, too, described the slums as having an absence of cleanliness and visual appeal. Upon visiting poor neighborhoods in the West and South Sides (although not Back of the Yards), Riis estimated that he had never encountered such desolation. Garbage boxes met the eye on every sidewalk, "overflowing with their nastiness." The dirt of the streets settled in residential lots and painted their houses. He spied backyards "filled with all manner of abomination," worse than what filled the gutters. The dirty landscape formed a "stain—a threat." The threat derived from the link between physical dirt and moral poverty. "Men are not going to help clean a city," Riis explained, "who cannot summon up spunk enough to clean their own backyards." The dirty streets endangered civic health. "You cannot," Riis insisted, "grow civic ideals out of such soil."[41]

Pullman bet that his model city would provide fertile soil for the growth of such ideals. Ground breaking took place three years after the railroad strike. Located fourteen miles south of Chicago, the town sat on a four-thousand-acre strip of land between Lake Calumet and the tracks of the Illinois Central Railroad. Though clearly based on earlier model towns in Europe and the United States, Pullman believed that his community would transform urban life. "Everything about the village," the historian James Gilbert writes, "was designed to create the impression of a special new urban culture."[42] Pullman hired one architect, only two years into his own practice, to design the buildings to reflect the railroad car manufacturer's personal vision. The town featured all the comforts of modern life, including paved streets, a reliable sewer system, indoor plumbing, and a central Arcade Building with a theater, library, and a full complement of retailers. The company announced that the town stood as nothing less than a work of art—"paintings and poems in brick, stone, landscapes and foliage"—born of the inspiration of a single person, Pullman himself.[43] The model community earned praise for what it lacked as well. Pullman dictated that no saloons, houses of prostitution, or gambling dens would darken the landscape. The Hotel Florence, a grand lodge with a visually commanding place at the town center, operated the only bar, one whose appointments and prices successfully discouraged the patronage of workers.[44]

The placement of the Hotel Florence at a central point in the town's visual landscape reflected well Pullman's conception of his model community (see fig. 5). The town served as his personal showpiece, one he offered to visitors as a spectacle of enlightened capitalism. Pullman's town, as the historian Stanley Buder put it so well, was "intensely surveilled" by visitors in its first decade.[45] The 1883 opening of the Arcade theater, a gala that brought visitors from around the nation, is a telling case. The theater embodied Pullman's idea that fine art served a therapeutic purpose against the corrupting effects of the city. "Earth is crowded and disfigured with unsightly forms," a company publicist wrote. Visiting the Arcade theater countered such ugliness because it provided the "opportunity for seeing beautiful objects" that served as a "physical as well as moral and intellectual tonic."[46] The theater further reflected the tight control that Pullman maintained over the town's institutions. The same publicist noted that Pullman personally oversaw its design, everything from the "elegantly furnished cloak and toilet rooms to the stage settings and the seating arrangement of the auditorium." He also retained control of the program to ensure that "no questionable performance and no company of second merit" reached his stage.[47]

On the evening of January 9 a special train left Chicago to carry Pullman and three hundred invited guests to the opening gala. According to a town publicist, the completion of the theater made "nearly perfect the ideal city, where the useful and the beautiful are so harmoniously brought together as to blend into a bright picture," one that "people have dreamed of, but never before seen realized."[48] At 8:30 PM the curtain rose to reveal a collection of Chicago dignitaries seated on stage, including Pullman and his special guest, Stewart L. Woodward, a leading Republican from New York, who was slated to deliver the dedicatory address. Having read much about the model town, Woodward told the audience that he welcomed the chance to travel there to "see and study it for myself, with my own eyes, and on the spot." Upon arrival, he reported, "beauty, grace, art met me on every hand."[49]

The landscape gardening flattered his sense of sight, rendering "eye and taste . . . content and glad." Equally impressive, the absence of filth— both actual dirt and corruptions of the saloon and brothel—stood as the "silent teachers that minister to [the] eye," promising moral uplift. Woodward celebrated how the town eliminated dirt in order to discourage sin: "The dirty tenement and the unwashed and uncombed wife and the dirty and unkempt children drive men from home to the groggery and the saloon." In their place Pullman put "the flower in the pathway; the tree by the sidewalk" as well as the "lighted and warm and graceful arcade [with its] reading room and library." The town's landscape appealed to the residents' senses to make clear to them the benefits of "more cleanly lives within as well as without."[50]

George Pullman must have been pleased with Woodward's address, because it so closely echoed his thinking on how the town transformed the sensory lives of its residents. While his factories buzzed with the sounds of productive labor—the company boasted that its shops "constitute a busy hive of human industry"—the residential section offered the cleanliness that set it apart from the typical Chicago street.[51] Pullman's waste disposal system kept the city's morally repulsive stench from its residents' noses. The company allowed no barns in the residential area, directing all horses to a central stable to keep manure from the streets.[52] It also cleaned the streets with great care and provided for the daily collection of garbage and ashes from residential lots. Early on, Pullman elected not to use the lake that abutted his town as a common sewer. He elected instead for a system that drained household waste to a cistern under the town's water tower, where it was pumped to a sewage farm three miles south and used to fertilize a productive vegetable farm.[53] "There is nothing offensive at this pumping station," the company pointed out, "and there are no odors that can be detected beyond those of the oil used about the pumps and the machinery," a scent that evoked healthy, productive labor.[54]

Residents lived in brick row houses that varied in size. The largest and most expensive—those reserved for management—stood closer to the center of town. Pullman steadfastly refused to sell any of the homes, a policy that permitted him to retain control over the property's appearance as well as his tenants' behavior. He offered one-year leases, but they included a stipulation that allowed the company to revoke the lease and evict with ten days notice. In the town's early days, the company deducted rent directly from workers' paychecks, arguing that the policy prevented men from endangering their family's security by misspending their wages in the saloons on the outskirts of town.

The regulations that renters faced inside their homes were equally constraining. The company controlled the visual profile of the residential area by limiting tenants' ability to decorate the exteriors of their homes, requiring written permission for significant alterations. It mandated neighborhood serenity with rules that outlined the appropriate time of day for music and the proper locations for smoking, and that reminded residents to "always enter or leave [their] building quietly."[55] Pullman saw none of the regulations as potentially irksome; instead he believed that arrivals from the city would naturally emulate their neighbors—those already schooled in middle-class sensory refinement—to fit into their new surroundings. Nor did he think that the heavy hand he used to keep residents from backsliding into the crude habits of the city streets was oppressive to their individual freedom. The careful regulation of the town constituted a necessary form of uplift, providing the sensorial features of middle-class life to people who otherwise lacked the resources and the inclination to do so for themselves.[56]

The dispatches from the observers who traveled to Pullman to study the model town largely supported its founder's thinking. In the summer of 1884 a group of state commissioners of labor statistics issued a glowing report on the model community. It noted that new arrivals, often bereft of the town's shared sensory values, could be easily spotted, "like a rubbish heap in a garden—out of place and unseemly." A tour around the town served as a quick visual corrective in which residents, fresh from the grimy city, spied only the "well kept lawns, tidy dwellings, [and] clean workshops" that embarrassed them into "setting their own houses to rights."[57]

The report emphasized that the town's women heaped the most praise upon Pullman, since it gave them the chance to keep a respectable, middle-class home. The "purity of air, cleanliness of houses and streets, and lessened household burdens are advantages over the former residences which brought out the heartiest expression of approval." The company maintained the type of healthy surroundings that made the outdoors a safe place for their children to play and to go to school; in addition, it provided security by making it more difficult for their husbands to waste the family's rent money on drink. The image that the commissioners drew of the women of Pullman could not have contrasted more sharply with the howling wretches who had fought with police during the railroad strike seven years earlier. Pullman trained working-class women to appreciate the comforts of middle-class home life, an accomplishment that reduced the chances that a dangerous inversion of gender roles born of labor protest would interrupt the serenity of the town. At the same time, the town transformed their husbands into a "magnificent class of workmen living under happy and moral conditions." Responding to criticism that Pullman's town looked like a "gilded cage," the report shot back, "If the workman at Pullman lives in a 'Gilded Cage,' we must congratulate him on it being so handsomely gilded."[58]

The commissioners' rhetorical shot may have been directed at Richard T. Ely, an economist who termed Pullman's town a "gilded cage" in his article in *Harper's New Monthly Magazine,* published months before they issued their report. Ely's critique represented one of the few critical appraisals of the town in its early years, but it attracted a great deal of attention, in part because of the magazine's wide readership. The logic of the critique, one that cast the town as an exercise that was antithetical to American values of individualism, is the best-known dissent from the celebratory analysis circulated by the company and observers. Ely understood that the model community served as a source of hope for the middle-class readers whose ears rang with the "dynamite bombs and revolutionary murmurings" of dangerous radicals. But his basic argument cast Pullman's model community as simply a different form of European extremism—a "benevolent, well-wishing feudalism"—that substituted the silence of political oppression for the roar of the mob.[59]

Ely agreed that the town maintained a pleasing visual profile, one that struck his wife from the opening moments of their visit. "What is seen in a walk or drive through the streets," he reported, "is so pleasing to the eye that a woman's first exclamation is certain to be 'perfectly lovely!'" Here Ely furthered the notion that the town offered something unique to women because it enhanced their efforts to maintain the appearances of middle-class respectability. The residential area looked entirely different from the usual working-class tenement districts, for "not a dilapidated door-step nor a broken window, stuffed perhaps with old clothing, is to be found in the city." Instead the economist's eyes studied perfectly clean streets, lined with the young trees that would soon provide tactile respite from the summer sun and bordered by neatly trimmed lawns, stunning in their rich greenness. Ely further praised the architectural forms that dotted the skyline to give it a pleasingly varied profile unlike the typical slum: "French roofs, square roofs, dormer-windows, turrets, sharp points, blunt points, triangles, irregular quadrangles, are devices resorted to in the upper stories to avoid an appearance of unbroken uniformity." He noticed that the least attractive housing remained out of sight, consigned to the least visited sections of the town, but even it looked superior to the worst tenements in New York.[60]

The visual aesthetic applauded by Ely differed most obviously from Chicago's slums in terms of cleanliness, but the varied architectural forms also contrasted sharply with the monotonous appearance of neighborhoods like Back of the Yards. The author of the most famous literary depiction of the stockyards neighborhood, Upton Sinclair, related such monotony when he described his protagonist's first trip through Back of the Yards in *The Jungle* (1906). "Down every side street" the Lithuanian immigrant Jurgis Rudkus could "see it was the same." "Never a hill and never a hollow," Sinclair wrote, "but always the same endless vista of ugly and dirty wooden buildings."[61] The commissioners of labor statistics' report applauded the visual contrast Pullman offered to the slums, writing that the "sameness [that] kills beauty" in the tenement districts appeared nowhere in the model town. The architectural design presented a pleasingly varied yet "harmonious" appearance that enhanced the beauty of the green lawns and clean streets.[62]

Ely's critique, however, penetrated Pullman's gilded surface. When he used his ears as much as his eyes, he discovered unpleasant aspects of the town that he believed moderated "the enthusiasm one is at first inclined to feel upon an inspection of the external, plainly visible facts." He noted that Pullman owned every square inch of the town; in addition, his company acted as the municipal government, responsible for every public service except the local school board. Even more disturbing, Pullman's representatives maintained what Ely termed "a needless air of secrecy" when it came to providing statistics about the town. He found that practices such as favoritism in the workplace forced residents to change jobs often. They also moved more than usual, making the town itself seem more like a "temporary oasis" than a permanent community.[63]

Part of the discontent stemmed from the company's practice of surveillance; it watched residents to make them feel as though they acted as players on a stage constructed by Pullman. Even in the ostensibly positive sections of Ely's article there are hints that he understood the weight of the company's gaze on the women who were responsible for maintaining their homes. He wrote of how company representatives sent women notes of approval when they kept a clean house; in one case an official sent a woman new plants from the town's nursery to complement the ones she placed on her porch, an act of generosity that could have easily been taken as interfering with her female prerogatives. Ely expressed his approval of the efforts to keep up the appearance of the town, but in a backhanded fashion, terming them an example of the "systematic persistence in little acts of kind thoughtfulness" that marked residents' encounters with the company.[64]

"The power of Bismarck in Germany," Ely concluded, "is utterly insignificant when compared with the power of the ruling authority of the Palace Car Company in Pullman." The residents' powerlessness left them at the mercy of the company, rendering them mute as political actors. Ely found it difficult to convince workers to give voice to their complaints, in part because many feared the company "spotters" might report their disloyalty.[65] He encountered a silent "population of eight thousand souls where not one single resident dare speak out openly his opinion about the town in which he lives." The economist pointed out that the silence stood in contrast to fundamental practices of American democracy, such as the citizenship training of the New England town meeting. "In Pullman," he argued, "all this disappears" because the "citizen is surrounded by constant restraint and restriction, and everything is done for him, nothing by him." Disturbed at the demoralizing effect of the silence, Ely found most residents defeated: "One feels that one is mingling with a dependent, servile people." In the final analysis he found Pullman's community a frightening expression of the power of capital to silence opposition to the detriment of democracy. "If free American institutions are to be preserved," he concluded, "we want no race of men reared as underlings and with the spirit of menials."[66]

The Pullman Strike

The 1893 World's Columbian Exposition, a fantasy of urban life that expressed Pullman's ideals with grander symbolism, represented the highwater mark for the model town as a spectacle of enlightened capitalism.[67] The visitors who came to the exposition grounds that summer could see a scale model of the town in the fair's Transportation Building. George Pullman further encouraged tourists to see his town up close. Thousands accepted his offer, satisfying themselves that the clean streets and green lawns constituted a successful approach to taming the "labor problem." The pamphlet that accompanied the exposition exhibit announced that the bucolic surroundings had transformed Pullman workers into a "distinct type—distinct in appearance, in tidiness of dress, in fact in all the external indications of self-respect." Visitors could see the transformation even in the residents' faces, distinguished as they were by the "clear complexions and brighter eyes" born of the "sanitary effects of the cleanliness and the abundance of pure air and sunlight" of the workers' homes. Just as George Pullman planned, town life transformed residents into workers who looked like ideal middle-class citizens, persons whose countenances reflected "the general atmosphere of order and artistic taste which permeates the town."[68]

The severe economic depression of the 1890s, however, exploded the sense of calm and contentment that visitors saw at Pullman. The world's fair delayed the worst effects of the economic slowdown in Chicago, but the situation worsened when it closed its gates in October. Workers who came to the city to build the fair competed with other Chicagoans for a shrinking number of jobs, spiking unemployment and homelessness. When orders slowed at the Palace Car Company, Pullman cut wages but refused to reduce rents or prices at the company store, arguing that the town functioned separately from the company, a position in contradiction to practical reality, as his employees saw it.

By the end of the year, the Chicago press reported suffering and discontent in the model town, a view that stood in stark contrast to the bright faces trumpeted by the company only months earlier. Employees staged a walkout in May and turned to the American Railway Union (ARU) for assistance in negotiations. Pullman made matters worse by refusing to arbitrate and by appearing remote during talks. The boss's behavior, following years of intrusions by the company into their homes, fueled residents' anger. By the end of June, with nothing to show from the negotiations, the ARU announced that its members would no longer service trains with Pullman cars. The ARU boycott halted railroad traffic and eventually gave rise to the same type of siege that middle-class Chicagoans faced in 1877, one of the developments that had compelled Pullman to build his town in the first place.[69]

Initially the strikers gained public support by invoking the sanctity of the gender norms Pullman promoted in the design of his model town. They argued that by cutting wages but not rents, and refusing to arbitrate, George Pullman prevented men from providing for their wives and children in the very fashion his town promised. As the historian Janice L. Reiff succinctly wrote, "If he deserved credit for creating the environment that made their lives better, then he also deserved the blame when their lives were worse."[70] Chicago's newspapers echoed the strikers' argument with stories of starving families in the town, casting its founder as unsympathetic and inflexible.

Nevertheless, as the sense of siege took hold of the city and as federal troops arrived in Chicago in July to break the strike, the public support faded. The Pullman workers acted with discipline and restraint in the opening days of the strike, but the arrival of the U.S. Army ignited the same type of violence that gave rise to fears of the irrational mob. The artist Frederick Remington, covering the army's arrival for *Harper's Weekly*, penned an account rich in the sensorial contrasts it drew between the troopers of the Seventh Cavalry ("a cleaner, decenter lot of young fellows can't be found anywhere") and the "raging, savage, unthinking mob" that protested their presence in the city. Much like their counterparts in 1877, the troopers marched through "howling mobs"—a "seething mass of smells, stale beer, and bad language." Remington echoed the earlier accounts by suggesting that dangerous radicals—people distinguished by their stench, a "malodorous crowd of anarchistic foreign trash"—caused most of the trouble. Although he feared that the "state of anarchy" that had taken hold of Chicago would worsen over time, the troopers restored train service by the end of the month, effectively defeating the boycott and the ARU's efforts in Pullman.[71]

Striking workers in the model town held out longer, but even their efforts eventually were painted as the actions of an irrational mob bent on challenging far more than their employer's position on wages and rents. Not to be outdone on the issue of gender norms, Pullman reopened his shops first to laundresses, generally younger women responsible for supporting widowed mothers and other family members who were unable to work.[72] The striking workers regarded the laundresses as scabs, so they turned out to express their rage at the end of the workday. In a refrain of the press coverage of the women warriors who battled federal troops during the 1877 strike, the *Tribune* ran its story of the conflict under the headline "They Cry for Gore: Amazons Menace the Holland Laundry Girls at Pullman."[73]

Once again the mob appeared all the more frightening because of its gender profile. While the newspaper reported that "howling, hooting mobs and men, women, and children swept through the streets" to vent their rage at the scabs, the gender-bending "Amazons" attracted the most sustained comment. As men stood in the background to provide verbal support, the women delivered "all sorts of violent demonstrations." At the height of the action, an elderly woman emerged from the mob to physically attack one of the young laundresses. "An old hag of a woman held the terrorized girl by one arm and clawed her face with long, bony fingers," the *Tribune* reported in language that made the attacker seem more like an evil witch than an Amazonian. Half a dozen other women, however, joined in to provide the masculine punches, "striking [the laundress] on the shoulders and head with their fists."[74] The strikers thus forfeited their claims as the protectors of women and children; further, they raised the specter of a radical class of women whose anger drove them to reject not simply those who crossed picket lines but also those who valued the home and women's proper role in it as the basis of the middle-class life.[75]

George Pullman defeated the strike, but he lost the larger war against labor. As the Federal Army once again occupied Chicago to battle with strikers, and as violent mobs brought disorder to his model town, the public saw his experiment not as a spectacle of enlightened capitalism but as the epicenter of the very conflicts it was intended to prevent. Pullman's reputation suffered in the aftermath, as many of his former supporters lamented his obstinacy during the strike and echoed a general sentiment that his model community had failed.[76]

Probably the most revealing example of Pullman's stubbornness is in the findings of the United States Strike Commission, appointed by President Grover Cleveland to investigate the causes of the upheaval at Pullman. Chaired by the same labor commissioner who praised the model town so highly ten years earlier, Carroll D. Wright, the commission presented a report that Buder termed "the most thorough examination of a labor disturbance in American history."[77] The commission found that Pullman's refusal to arbitrate concentrated power in the hands of capital, robbing workers of the legitimate leverage afforded by a union. Pullman's position on unions placed his company "behind the age," a judgment that must have stung the man who had so recently been celebrated as a pioneer in industrial relations. The report further expressed doubts about the ultimate wisdom of the model community itself. Pointing out that rents in the town exceeded similar prices in Chicago (excluding the cost of the town's amenities) by as much as 25 percent, it concluded that Pullman placed the smooth functioning of his stage show over the material needs of his employees: "The aesthetic features are admired by visitors, but have little money value to employees, especially when they lack bread."[78]

The commission ultimately suggested that the company's effort to immerse its employees in an environment rich in middle-class refinement to transform them into compliant and productive workers created as much alienation as it did serenity. The residents of Pullman felt no real stake in their community, because the company would not allow them any substantial role in its development. When the strike began, the company faced discontented workers of "comparably excellent character and skill, but without local attachments or any interested responsibility in the town, its business, tenements, or surroundings."[79] Even the most celebrated features of the town such as the library and theater were not really intended for them to enjoy; rather, Pullman provided them for the local elites who already shared his sense of the beautiful. The commission pointed to the library as one example of a local institution whose "air of business" prevented a "more universal and grateful acceptance of its advantages by employees."[80]

The report implied that Pullman's town highlighted differences of social class as much as it bridged them. William H. Carwardine, pastor of Pullman's First M. E. Church, agreed. In *The Pullman Strike* (1894) he went even further than the commissioners to suggest that George Pullman intended the amenities like the library to serve as mere props in his show of enlightened management. To the "passing student of the industrial problem," Carwardine wrote, the town "has a fascinating appearance," but it was a misleading one. Much like a play, "there is a good deal of tinsel and show about it." To him the town amounted to a "hollow mockery, sham . . . and as a solution to the labor problem a very unsatisfactory one."[81]

The town of Pullman and its founder expired soon after the 1894 strike. George M. Pullman died in October 1897. Obituaries celebrated his accomplishments as a business leader, but his burial at Chicago's Graceland Cemetery was equally suggestive as a last word on his relations with labor. His family, fearful that former employees would desecrate the corpse, buried him at night. They sank his coffin in a thick concrete block, further reinforced with a covering of steel rails, and topped the grave with a massive Corinthian column.

The next year the Illinois Supreme Court delivered the final blow when it ordered Pullman's company to put the town property up for sale. The Arcade theater, the site of Woodward's celebratory remarks about the beauty and promise of Pullman, limped on for another four years, eventually closing its doors in 1902. The Hotel Florence, the visual centerpiece of Pullman's experiment that embodied his call upon visitors to look over his experiment in retraining workers as refined middle-class actors, became a cheap boardinghouse.

CHAPTER 4

A REVOLUTIONARY AND A PURITAN

Upton Sinclair and *The Jungle*

The Jungle is the best-known literary evocation of industrial Chicago. One hundred years after the novel first disgusted readers with its descriptions of the city's meatpacking plants, it continues to inform discussions about food politics. Upton Sinclair's gastric prose and his eye for revolting detail echo in contemporary exposés about industrially produced meat.[1] Much like those exposés, *The Jungle* shocked readers' senses, famously turning their stomachs with descriptions of rats tossed into sausage hoppers. However, Sinclair's novel also had much to say about how the meatpacking industry robbed the senses of workers. This chapter analyzes *The Jungle* to explore the sensory politics of its author and the indictment of industrial capitalism he proposed. It traces how the author drew lines of class, ethnicity, and race in sensory terms in order to simultaneously express sympathy and solidarity as well as repulsion and social distance from immigrant workers in Back of the Yards.

A good example of Sinclair's discussion of how work in the meat factories dulled the senses of workers takes place about halfway through *The Jungle,* when the protagonist, the immigrant laborer Jurgis Rudkus, decides that his mother-in-law must take work in a sausage factory. Life and labor in Chicago's stockyards district is tougher than Jurgis imagined when he left Lithuania, and things keep getting worse. It is a regrettable decision, but necessary, as more and more members of the extended family are forced to take jobs in the packing plants to help make ends meet.

Elzbieta is no stranger to hard work, but she is tested when she becomes, as Sinclair put it, a "servant to the sausage machine." The job requires her to stand in the same place for ten hours, with only a forty-five-minute break in the middle of the day. Worse, the room where she works amounts to a "dark hole," lit dimly by electricity and constantly wet. "There were always puddles of water on the floor," Sinclair wrote, "and a sickening odor of moist flesh in the room." The meatpackers allowed tourists to pass through, but quickly. The machinery impressed tourists, especially the stuffing machines and their multiple nozzles, over which female workers like Elzbieta held casing. With the simple pull of a lever, the ground meat shot out into the casings like a "wriggling snake," to be caught and twisted into links, an operation the women executed "so fast that the eye could literally not follow."[2]

The wondrous sight lost some of its appeal, however, when the tourists looked at the women's faces, "tense set, with the two wrinkles graven in the forehead, and the ghastly pallor of the cheeks." The work paid by the piece, so the women focused intensely on it, seldom glancing at the passersby who stared at them "as at some wild beast in a menagerie." Elzbieta probably cared little about the tourists anyway. The work itself—stupefying in its repetitiveness and speed—"crushed out of existence" all of her sensory faculties that were "not needed for the machine." The "only mercy about the cruel grind," Sinclair lamented, was "the gift of insensibility," a numbness that inoculated her during the day and followed her home at night.[3]

Attention to sensory denial in *The Jungle* underscores Sinclair's central argument that work in industrial capitalism dulled workers' senses. The argument rested on a fictionalization of Karl Marx's ideas about the alienation of labor, including the German philosopher's claim that capitalistic production transformed workers into insensate cogs in mass production machines. The scholarly literature on Sinclair is strangely silent on the author's intellectual debt to Marx.[4] Sinclair's theoretical orientation is crucial, however, because it underscores his intention to write a story about immigrants from a bottom-up perspective at a time when middle-class readers often viewed immigrants from Eastern Europe with suspicion and fear.

Sinclair's fictionalization of Marxian theory makes sense when we consider his background as an intellectual who distrusted sensory knowledge. Throughout his life the author spurned sensory pleasure as antithetical to the pursuit of reason. He saw himself as a rationalist who made decisions through cool, objective thought, not crude sensory desires. He often told his first wife that he viewed his mind as a "machine" he could control through force of will and a strict diet regimen.[5] In other words, Sinclair associated himself with the objective, scientific eye. He wrote to expose readers to the truth, as he saw it, so that they could make rational judgments. He said as much in *The Jungle* when he likened the horrors of the hog abattoirs to "some horrible crime committed in a dungeon, all unseen and unheeded, buried out of sight and memory."[6]

Historians have long considered *The Jungle* a useful depiction of Chicago's slaughterhouses and their environs. Many emphasize how the novel raised public concern about the state of their food. This is the familiar story referenced in *Puck* whereby *The Jungle* disgusted readers, including President Theodore Roosevelt, to spur federal regulatory legislation (see fig. 6). In these cases *The Jungle* is a prime example of the Progressive impulse to publicize the danger of concentrated industry and to remedy it with governmental oversight.[7] Social and labor historians have likewise seen *The Jungle* as useful by emphasizing how the novel accurately reflected the living and working conditions of the city's stockyards district. The sensory dimensions of the stockyards—"the sight and smell of mass-produced death," as the social historian James Barrett writes—are treated well in these studies. Blood, noise, stench, and cold come through as features of the industrial workplace that strained workers' senses.

Attention to the complex sensory politics of *The Jungle* furthers the scholarly conversation by exploring how its author, and the socialist movement that he promoted, struggled to portray a diverse, theoretically debased working class. Sinclair wrote with sensitivity about the conditions that immigrants faced in the stockyards, including how the packing plants assaulted workers' senses. Yet he conveyed a flawed understanding of workers' lives by describing them as completely dominated by the sensory landscape of the factory and the slum. The characters in *The Jungle* are set apart from middle-class readers as animalistic sensory beings; their coarse senses embody their class, ethnic, and racial identities. At the same time, Sinclair describes their salvation—socialism—in non-sensory terms. He closes his novel by describing an oddly disembodied socialist revolution, one limited to the intellectual terrain on which he was most comfortable.

Upton Sinclair and the Senses

Upton Sinclair described himself as a "revolutionary and a puritan," a propagandist for the working class who "hated drink and lust."[8] Born in Baltimore in 1878, the author hailed from a family of gentile, Southern roots. In the decades following the Civil War, the family lost stature, in large part because of his salesman father's alcoholism. Sinclair spent a good part of his childhood in rundown boardinghouses in New York City, dragging his drunken father, who eventually died from excessive alcohol consumption, from neighborhood saloons. The experience nurtured a lifelong hostility to alcohol and provided glimpses of the urban filth and privation that he later wrote about in *The Jungle*.

Sinclair's mother took him to live with her wealthy family in Baltimore when his father's drinking made it impossible for him to support them, a regular circumstance that presented the young man with the contrasting images of wealth and poverty that also appeared in his 1906 novel. Sinclair's mother, a devout Methodist with whom he enjoyed a close relationship, further pushed him toward sensory self-denial. She never took coffee, tea, or tobacco, prohibitions he continued to uphold. The intimate relationship with his mother also bred an early sympathy with feminism and a tendency to idealize women, the latter of which helped account for his discomfort with lust.[9]

Sinclair came of age hopelessly ignorant in matters of the flesh. Neither his father nor his mother provided any guidance, leaving him to face the trials of puberty alone and confused. As late as age sixteen he spent a great deal of time speculating about the concept of prostitution, the truth of which, he later wrote, "shocked me deeply."[10] Later, as a student at Columbia University, Sinclair's discomfort with sexual matters even hindered his ability to study classical art. Columbia's library held great volumes on Renaissance art, to which a curious Sinclair turned with interest, hoping to pick up a complex subject with great dispatch, a habit he continued throughout his life. Instead he found himself dumbfounded by what he termed a "mass of nakedness." His "senses reeled" and he had to drop the subject. As an older man he regretted that the lack of maturity had stifled his education, but he still begged off, insisting that he was "too busy trying to save the world from poverty and war" to revisit the Renaissance nudes.[11]

Sexual puritanism also weakened Sinclair's first marriage. The young author remained chaste until age twenty-two, when he married Meta Fuller, whom he knew through a friend of his mother. He later described their courtship in less than romantic terms: "they gazed at each other across a chasm of misunderstanding."[12] He explained the origins of the marriage as a sad matter of proximity in which both parties knew nothing about physical intimacy.[13] The mismatch also suffered from incongruent attitudes about the value of sexual pleasure, which Meta viewed far more positively than her husband. At one point early in the marriage, Sinclair, terrified of the financial burden and distractions from writing that would follow pregnancy, suggested that he and his wife live as "brother and sister" to avoid sexual temptation. "Since caressing led to sexual impulse, and therefore to discontent," he explained, "it was necessary that caressing should be omitted from the daily program, and love-making be confined to noble words and the reading aloud of Civil War literature." The distinction between base pleasures of the flesh on the one hand and the noble pursuit of Civil War literature on the other hand highlighted the broader contrast that Sinclair drew between the value of sensory pleasure versus intellectual enlightenment. His wife's understandable objection to a marriage based on that contrast (he later complained that "she *had* to" have sex) further poisoned the relationship, which soured Sinclair's attitude about marriage in general.[14]

Meta more willingly participated in the dietary experiments that reflected her husband's wishes to tame gustatory desires so as to elevate the intellect. He often bemoaned the diet of his Southern boyhood, one replete with fried foods, gravy, and sweets. Sinclair told Meta that it had made him forever prone to becoming a slow-thinking "food drunkard."[15] A healthy body and quick mind, he insisted, could be developed through strictly controlled eating habits. An early example of the practice unfolded in the spring of 1905 as Sinclair faced the first editorial comments on his draft manuscript of *The Jungle*. Suffering from physical signs of overwork and anxiety, he and Meta turned to Horace Fletcher, a turn-of-the-century food faddist who believed that digestive and other health problems (including cancer) developed when eaters failed to properly chew their food. Fletcher advised extreme mastication. He told his followers to swallow their food only after it turned to liquid, a habit that he said would curb their overall appetite, ease digestion, and improve their general health. Sinclair and his wife abandoned the diet before too long (they lost excessive amounts of weight), but the idea that the mind could discipline the tongue appealed to the author throughout his life. After the publication of *The Jungle*, he experimented with vegetarian diets, including one raw food program in which he consumed chiefly nuts, olives, and fresh fruit and another that revolved around daily doses of yogurt and buttermilk.[16]

Another source of the author's austere lifestyle grew from his personal sense that artists are doomed to sacrifice physical comforts for their work. The belief came through in the days preceding the invitation to write *The Jungle*, when Sinclair took his wife to live with him in Princeton, New

Jersey, so that he could conduct research in the university's collection of Civil War materials for a war novel. Having suffered multiple rejections of his first serious literary efforts, Sinclair had little money, compelling the couple to set up residence in a tent he pitched on a local farm. Although the later commercial success of his Civil War novel, *Manassas* (1904), gave the couple the resources to purchase a permanent dwelling, Sinclair continued to live in tents at various points in his life, even after *The Jungle* made him an international celebrity. As one of his recent biographers has suggested, Sinclair welcomed personal financial gain, but not because it bought creature comforts; instead, money meant freedom to pursue his chosen work and to live as he saw fit.[17] The author later honored the commitment to creative freedom by using the proceeds from *The Jungle* to start a utopian artists community called Helicon Hall in a former boys school outside Manhattan. In 1907 it burned to the ground, only months after its founding.

Sinclair's conversion to socialism in 1902 provided the theoretical framework to structure his ideas about how immigrants like Jurgis engaged the industrial work process through their senses. The conversion began not as visceral witness to inequality, but as an intellectual journey that was initiated when he discovered the writings of two influential socialists—George D. Herron, a minister, and Gaylord Wilshire, a land developer and publisher. In November, Herron invited Sinclair to dinner at a fancy residential hotel in New York City, having earlier received a letter of praise from the young author. The dinner conversation impressed Sinclair, who was looking for an intellectual framework to understand his own economic and professional frustrations.[18]

The young author admitted, somewhat shamefacedly, that he held no deep understanding of the thinkers discussed by his hosts, including Karl Marx. (He later placed the gap in his education squarely at the feet of the faculty at Columbia, whose lectures on socialism he lamented as superficial.)[19] Soon after the meeting, Sinclair began an intense course of self-directed reading in socialism. Throughout the spring and summer of 1904, he read the German socialist Karl Kautsky (a "giant of the mind"); Karl Marx (whose *Communist Manifesto* he termed a "milestone in the progress of civilization"); Thorstein Veblen (whose *Theory of the Leisure Class* he read in a "continuous ebullition of glee"); and various socialist newspapers, including *The Worker* (New York) and the *Appeal to Reason* (Kansas).[20] The experience fundamentally changed Sinclair's understanding of the roots of economic inequality, an intellectual transformation he later described in grand terms: "Not since [I] had discovered the master-key of Evolution had [I] come upon any set of ideas that meant so much."[21] Sinclair wrote admiringly about the "scientific" basis of socialist thought, praising the "mathematical precision" in which Marx and company had diagnosed social problems and outlined remedies.[22]

Sinclair's most recent biographer minimizes the influence of Marx in shaping the author's ideas about socialism. He argues that Sinclair, like many American socialists, chiefly drew inspiration from domestic and Christian sources.[23] While such influences are clear, it does not follow that Sinclair ignored, or rejected, the work of the most influential political radical in nineteenth-century Europe. In fact, Sinclair's fictionalization of the alienation of labor dovetailed with broader intellectual currents in turn-of-the-century socialism, particularly the attempt of Chicago's radical publishing house, Charles H. Kerr and Company, to "Americanize" Marxian thought.[24] Marx's precise influence on Sinclair must be gleaned from autobiographical accounts and inferred from works like *The Jungle* (the fire at Helicon Hall destroyed Sinclair's personal papers for the period before 1907), both of which show a clear debt to Marx.

Sinclair acknowledged the German philosopher directly in his autobiographical novel, *Love's Pilgrimage,* but *The Jungle* evinces the debt in far richer detail. Marx set out the basic terms of alienation as a physical phenomenon in his key work, *The Communist Manifesto* (1848). In it he argued that workers like Jurgis became an "appendage of the machine," called upon to exercise the "most simple, most monotonous, and most easily acquired knack," the wages of which "prolong and reproduce a bare existence." The laborer, Marx wrote, "lives merely to increase capital."[25] The labor process culminated in what the sociologist Anthony Synnott terms the "bestial barbarization of the worker in the capitalist system."[26] The mass-production workplace—meatpacking plants were among the first, as we shall see—transformed workers from human beings into insensate beasts of burden.

The emphasis on the sensory nature of alienation continued in Marx's massive study *Capital.* Tellingly, the *only* selection from *Capital* that Sinclair included in a lengthy collection of classic texts in socialism that he compiled in 1914 described how capitalism's appetite for surplus value exhausted workers' senses. Capitalist production drained workers' strength, extending the evil system's reach into their homes to usurp "time for the growth, development, and healthy maintenance of the body." The selection also included a discussion of sensory respites (meals) that Sinclair would return to in *The Jungle.* On workday meals, Marx argued that industrial labor dulled the tongue, taking the gustatory pleasure from eating so that it became a "mere means of production, as coal is supplied to the boiler, grease and oil to the machine."[27]

Key differences, no doubt, distinguished Marx's and Sinclair's views on the senses. Marx portrayed workers as sensory beings, but, unlike Sinclair, he saw the senses as the instruments through which workers affirmed their humanity. Synnott terms this attitude a "materialist sense-positive philosophy."[28] The view is treated most directly in Marx's *Economic and Philosophical Manuscripts of 1844,* a work that was not available to Sinclair when he wrote *The Jungle.*[29] The 1844 manuscripts make the claim, embedded in later works like *Capital,* that "man is affirmed in the objective world not only in the act of thinking but with *all* his senses," and further propose the senses as historical constructs by arguing that "the *forming* of the five senses is a labor of the entire history of the world down to the present."[30] For Marx, workers' affirmation in the world through their senses made them human and noble, not animalistic and base.

Sinclair also differed radically from Marx on the revolutionary process. Throughout his life the author rejected violence as an instrument of political change, arguing that the ballot box provided the most effective tool for radical reform. In the fall of 1904 he wrote two articles for the *Appeal to Reason* that highlighted his emphasis on democratic change. The first dealt with a recently defeated strike in the Chicago stockyards.[31] The article expressed Sinclair's discomfort with labor unions and insisted that workers could transform their lives simply by voting for the Socialist presidential candidate, Eugene V. Debs. Sinclair resisted the idea that unions—portrayed in *The Jungle* as ineffective at best, corrupt at worst— effected positive change, seeing strikes as too often degenerating into the type of loud, chaotic mobs that middle-class Chicagoans associated with the labor violence of the late nineteenth century. Sinclair implored readers to resist that idea that the solution to their problems lay in "mobs, insurrections, dynamite, and gatling guns"; instead he appealed to sweet reason by promising a socialist utopia where unemployment, political corruption, crime, prostitution, drunkenness, and war no longer ruined their lives.[32] The vehicle of change—the voting booth—symbolized the author's emphasis on the rational, intellect-driven transition to socialism.

The second article—titled "Farmers of America, Unite!"—further underlined Sinclair's emphasis on the voting booth as a vehicle of change, but did so in ways that revealed the author's tendency to express nativism in sensory terms. Obviously attempting to appeal to Midwestern populists—and the racial attitudes that rent the overall movement—Sinclair warned readers that capitalists' need for cheap labor had them "raking out the sewers and gutters of Europe today and shipping their degraded outcasts here." Immigration had more than doubled since 1899, bringing to America, he wrote ominously, immigrants "from Hungary, Russia and Southern Italy." The flood of Eastern European immigrants fueled the corrupt political machines that ran the nation's cities. In Philadelphia the electoral puppet masters "keep the names of dead men, dogs and negro babies on the voting lists" to shape the results to their corrupt ends.[33] The author's comparison of black infants to "dogs" represented an example of the crude antiblack racism that he probably carried forward from his Southern boyhood. In broader terms, the reference underscores how the socialist movement suffered from the prejudices of racism as well as nativism that were prevalent in the era.[34]

The article on the 1904 stockyards strike led directly to the invitation to write *The Jungle*. Sinclair's full-throated endorsement of Debs—a figure with a heroic reputation among Chicago's workers for his participation in the Pullman strike a decade earlier—made the article of special interest in Back of the Yards. The *Appeal* printed thousands of copies for direct distribution there. The newspaper's editor, Fred Warren, suggested Sinclair consider writing an exposé to raise public awareness of the conditions that the workers faced in the meatpacking plants.

Chicago had already been the subject of muckraking exposés on topics such as commodity speculation, and the meatpacking industry itself had been targeted by an 1899 pamphlet written by the socialist A. M. Simons. The reading public, however, still regarded the stockyards and their factories as a great success story in mass production.[35] Warren, who had read *Manassas*, believed that Sinclair commanded the narrative abilities to write a compelling challenge to the success story. He had in mind the "*Uncle Tom's Cabin* of wage slavery," a work that tugged at readers' emotions to generate sympathy for labor in the same way Harriet Beecher Stowe's 1852 novel bolstered support for the abolitionist movement.[36] Sinclair took the assignment, traveling to Chicago in October 1904 to begin research. He accepted a five-hundred-dollar advance from Warren, who agreed to publish the results as a series of articles in the *Appeal*. A novel, with a commercial press, would follow.[37]

The Back of the Yards Jungle

Thirty years before Sinclair arrived in Chicago, the city's meatpacking industry undertook a major expansion around the Union Stockyards. Chicago's packers traditionally processed pork (salted or smoked) during the colder winter months. Chilling technology, especially the perfection of refrigerated railroad cars, eventually allowed them to operate year round; to reach the urban markets of the East; and to bring a wider range of live-stock to buyers. Corporate mergers in the second half of the nineteenth century concentrated the industry, paving the way for the domination of the large packinghouses Sinclair targeted in his novel (Armour, Swift, and Morris). By 1900 the six largest packers slaughtered more than 95 percent of all livestock at the stockyards. The sheer number of animals killed each day attests to the size, complexity, and speed of the production system those corporations developed. The *daily* volume of the stockyards in 1900 reached seventy-five thousand cattle; eighty thousand sheep; and three hundred thousand hogs.[38]

Handling thousands of livestock units forced the packing companies to develop a production mechanism that ran continuously and to organize it down to the last detail: the disassembly line. Long before Henry Ford perfected assembly lines for automobiles, the meatpacking industry had developed what Barrett terms the "most sophisticated production process in the United States before the turn of the century."[39] Disassembly took place on a factory floor with a seemingly incongruous organizational scheme. Within giant factory buildings, management controlled both the speed of the line and methods for the smallest tasks on it. The entire process relied on the hands of the individual workers who broke down the carcasses. One of Sinclair's accomplishments in *The Jungle* is to capture the feverish sensory environment that workers on the line faced each day. His description of the gritty sights, sounds, smells, feel, and even tastes of the line is richest in the case of Jurgis himself, which we will soon consider in detail.[40]

The bulk of the work on the disassembly line required no special skills, so the packing companies hired corps of unskilled immigrant laborers.[41] Back of the Yards housed a great deal of that workforce, growing by 75 percent in the first decade of the twentieth century, when Sinclair wrote *The Jungle*.[42] Population growth also changed the ethnic makeup of Back of the Yards, transforming the neighborhood from an enclave of Irish and Germans to a diverse collection of immigrants that included Poles and Lithuanians.[43] Sinclair's decision to settle Jurgis and his family there reflected the diverse ethnic character of the neighborhood. The family's initial housing, a crammed tenement, also captured the density within residences.[44] In 1910 researchers found that more than half of the people it surveyed in Back of the Yards slept in rooms that exceeded the minimum standard in local code, four hundred cubic feet per person.[45]

Crowding also inflamed the pollution of Back of the Yards' physical environment and bred disease. In *The Jungle*, Jurgis and his soon-to-be wife, Ona, are overwhelmed by the noxious sights and smells of garbage on their first tour of their neighborhood. They stroll with some difficulty, as potholes mark the unpaved streets. Pitted with "great hollows full of stinking green water," the streets resemble "a miniature topographical map." Soon Jurgis smells a "ghastly odor, of all the dead things in the universe," wafting from one of the neighborhood's four garbage dumps, where the refuse of six South Side wards accumulated.[46] Combined with the stench of Bubbly Creek and other receptacles of packinghouse waste, the odious smell earned Back of the Yards a reputation as a world apart from nearby, middle-class neighborhoods like Hyde Park. The historian Thomas Jablonsky described Back of the Yards' olfactory reputation well—"blue collar, ethnic, aesthetically unappealing"—though he might have gone further to say that residents of Hyde Park believed they whiffed an alien world when they turned their noses toward the stockyards.[47] The stench also signaled the unsanitary conditions that created high rates of death from disease, figures in which Back of the Yards well outpaced Hyde Park.[48]

Sinclair described the working and living conditions of the stockyards district accurately, but he erred when he suggested that the sensorially oppressive environment drained people like Jurgis and Ona of their humanity. Barrett has demonstrated that workers in the stockyards enjoyed a rich religious and associational life. He also notes that the hundreds of local saloons served up not just alcohol but also a convivial retreat from the workplace and the tenement.[49] For Sinclair, whose personal background made him deeply suspicious of alcohol, the saloon served only the negative ends of addiction and debt. In addition, the socialist author seldom allowed Jurgis and family much fun. Their engagement with Chicago's consumer culture is brief and menacing.[50] The author's ideological commitments account for the silence on the issue, but those must be linked to his distrust of sensory pleasure. The anthropologist David Howes has made the intriguing argument that Marx's analytical neglect of the sensual appeals of consumer culture may have stemmed from health problems that made his later life distinctively painful.[51] Sinclair's discomfort with pleasures of the flesh indicate a similar sensory alienation, in this case leading to neglect of what the growing, urban consumer culture offered to Chicago's working classes.

Writing *The Jungle*

Sinclair spent seven weeks in the stockyards district to research *The Jungle*. Scholars typically associate Sinclair's personal study of Back of the Yards with the journalistic muckrakers of the Progressive Era, and for good reason. It should also be noted, however, that *The Jungle* rested on the undercover mode of reporting that animated the popular "down-and-out" literature of the turn of the century.[52] In works like Stephen Crane's "An Experiment in Misery" (1894) and Jack London's "South of the Slot" (1909), down-and-out authors literally joined the lives of the urban poor, because they believed it was the only way to fully comprehend their lives. Such authors often disguised themselves as members of the community they studied, a deception they justified for the larger good of articulating the problems of people with little public voice.

Sinclair's foray into Chicago's stockyards no doubt differed from other down-and-out projects because only once did he disguise himself as a member of the Back of the Yards community. Nevertheless, he shared down-and-outers' tendency to combine fiction and nonfiction in narratives that portrayed the urban slum as a foreign land through which authors guided middle-class readers as tourists. In reflecting on Sinclair's description of the actual tourists who visited the stockyards, the labor historian Daniel Bender observes that Sinclair's narrative "blurred the line between his own socialist sojourn in Packingtown and class tourism."[53]

Sinclair's arrival at Back of the Yards demonstrates another feature of down-and-out narratives that relates to the class backgrounds of their authors: a sense of fear and sensory disjuncture upon their initial "descent" into the slum. As Sinclair later wrote, the stockyards district shocked his senses, hitting him like a "sudden violent blow." He explored the neighborhood "white-faced and thin, partly from undernourishment, partly from horror."[54] The historian Mark Pittenger describes a similar reaction by the socialist author Jack London when he arrived in London's East End to write the down-and-out classic *People of the Abyss* (1902). A friend and comrade of Sinclair, London reacted with fear because the East End slum mirrored the meager circumstances over which he had triumphed to become a successful writer.[55] Sinclair may well have experienced the same kind of dread, as Back of the Yards recalled his boyhood in New York City. In any case, his visceral reaction illustrates how down-and-out authors could be at once repelled and sympathetic, perspectives that both shape *The Jungle*.

The particular horrors of the stockyards quarter became apparent as Sinclair began talking with the people there—settlement house workers, labor activists, and a medical writer and workers. Ernest Poole, a volunteer publicity agent for the meatpackers union, served as the author's initial contact. Poole resided in the neighborhood, at the University of Chicago Settlement House, where Sinclair took his meals. An accomplished writer, Poole had recently published a fictional autobiography about a Lithuanian immigrant who worked his way up in the stockyards through the good works of the union.[56] It appeared in the magazine *The Independent* two months before Sinclair arrived. Much like *The Jungle*, Poole's "autobiography" attracted the attention of President Theodore Roosevelt, who asked an acquaintance to investigate its verisimilitude.[57] Sinclair later drew from the autobiography when he wrote *The Jungle*, but the details of the two men's cooperation during the October visit remain unclear.

A more substantial collaboration developed with A. M. Simons, a socialist organizer and journalist, who had worked as a charity agent in the stockyards. The author of an 1899 exposé on the meatpacking industry, *Packingtown*, he put Sinclair in touch with other socialist organizers in the neighborhood in order to help him gain undercover access to the packing plants.[58] Sinclair eventually made at least three personal visits to the plants. The first consisted of an official tour, which later appeared in *The Jungle* as part of Rudkus's introduction to Back of the Yards. Sinclair also took up Simons's offer to go undercover, posing as a worker to see the parts of the plants that the packers wanted to keep from the prying eyes of journalists. The investigative coup allowed the author moments of unfettered access, constituting the point at which Sinclair most directly emulated the undercover strategies of the down-and-out authors.[59]

Sinclair's third contact in the stockyards—and the person with whom he took his third tour of the packing plants—proved especially influential. Adolph Smith was an English medical writer and socialist who was visiting Chicago to investigate the packinghouses. Sinclair first met Smith through Jane Addams, the Progressive reformer and founder of Chicago's best-known social settlement, Hull House. Addams met Sinclair briefly after he arrived in Chicago, finding him naïve and irritating—a "wild-eyed theorist," according to one of his recent biographers. She bristled when he announced that the work of the settlement houses paled in comparison to the conversion of the poor to socialism, leading her to say later that she saw him as a "young man with a good deal to learn." Addams directed Sinclair to Smith nonetheless, hoping that the medical writer might provide concrete data to inform his theoretical excesses.[60]

The introduction served its purpose, as Sinclair later wrote that Smith offered some of the most substantial guidance about the dangers of the meatpacking plants. He explained to Sinclair the differences between the American and European techniques for meatpacking, demonstrating that the municipal slaughterhouses across the Atlantic offered a more sanitary, safe, and humane alternative.[61] The following summer Smith's researches appeared in the British medical journal *The Lancet* just in time to serve as key reference sources.[62] For Sinclair the relationship with Smith provided the expert knowledge that grounded his idealism. "When I wondered if possibly my horror might be the offensiveness of a young idealist," he later wrote, "I would fortify myself by Smith's expert, personal horror."[63] Smith's article proved important after Sinclair drafted *The Jungle* as well, serving as one of sources of substantiation demanded by Doubleday, Page, and Company before it agreed to publish the novel.[64]

The commercial success of *The Jungle* derived in large part from Sinclair's ability to craft a novel with shock value. The author's literary style combined the graphic realism of the naturalist authors he admired with the reportage common in muckraking and down-and-out works.[65] Sinclair's literary agenda was not as bold as that of the author Stephen Crane, who disguised himself as a drifter in an attempt to actually adopt the subjective perspectives of the transients of New York's Bowery district.[66] Although Sinclair saw himself as a sensitive artist and hoped *The Jungle* would be regarded as great literature, he viewed his purpose as presenting an accurate sketch of the conditions workers faced in industrial capitalism to effect their liberation. Still, as Sinclair famously put it, he aimed at his reader's heart by relating what he found most horrifying and tragic in Back of the Yards. Those judgments sometimes reflected what Pittenger terms a "dialectic of attraction and repulsion" in down-and-out writing, in which an author's commitment to social reform was "cross cut by disgust and repulsion stemming from actual contact."[67] Sinclair, an ideological ally of stockyards workers like Jurgis, similarly drew lines of social class and ethnicity in the sensory terms that both engaged and repelled his elite audience.

The novel's description of Jurgis and Ona's Lithuanian wedding feast (*veselija*) is a telling example. Sinclair opens the novel with this scene, but it is understood to take place six months after the family's arrival in Chicago.[68] Most family members have found work in the stockyards and its packing plants by this point, but they had not yet suffered the type of sensory degradation that awaits them in later chapters. With the exception of Jurgis's father, everyone is healthy and robust.

The sensorial richness of the celebration—the lavish banquet and the Lithuanian folk music—is a testament to the persistence of ethnic tradition.[69] The scene conveys how the feast bolstered the family's self-respect by allowing them to host a cherished and expensive ritual of home in the shadows of the meatpacking plants.[70] (As the novel unfolds, Sinclair tracks the family's decline by noting how they become increasingly unable to pay the funeral expenses for their dead relatives.) One of the most perceptive students of the wedding scene, the literary critic Orm Øverland, has argued that Sinclair's treatment of the folk music evinces the author's sensitivity to his subjects' cultural values. He argues that the earnest fiddler Tamoszuis Kuszleika symbolizes an ever slipping grip on the sounds of home. Tamoszuis's squeaky fiddle alludes to how the muting and replacement of those sounds by Chicago's strange aural landscape was a confusing and emotionally wrought transformation for the Rudkus clan and their fellows.[71]

At the same time, Sinclair's discussion of the scene's origins in his autobiography underscores the author's detachment from the lives of his subjects. Sinclair drew the scene from personal observation, happening upon an immigrant wedding on an evening stroll in Back of the Yards.[72] The author anticipated an event that would be rich in character models, so he "slipped into the room, and stood against the wall," watching the married couple, their parents, and the other guests with interest.[73] His stomach growled. *The Jungle*'s description of the veselija indicates that all comers may eat as they please, but Sinclair decamped: "I went away to supper, and came back again, and stayed until late at night, sitting against the wall, and not talking to anyone."[74]

Sinclair's personal discomfort with feasting may account for his gustatory restraint, for *The Jungle* describes a banquet of rich, mouth-watering food and drink—"a big yellow bowl of smoking potatoes, . . . ham and a dish of sauerkraut, boiled rice, macaroni, bologna sausages, great piles of penny buns, bowls of milk, and foaming pitchers of beer."[75] The author's autobiographical reflections, however, do not say why he avoided conversation. He may have been uncomfortable with the noise levels, as *The Jungle* presents a loud, even deafening, affair. The attendees rejoice with "laughter and shouts and endless badinage and merriment," a hub-bub that combines with the music to create a "deafening clamor." The raucousness continues as the partygoers drink and dance to exhaustion, some passing out in chairs or on the floor. By the end of the night, the "heavy scent in the room," a mixture of lamp oil, alcohol, food, and sweaty bodies, is practically visible, a physical marker of the feast as working-class and ethnic.[76]

For Sinclair the veselija is both moving and exotic. It is one of the few points in the novel when Jurgis and his family manage to control the shape of their lives in Chicago. Their wedding traditions are not stamped out by the rigors of the workplace and the putrid industrial landscape; on the contrary, the celebration is notable for its sensory vitality. At the same time, however, that sensory vitality—the clamor, the rich food, the sweaty musicians and inebriated dancers—underscore the cultural distance that Sinclair drew between his elite readers and working-class immigrants. The Rudkuses rejoice with little of the restraint and civility that signaled social distinction to members of Chicago's middle and upper classes. Jurgis and Ona's wedding celebration is thus poignant, in both senses of the term. It is a touching evocation of the importance of ethnic tradition in Back of the Yards, but it is also marked by sharp smells and flavors that set the attendees apart as sensory beings with coarse tastes.

The wedding feast is where readers first meet Jurgis. In many ways *The Jungle* is the story of the protagonist's physical decline and sensory degrada-tion. Working in the packing factories debases Jurgis's senses, which even-tually grow numb. He is steadily driven to satisfy only his lowest sensory desires, a model of Marx's notion of alienated labor. As a socialist, Sinclair blamed the packers for the degradation, challenging earlier middle-class critics of Chicago's working class who conflated sensory difference with poor character or moral turpitude. At the same time, however, the author betrayed his social remove by portraying the meatpacking factory and the slum as sensory worlds that totally consumed Jurgis's humanity. As the protagonist begins to embody his ever more repulsive workplaces, he becomes a stinking beast of burden, a walking counterexample of middle-class social distinction.

In *The Jungle*'s opening chapter, Jurgis is defined by his powerful build and robust senses. The contrast with his delicate bride, Ona, is rendered, literally, in black and white terms. Ona's visage—a "wan little face . . .

blue-eyed and fair"—seems a natural reflection her petite, sixteen-year-old form, which is outfitted in a "conspicuously white" muslin dress complete with a veil holding five pink paper roses. Her face, flushed red with nervousness, betrays her wonder at marrying the bridegroom, a man with "great black eyes with beetling brows, and thick black hair that curled in waves about his ears." If Jurgis's brow looks husky, his chest and arms define him as the type of workhorse that just might survive the rigors of the packing plants. Jurgis's "mighty shoulders and . . . giant hands" gave him the strength to "take up a two-hundred-and-fifty-pound quarter of beef and carry it into a car without a stagger, or even a thought."[77] As the celebration winds down, and as Ona becomes more and more worried about the expense, Jurgis carries her home, promising to "work harder" to solve their problems.[78]

Jurgis's first job in the packing plants requires him to do one thing, all day: sweep up guts from the cattle slaughtered on the "killing beds." Sinclair's account of the work, like his description of Elzbieta's stint in the sausage factory, captures how it focused workers' senses around one minute, repetitive task. The killing, conducted at a frenetic pace in unheated rooms with slippery floors, "called for every faculty of man" to keep up, providing "never one instant's rest . . . for his hand or his eye or his brain."[79] Jurgis seems uniquely suited to the job. At first he even enjoys it. The work serves as an outlet for the "overflow of energy that was in him," a natural spiritedness that made him fidget and dance when asked to stand still.[80] He "would laugh to himself as he ran down the line, darting a glance now and then" at his fellow workers, many of whom seem to hate their jobs, an attitude that leaves Jurgis nonplussed.[81] Here Jurgis's energy renders him childlike and naïve, so gleeful in physically exerting himself that he is unable to see why others detest the work.

Before too long, however, he starts to understand how the work coarsened the sensory faculties of his coworkers. The packers keep the killing beds unheated, so the men must use the materials at hand to keep their extremities warm. Some wrap their feet in newspapers, but the wrapping becomes soaked in blood and frozen solid, a process that repeats itself until "by night-time a man would be walking on great lumps the size of the feet of an elephant." Others thrust their feet into the carcasses of slaughtered cattle for relief. The men who carve up the carcasses do so without the benefit of gloves, so their hands and arms become numb, making knife accidents on the line frequent. The heat of the blood creates steam, so those same workers find it difficult to see, which further increases the possibility of accidents, especially when they face an animal that has been insufficiently stunned before slaughter. "It was to be counted as a wonder," Sinclair wrote, "that there were not more men slaughtered than cattle."[82]

Even worse than the cold is that the packers deny the men the most basic sensorial respite, the midday meal. Equating it, as Marx did, with shoveling "coal to the boiler," the bosses refuse to set aside a clean place for the men to eat. They force Jurgis to "either eat his dinner amid the stench in which he worked, or else to rush, as did all his companions, to any one of the hundreds of saloons which stretched out their arms to him." Sinclair's view of "whiskey row" is predictability scornful. He acknowledged that the workday saloons offered refuge—free food, a warm stove—but he cast them as mere traps that lulled workers into wasting their lives on drink. "If you went in not intending to drink," he averred, "you would be put out in no time, and if you were slow . . ., like as not you would get your head split open with a beer-bottle in the bargain." When Jurgis drinks, the alcohol inoculates him so that he might better stand his work—"the deadly brutalizing monotony of it did not afflict him so"—but the numbness lasts only moments. It wears off even before the end of the day, starting him down the road to addiction, a tragedy that Sinclair knew all too well.[83]

Sinclair wrote with greater insight about the seasonal nature of the work on the killing beds. In the summer the heat made the plants stifling and malodorous in the extreme. "All day long the rivers of hot blood poured forth," the author explained, "until, with the sun beating down, and the air motionless, the stench was enough to knock a man over." The packers give little attention to keeping the killing beds clean, so as the blood from the slaughter cakes upon them and bakes, "the old smells of a generation would be drawn out." The men's skin absorbs the stench, rendering their bodies offensive to the nose, even at long range. The work proceeds with such speed that it is simply impossible to keep the blood at a distance: "There was simply no such thing as keeping decent, the most careful men gave it up in the end, and wallowed in uncleanliness." The summer brings no improvement to the mealtime respite, either. The men who avoid whiskey row have no place to wash their hands, forcing them to eat "as much raw blood as food at dinner-time," a workplace reality that echoed Marx's assertion about how industrial work grew ever more repulsive, reducing wages as well as standards of personal decency.[84]

Jurgis's own fall from decency is hastened by a workplace injury that costs him his place on the killing beds.[85] The man, once so vigorous, is bed-ridden and sapped of spirit. "They say that the best dog will turn cross if he be kept chained all the time," Sinclair wrote, "and it was the same with the man." Jurgis becomes an angry beast, so trapped and threatened that he snarls and curses all day, reducing his wife to tears. The most devastating aspect of his convalescence, however, is that it weakens his robust body. The robust visage of the wedding feast slowly transforms into that of a "homeless ghost, with cheeks sunken in and his long black hair straggling into his eyes." Without exercise, his muscles grow flabby and waste away, a problem made worse by his refusal to eat an unearned share of the family's food. The condition makes regaining the job on the killing beds impossible. Jurgis—"thin and haggard"—enjoys none of the preferences that his formerly powerful body earned for him among the hiring bosses. At this point Jurgis reaches a new stage in the alienation process, going from cog in the killing beds machine to a worn-out and discarded machine part. "They had worn him out," Sinclair explained, "with their speeding up and their carelessness, and now they had thrown him away!"[86]

Yet Sinclair has even worse in store for Jurgis's senses. After an unsuccessful hunt for a new job, Jurgis is forced to take work in the most dreaded of places: the fertilizer plant. Sinclair sets the fertilizer plant apart from the worst of the killing bed and sausage room horrors, casting it as the innermost circle of the stockyards hell. The place where the last remains of the livestock are transformed into bone phosphate and other by-products, it is filled with a blinding dust and sickening fumes. Jurgis is charged with shoveling fertilizer into carts, a job that quickly covers him in the dust. A wet sponge tied over his mouth provides his only protection from inhalation. He is unable to see, so he knows that he works alongside others only because he hears the sound of their shovels. Yet even that sound is dulled when his ears fill with dust. As it seeps into his skin, Jurgis's face and hair become the color of the fertilizer. His senses reel, leading to a pounding headache and tremors: "The blood was pounding in his brain like an engine's throbbing," Sinclair wrote, "there was a frightful pain in the top of his skull, and he could hardly control his hands."[87] He is reduced to vomiting after an hour; by the end of the first day, he can barely keep himself upright.

The malodorous dust bores deep enough into his skin to escape the cleansing action of soap and water, so the smell follows him all the time. When he rides home on the streetcars, Jurgis smells so rank that it forces the other passengers to "gasp and sputter, to put handkerchiefs on their noses and transfix him with furious glances." At first he is so dazed that he barely notices as the other riders clear from the car. After a few shifts, however, he sees riding the streetcars as a kind of game. Indifferent to his own stench, Jurgis amuses himself by observing the reactions of the other passengers. The situation at home is less amusing, because the stench seeps into the family's clothing and even their food. With their home smelling as a "miniature fertilizer mill," the other members of the family are barely able to eat, retching and vomiting at mealtime.[88] Jurgis must continue the work for the much-needed pay, even as the stench infiltrates the family kitchen to deny the Rudkuses the most basic separation of work and home that middle-class readers identified with a respectable domestic life.

Weakened and reduced to working in what Sinclair labels "the steam-ing pit of hell," Jurgis's sensory degradation reaches its apogee. The urge to inoculate himself with drink haunts him constantly, further alienating him from the other members of the family, including Ona. She shows increasing signs of emotional distress, but her husband is so numbed that he relegates the worries to the back of his mind. While the packing plants work overtime for the holiday rush, Jurgis and Ona toil from early morning to late at night, meeting at the end of the day to walk home in silence. Having fallen into a constant torpor, they no longer talk to each other. Their lives are entirely consumed with work and sleep: "And they would eat what they had to eat, and afterwards, because there was only their misery to talk of, they would crawl into bed and fall into a stupor and never stir until it was time to get up again, and dress by candle-light, and go back to the machines."[89] Jurgis has become a model of the alienated, insensate worker, "a dumb beast of burden, knowing only the moment in which he was."[90]

Sinclair might have ended his story there, but, much to the chagrin of literary critics, he turned it into an ever more implausible tale of Jurgis's flight from the stockyards and his family.[91] After discovering the source of his wife's emotional distress—sexual abuse at the hands of her boss—Jurgis attacks the offender. He ends up in jail and blacklisted from work in the stockyards. A parade of horribles follows: the family loses their house; Ona dies in childbirth; Elzbieta's thirteen-year-old-son is killed by rats; Jurgis's baby son drowns in the street; and Ona's cousin is reduced to drug addiction and prostitution. Jurgis takes flight on a train to live as a hobo. He eventually returns to the city, but stays away from the family to work as a thief, both literally (as a mugger) and figuratively, as a cog in the stockyard's corrupt political machine.

It is at this point in the novel that Sinclair turned to race. He did so when he fictionalized the 1904 stockyards strike, which he knew well from his earlier writing for the *Appeal*. The strike capped a long period of labor organizing in the stockyards. The packers, in part through the use of strikebreakers that included black migrants from the South, defeated it. The version of the strike in *The Jungle* conveys how such divisions of race divided the working classes in Back of the Yards. At the same time, Sinclair's treatment of the episode suffered from historical half-truths and racial stereotypes expressed in sensory terms. The author failed to mention that black workers struck alongside their white fellows in 1904; in addition, he neglected to explain how labor unions' exclusionary practices contributed to racial division.[92]

Jurgis encounters black strikebreakers when he takes a job as a boss on the killing beds as a strikebreaker. He crosses the picket line secretly, having been ordered to do so by a corrupt local politician. The gang under Jurgis's supervision—a "throng of stupid black negroes"—has come to the stockyards chiefly to run riot. Giving vent to their crude instincts, they drink and fight late into the night. The black workers resist orders with contempt and threats of violence, bolstered by the knives they have stolen from the mess hall and stored in their boots.[93]

Sinclair's depiction of the strikebreakers as criminal and depraved echoed the sensory stereotypes that Southern whites had long used to reinforce the racial divide. As the historian Mark M. Smith has argued, white supremacists dodged tricky questions about their inability to "see" race in an increasingly mixed society by insisting that they could detect "blackness" with their nonvisual senses.[94] Sinclair applied similar racial stereotypes, perhaps picked up during his Southern boyhood, to a Northern, industrial context. The stereotypes—extreme versions of the sensorial lines of class and ethnicity drawn earlier in the novel—demonstrate how languages of sensory disgust sketched varied notions of social differentiation in *The Jungle*. In this case Sinclair tapped into the existing discourses of racial savagery.[95]

The author's view that blacks threatened white "civilization" is clear when he explains that the strikebreakers' ancestors "had been savages in Africa" whose debauchery had been wisely contained by slave owners and, more recently, by Jim Crow segregation. Sinclair feared that Chicago lacked the restraints that kept blacks from feeding their primitive instincts in the South. Black migrants in the stockyards had been set "free to gratify every passion, free to wreck themselves," a natural instinct that expressed itself in the noises of the men's "fighting, gambling, drinking, and carousing, cursing, screaming, laughing and singing, playing banjoes and dancing!" The noise of the strikebreakers' religious worship was equally vulgar to Sinclair. He described a priestess standing before a bonfire in the yards of the packing plants: "an old, gray-headed negress, lean and witchlike, her hair flying wild and her eyes blazing." The priestess exhorted her spellbound listeners, who "moaned and screamed in convulsions of terror and remorse," demonstrations that expressed racial savagery in dramatic terms.[96]

Sinclair's use of sensory stereotypes cast blacks as depraved sensory beings. His depiction of the 1904 strike reflected the racial tensions that divided Back of the Yards at that time, giving voice to the prejudices that inhibited class unity across the racial divide.[97] In broader terms the depiction revealed how the racial prejudices of the era ran through socialist discourse. Sinclair saw himself as politically enlightened, but, like other socialist authors, he rejected social equality among blacks and whites. The racial division he underscored bedeviled labor organizing in Chicago for decades to come.[98] It also ominously foreshadowed the most infamous expression of racial discord in Chicago's history, the race riot of 1919.[99]

A final point to consider is *The Jungle*'s conclusion. Sinclair resolves the story abruptly by introducing Jurgis to socialism, an evangelical conversion much like his own. Featuring a long speech on socialism by a character resembling Debs, the story concludes with a dinnertime seminar on socialism, modeled on the 1902 affair with Gaylord Wilshire and George D. Herron. The final scene—a rousing election-eve speech that ends with "CHICAGO WILL BE OURS!"—sums up Sinclair's emphasis on the voting booth as the vehicle most likely to transform American politics. The ending is didactic and unsatisfying, but it captures well his attitude about the distinction between sensory knowledge and reasoned judgment. After a long, emotional appeal to readers about how capitalistic production degraded workers' senses, Sinclair made his final appeal to their minds. Studying socialist texts and voting the ticket—strategies rooted in the rational eye he so valued—was his best advice about how they might further the cause. As one of his reviewers put it, Sinclair "begins in the fiercest light of melodrama and ends like a lyceum lecturer."[100]

Sinclair's hope that reading would spark radical political change reflected his tendency to privilege the mind over the senses, but it was not incongruent with the socialist movement's recruitment strategy. To the contrary, the creation of a "print culture of dissent" was one of its leading strategies, as the historian of socialist literature Jason D. Martinek has observed.[101] *The Jungle* followed in that tradition by using literacy to effect change and by presenting radical material in broadly accessible terms, unlike Marx's theoretical works. In this sense *The Jungle*'s indictment of the sensory alienation wrought by industrial capitalism served the author's political intentions well.

A sensory reading of *The Jungle* underscores how the conclusion failed to amplify the novel's compelling treatment of industrial labor, the senses, and alienation. Sinclair concludes the novel with a broad and sterile picture of the socialist future. He neglects to explain how socialism promised to rejuvenate the senses, making only passing references to art and music. He implies that good socialists are ones who chew their food "scientifically," much as the diet guru Horace Fletcher recommended.[102] Even Jurgis's salvation is limited to the intellect. "In the realm of thought," Sinclair explains, the protagonist's new life was a "perpetual adventure," but outwardly it was "commonplace and uninteresting."[103] Here Sinclair's novel compares unfavorably with two of the other best-selling socialist tracts of the era, both of which delivered vivid—if quite different—pictures of a socialist alternative in which the senses enriched the lives of regular people: Robert Blatchford's *Merrie England* (1893) and Edward Bellamy's *Looking Backward* (1888).[104] Sinclair's much vaunted appeal to the emotions could only register with greater force had he been willing to celebrate sensory rejuvenation as much as he condemned alienation.

CHAPTER 5

SENSORY REFRESHMENT

The Other White City

Joseph Beifeld, president of the White City Construction Company, visited Coney Island in the summer of 1904. Witnessing what he described as the "intense enjoyment" of the New Yorkers who fled the city proper for the seaside resort, he resolved to bring a similar set of attractions to Chicago. Much like the architects of Coney Island, he saw potential profit in the multiplying urban population, with its growing leisure time and spending power, all of which Chicago's streetcar lines would deliver to his doorstep. Yet Beifeld had more than dollar signs on his mind. He believed that a respectable amusement park would enhance Chicago's civic health by enlivening the senses of its residents. White City promised to countervail the monotony of factory work and the squalor of the vice district to make better, healthier citizens. It was a commercial venture, he announced with little sense of hyperbole, based on "humanitarian principles."[1]

The "White City" in the amusement park's name referenced the centerpiece of the 1893 world's fair, architect Daniel Burnham's classically designed model city, the buildings of which were covered in bright white stucco. Like the landscape architect Frederick Law Olmsted's Central Park in New York, Burnham's White City represented an effort by nineteenth-century cultural elites to lift up the sensibilities of the working and middle classes by surrounding them with beautifully designed spaces. The project resembled the efforts of George Pullman's model town, but the goal had less to do with turning a profit and more to do with raising social and cultural standards for political purposes. Burnham's White City, when contrasted with the "black city" that was Chicago's dirty business district, represented a utopian ideal in which the cultivation of aesthetic values gave rise to a more civilized, healthy urban order.[2] As the historian John Kasson writes, White City's classical design stood for an "architecture of responsibility," one that its practitioners associated with "public order, cultural unity, and civic virtue" in an era characterized by "disorder, strife, and vulgarity."[3]

In its initial conception, Beifeld's White City mimicked the cultural mission of Burnham's urban utopia, but in far more vernacular terms. It might be said that Beifeld and his partners attempted to synthesize the two main sections of the 1893 world's fair. They imagined placing the excitement of the popular Midway Plaisance (with its Ferris wheel and theatrical spectacles) in a refined setting that resembled Burnham's model city.[4] "Management proposes to supply amusements and entertainment for all of Chicago's citizens," the company's official magazine announced in 1905, a commitment that meant "catering to the artistic and love of the beautiful as well as the hilarious and more boisterous" attractions desired by thrill-seekers.[5] The design of Beifeld's White City reflected how the park invited consumers to abandon the self-restraint required in other public places without sacrificing cultural respectability. One of the most telling design decisions was the liberal use of the color white, which evoked both moral purity and physical cleanliness, much as it did in Burnham's model city.

Beifeld cast White City as an alternative to the disreputable culture of the city streets, especially the South Side's vice district. His decision to bar the seedy sideshows associated with street culture evinced his promise to further his customers' sense of respectability and morality. "Frightful monstrosities" and "hideous dwarfs," he explained, attracted indecent patrons. White City was a "fairy-like place." There was to be "nothing suggestive, nothing terrible, nothing disagreeable, or nothing questionable" if the park was to refresh the senses of consumers to nurture civic health.[6]

After the park's first few seasons, however, Beifeld's uplifting vision dimmed. White City faced slumping ticket sales, compelling his company to offer some of the more popular but morally questionable attractions of the city street and vice district. Moral reformers noticed. They questioned the amusement park's contributions to Chicago's civic health, eventually bringing legal charges of indecency. The charges represented one of the clearest indications that Beifeld's attempt to refresh the senses of Chicagoans had floundered. As more and more Chicagoans turned to the emerging national consumer culture for the sensorial thrills of modern urban life, they left White City behind.

Multisensory Amusement in the City

The entrepreneurs who built the fun parks that dotted Chicago in the early twentieth century participated in an emergent culture of amusement that has long attracted the attention of historians.[7] Those entrepreneurs may have bristled, however, at historians' long-running emphasis on vision as the dominant modality of the larger consumer culture they helped to create. Consumer historians, in particular, have emphasized seeing, looking, and spectacle to portray turn-of-the-century society as a reflection of a visual modern age, one in which the other senses declined in prestige and influence.[8] The emphasis on sight in the scholarship on consumerism makes sense in some crucial ways; indeed, it is impossible to understand the sensory politics of White City without surveying its displays of electric lights and reenactments of spectacular urban disasters.

It is equally clear that White City defined itself as a resort that appealed to all five senses. Unlike other popular amusements of the age—nickel-odeons, baseball games—the patrons who visited White City were not understood chiefly as "spectators."[9] "Audience and activity frequently merged" at turn-of-the-century amusement parks, Kasson explains, so consumers engaged commercial attractions in a hands-on fashion.[10] White City exemplifies how the architects of mass consumer culture provoked the senses to further their own financial and political agendas, a situation that was quite different from the one described by Karl Marx and Upton Sinclair in the previous chapter, in which capitalism inexorably drained the senses.

The performance scholar Lynn Sally's study of Coney Island is a good starting point to discuss a multisensory history of White City amusement park. At Coney Island, she argues, the pleasure merchants "reconfigured the consumption of leisure as participatory and kinesthetic." The spectacle often highlighted by historians as indicative of modern consumption became "not solely a visual experience but a corporeal one, an experience that catapulted pleasure seekers out of their everyday experiences into unexpected and fantastic circumstances."[11] In this way, she reasons, the attractions at Coney Island turned the alienating effects of the industrial machine back on itself. The workers who visited the seaside resort rode the "Leap Frog Railway" and the "Flip-Flap" to stimulate their senses, an inversion of the relationship between people and industrial machinery as described by Marx. Even more, Coney Island sold the various "shocks" of urban life—defined broadly by Sally as new sensory stimuli—back to consumers as "fun" in order to help them adjust to the modern age.

Kasson's study of Coney Island demonstrates that the New York resort offered consumers of various backgrounds a holiday from the strictures of social convention too. Patrons shed the self-control and reserve that marked social distinction without the consequences that attended similar behaviors on the city streets or the workplace. They clowned around, laughed when rides knocked them off balance, and generally reveled in the lack of predictability and routine. They also enjoyed ample opportunities to socialize with members of the opposite sex. Young men and women, outside the gaze of chaperones, floated through darkened tunnels of love or took mechanical rides that jostled them together in titillating ways. The urban historian Eric Avila takes the sexual thrills of Coney Island as its defining attraction. His interpretation underscores how amusement parks facilitated new forms of touching that playfully violated the middle-class standards of "privacy in public" to enliven a day at the park.[12] Coney Island, Avila suggests, might be understood as a precursor to late twentieth-century theme parks like Disneyland in so far as "sex, romance, and titillation" served as Coney Island's main "themes."[13]

Kasson best captures the essence of Coney Island when he writes that the park promoted a sense of "vulgar exuberance" that contrasted with the cerebral, uplifting cultural politics of Burnham and Olmsted.[14] Coney Island provided immigrants and working-class groups a chance to participate in "American" life on relatively equal terms. It also gave its visitors an opportunity to engage an increasingly modern world—one of machines, electricity, and crowds—as a form of pleasure. The resort succeeded because it struck a proper balance between exuberance and respectability. Coney Island offered respite from the era's restrictive social mores, but it never brazenly peddled vice.

Other purveyors of mass amusement understood their mission as more congruent with the goals of cultural uplift and civic health. A case in point from Chicago's South Side is Charles Comiskey, owner of the city's White Sox baseball team. The urban historian Robin Bachin's analysis of Comiskey traces how he built his eponymous ballpark, opened in 1910, to exude an "aura of respectability." Architecturally, Comiskey Park followed the lead of Chicago's City Beautiful movement, featuring a classical design that visually signaled the contributions of the White Sox's owner to the city's public culture and the respectable nature of baseball in general.[15] "The classically designed physical space of the ballpark," Bachin explains, "pronounced it a place where codes of decorum were observed," even among fans divided by class, ethnicity, or team loyalty. Like Burnham's White City, Comiskey's ballpark "encompassed ideas about properly ordered space and its ability to control behavior."[16]

The entrepreneurs who created White City amusement park argued that it advanced Chicago's civic health by refreshing visitors' senses. They believed that the larger city of Chicago offered few affordable and decent amusements for people of meager incomes. Chicago boasted a range of attractive public spaces, but none that catered to wage earners. The fine boulevard system, for example, chiefly benefited people with the means to spend a day riding, cycling, or automobiling. Hardworking men and women faced a "lamentable lack of opportunities for clean, healthful amusements and innocent pleasures of the inexpensive kind." This claim neglected existing ethnic and neighborhood sources of leisure, but it also tellingly highlighted White City's cross-class appeal as well as its owners' paternalistic cultural mission.[17]

Beifeld made the case for the political benefits of healthy commercial play for workers by arguing that refreshing the senses diffused class resentment. If circumstances forced toilers to "spend the hot evenings and sultry afternoons in [the] sulkiness" of the factory or the slum, poor people would only "bewail their lack of fortune" and envy those who maintained the "faculties for purchasing immunity from ennui." He pointed to the carnivals of the Old World as wisely designed social safety valves. The carnivals prevented the eruption of riots, the radical political tenor of which he illustrated by invoking the Terror of the French Revolution. Amusement park operators, then, were best understood as "public benefactors." The bigger the amusement park, the more its attractions released workers from the "labor exhaustion" that alienated the senses. The key was that White City provoked workers' senses in "the utmost orderly way" to ensure that the park did not simply give rise to a different form of working-class riot.[18]

White City also addressed a wider cultural concern about the urban middle classes: that they lacked invigorating experiences. The self-control and repose that signaled social distinction could lead to listlessness and a lack of resolve. Broadly echoing the critiques of sensory alienation among the working classes, medical professionals held that white-collar work taxed the body as well as the mind.[19] It sapped desk-bound men of the physical strength and the rugged independence of the frontier days. The popular concern with "neurasthenia" indicated that the urban middle classes desperately needed to remedy their psychic and physical health.[20]

The historian Jackson Lears has argued that the emergent consumer culture provided therapeutic avenues to reinvigorate middle-class life.[21] White City demonstrates how amusement park operators stimulated the senses to alleviate what some determined to be the dullness of the urban age. "The stiff-necked businessmen" and the "haughty society dame," the park's operators announced, "will find themselves benefitted by a few hours of relaxation." Yet not just any relaxation would do. White City offered the kinetic thrills that provided sensory release. The park's mechanical rides, for example, delivered "those thrills which are the result of swinging, riding in a rapidly moving elevator, coasting, or similar quick unexpected movements." Kinetic activity reestablished the balance of the senses demanded by nature, one knocked askew by urban lifestyles. White City proposed to stimulate the "equalization of use of every faculty," much like a course in physical education for schoolchildren, a claim that further illustrated the park's public mission.[22]

White City, South Side

In its opening season in 1905, White City invited consumers to rejuvenate their senses in a physical space set apart from the more questionable South Side streets and their leisure resorts. The downtown State Street shopping corridor, home to Marshall Field's department store among others, attracted bunches of middle-class consumers. Negotiating the retailing district, however, required keeping the senses on high alert to avoid tawdry street scenes. Three years after White City's debut, for example, the *Tribune* lamented the steady expansion of the South Side's "levee," a collection of saloons, gambling dens, and brothels that were generally tolerated by city authorities as a red-light district a few blocks south of downtown. Identifying an "encroaching gateway" to the vice district on the west side of State Street, around the Loop station at Van Buren Street, the newspaper described "inharmonious levee characteristics" that offended the eyes and ears of shoppers.[23]

The *Tribune* expressed the contrasts between the gateway to the levee on the west side of the street and the middle-class stores on the east side in languages of sensory distinction. The west side had transformed into "one of the noisiest, flashiest and most impressive of the highways of the South Side levee." It contrasted with the "solid wall of respectability" on the east, with its "sedate" and "well-groomed" commercial establishments, open to consumers of all ages. Those shoppers had to avert their eyes and even plug their ears to avoid the vulgarity just across the way. Their senses assaulted by a "strident, blaring line of cheap amusement places," respectable consumers were forced to, as the newspaper put it, "keep eyes, Moslem like, to the east." Even worse were the entrances to saloons, "questionable hotels," and suggestive "museums of anatomy," which, the *Tribune* griped, "must offend every passing eye not schooled to sights characteristic of the levee."[24]

Those establishments offended the eye because they operated during regular business hours, in broad daylight. Passersby were not even granted the courtesy of darkness, a dimming of the street scene and the persons who frequented it, including middle-class slummers who wished to remain anonymous.[25] The gateway to the levee, the *Tribune* explained, "wakes early to the orchestration, the barker, and the flotsam of humanity which is attracted to it," loud, garish, and smelly indications of moral poverty. By mid-afternoon the street's sexual culture intruded on the ear, as "the sharp clicking of exaggerated French heels" stood out among the shuffle of business shoes and work boots. Consumers risked catching a glimpse of shocking displays of indecency, as the habitués of the questionable hotels sometimes opened their street-level windows suddenly. The entire scene was laid bare "in its tawdry flashiness or its dull squalor, a blot upon the great retail district" of Chicago's proud State Street.[26]

The owners of White City used visual effects to set the park apart from such indecorous street scenes. They made much of the park as a world apart—a "fairy-like place"—precisely because the seedy temptations of the larger city were nowhere to be found inside. A large gateway ushered visitors into White City. The historian David Nasaw's analysis of electrical lighting and urban nightlife indicates that such grand entryways served as "intermediate buffer zones"—essentially, elaborate vestibules—between the regular world of the street and the pleasure zones within.[27] Dazzlingly lighted and often monumental in size, they signaled a safe zone of merrymaking that was distinct from the city streets.

Inside, the managers of White City kept control over physical space and the crowds. The park's chief partners owned all the major attractions, giving them veto power over proposals for suspect ones. The files of the White City Construction Company are filled with requests, many denied, from traveling sideshow artists.[28] The park had its own sewer system and provided customers with toilet rooms complete with attendants. "The most fastidious person will have no occasion to complain of the conveniences furnished," the management assured bathroom visitors.[29] Management also pointed out that it closely monitored its employees. Food servers were given a detailed list of rules that demanded personal cleanliness and decorous manners. White City kept a private fire department and police force commanded by retired Chicago officers. "Visitors can come with perfect assurance that they are better protected at White City," the park announced, "than almost anywhere else they may go."[30] The officers were trained to spot shady characters before they made trouble, helping to keep the outside world from creeping into White City.[31]

Electrical lighting also helped block out the city beyond. When White City opened in 1905, electrical lights were still something of a novelty, though they were becoming less so. The 1880s saw the construction of Chicago's first central power stations, which were built mostly to service the mansions of the business elite. By the time the lights at Burnham's model city dazzled in 1893—a visual effect that some nighttime observers found the most spectacular of the world's fair—electricity had emerged as a key feature of the commercial landscape. Existing gas lamps made a sooty glow, but the electric bulbs on the department stores and theaters downtown transformed the business district with their radiant "daytime" illumination. The brightness helped make a night on the town respectable by eliminating the metaphorical "darkness" associated with vice districts. It also enhanced the safety of those who took their leisure after dark. In a broader sense, however, electrical lights conveyed a type of splendor that contrasted with the dim tenement and the darkened offices of the after-hours city. Around the turn of the century, Nasaw argues, "electric" became a term that referred to the lights on downtown streets as well as the pleasures of a night on the town.[32]

The White City Construction Company built a 250-foot Jewel Tower, lighted with twenty thousand incandescent bulbs, as the visual center-piece of the park (see fig. 7). The park's electrical demands were so great that the closest Commonwealth Electric powerhouse could not generate enough current to suit its needs. White City negotiated a special contract with the Chicago Edison Company for its electricity, the power company's largest contract to that point. The Jewel Tower, the tallest structure south of the downtown business district, shined so brightly that it could be spotted by people across the South Side as well as passengers approaching Chicago by train.[33]

Yet the tower served as one of the park's key attractions, because it was something to be seen up close. One visitor, John S. Reid, quite literally illustrated the visual spectacle in a letter he wrote to a female friend living in New York. The 1908 letter described his route from his apartment on Dearborn Street to White City via streetcar. Reid pasted dozens of small photographs in the text so that his reader saw the attractions as he described them. The electrical tower caught his eye when White City came into view from the streetcar window. It was a "wonderful thing," he explained, made even better at night. Reid closed the letter with five small photos, one of which pictured the tower covered in dazzling lights (see fig. 8). Another captured a surprisingly clear picture of the moon as it shined over some of the park's main rides, also lit brilliantly. For Reid the lighting represented something novel and noteworthy, a commercial spectacle that characterized leisure in the big city. Nasaw terms such beaming displays the "new landscape of modernity."[34]

It must be observed, however, that the visual spectacles at White City constituted but one aspect of a multisensory "landscape of modernity." Advertising trumpeted the park's impressive sights, but it went on to explain how aural and olfactory pleasures enhanced the views. On the park's boardwalk, the pleasant "sounds of laughter and merriment come to the ear." The audible merrymaking joined with the "alluring strains of music" from the outdoor band as the "delicate fragrance of beautiful flowers" planted alongside delighted the nose. The park's main avenue provided visitors with "scintillating surroundings that appeal to every sense." In short, simply walking along White City's boardwalk rejuvenated the senses by washing away the industrial ambience of the city. Advertising boasted that the scintillating surroundings refreshed the senses by boosting "blood circulation" and delivering the "tingling of the nerves" for the sedentary urbanite or wearied factory operative.[35]

The mechanical rides provided the most bracing kinetic thrills. White City followed Coney Island in the design of some of its rides, either purchasing used equipment directly from the New York resort or ordering duplicates that were manufactured elsewhere. Visitors to White City had the opportunity to thrill from the same kind of mild sexual suggestiveness found in Coney Island too. One of White City's more popular rides, "Squeeze-Her," placed patrons in two-person seats within a wide bowl, elevated twenty feet from the ground. When the bowl revolved (as much as twenty-five times a minute), the force pushed the two riders together, creating a "squeeze" that otherwise might have strained modesty. Much like the rides at Coney Island, Squeeze-Her playfully violated middle-class standards of privacy and self-control. The kinetic sensation—a rush indicative of modern times that the historian Constance Classen has associated with the railroad—delivered a haptic thrill.[36] Unlike the other haptic pleasures of the emergent consumer culture—for example, the tactile browsing that department stores encouraged—Squeeze-Her disseminated sensation throughout the body, no doubt tingling the nerves and exciting multiple senses in suggestive ways.[37]

"The Bumps" offered similar types of kinetic thrills but to a larger group of riders. Essentially a giant slide, the Bumps originally appeared at Dreamland, the more sedate of Coney Island's three amusement parks and the one most closely emulated by White City. When the *Tribune* covered White City's opening night in May 1905, for which twenty-five thousand Chicagoans paid admission, its reporter described how visitors swooshed downward from a platform, twenty feet from the ground, to be tossed around by a series of embedded bumps. "The percentage of dignity observed last night was of negligible quantity," the paper reported about those who bumped the Bumps.[38] Riders slid as singles and in pairs, both men and women, most of whom seem to have enjoyed what White City termed a "veritable craze" its first summer.[39] Unlike other mechanical rides, no car or boat mitigated the contact between the sliders and the smooth incline, finished as it was with satin. The sensation to the lower extremities rejuvenated wearied bodies, prompting White City to suggest the ride—tongue in cheek—as a palliative for the indigestion created by wearying days in the city.

Another ride reveals how amusement parks excited the eye by making a spectacle of other patrons. "Shoot the Chutes," a flume ride, delivered a haptic rush for riders and pleasing views for onlookers. Other attractions, including the Bumps, invited spectators to enjoy the sight of people abandoning restraint, but Shoot the Chutes offered a full-blown spectacle. As the boats traveled through the flume to hit the lower lagoon, they skimmed over water that reflected the thousands of electric lights on the Jewel Tower. The dazzling water framed the spectacle as the boat's impact created "great waves of liquid fire" to please the eye.[40] At the same time, the spectacle was multisensory, complete with the gleeful sounds generated by the descent and the crash of the lapping waves. White City advertised the ride as appropriate for older customers and young, boasting that a trip down the slide "toned" the nerves more effectively than medicine. Mindful of safety concerns that surrounded the novel forms of amusement, White City offered a physician's testimony that "no person in the world could possibly be injured or hurt, in morals, disposition, or in a physical way" from the rush of the water slide or the mild touching of the "Squeeze-Her."[41]

The biggest spectacle at White City played on the fascination with urban disasters that colored witnesses' accounts of Chicago's 1871 fire. The 1906 season saw the opening of the "Chicago Fire" building, where visitors were shown a panoramic display of the famous disaster, complete with the peals of alarm bells and smoke effects. The park's advertising stressed accuracy, pointing out that the designer, Morris Beifeld, vice president of the White City Construction Company, had weathered the Great Fire personally. Promoting the show as edifying as well as thrilling, its designers ignored the visual disorientation that witnesses described as a key feature of the disaster, a sooty mess that made for an unpleasant spectacle. Instead, visitors were promised a "scenic holocaust" carried out with "absolute fidelity" to historical accuracy.[42] White City indulged the fascination articulated by actual witnesses of the fire, but in a controlled setting that furthered the narrative of Chicago's "Phoenix-like" recovery. Spectators watched a celebrated moment in the city's history with far greater clarity than its original victims, a reversal of the difficulties of "seeing" the actual blaze created to satisfy the logic of a consumer culture.

If the Chicago Fire exhibit was at least partly didactic, the other disaster spectacle, "Fighting the Flames," provided sheer excitement to the senses. Here the park performed a safe demonstration of a common urban danger to titillate consumers. "Fighting the Flames" involved 250 actors spread over a city block that included a six-story hotel that appeared to be burned down at every performance. White City's description of the sight resembled the account of John Shorthall, the Chicagoan who had darted through his burning office to save business papers on the night of October 8–9, 1871. Would any right-minded person, White City's promoters asked, resist the desire to "see a fire," or, "even at the loss of dignity run with the crowd to see, with great enjoyment, the other fellow's place burn up," much as Shorthall had?[43]

The answer was clearly no, but White City created a multisensory spectacle to expand the visual pleasures of watching a neighbor's house burn down. John S. Reid enjoyed it as the sudden clang of a fire bell wrenched his attention from a sedate balloon ascension elsewhere in the park. A hook and ladder company arrived to "rescue" one of the hotel residents, who, according to Reid, "set his clothes on fire" before jumping six stories into a tank of water.[44] Again, the emphasis was on the vicarious nature of the sensory experience, despite claims in advertising that some visitors were fooled into thinking an actual fire threatened the park. Reid assured his reader that the fire came from gas jets that ran throughout the hotel; he also pointed out that ignitions of black powder created the richly smelling smoke. The show was something to be absorbed with the ears and nose as well as the eye, all to help visitors transcend the daily routines of city life in a safe and controlled environment.[45]

White City also featured spectacles of foreign peoples in "native" villages, much like the Midway Plaisance. The park put various nonwhite groups on display to provide customers with glimpses of the exotic. The opening season included a "Gypsy Camp," complete with "olive complexioned maids attending to the duties of camp life" and men dressed in velvet, silk, and gold earrings. The camp's "Gypsy Queen" served as a focal point, enthroned as she was in the "splendor of barbaric affluence" that marked the gypsy's gaudy appearance. The park's management was at great pains to assure patrons that its gypsies were not to be confused with the rogues that might be encountered in the seedier parts of the city. The gypsies at White City hailed from Spain, having been hired by the park's traveling envoys. Unlike the "graceless, ragged and dirty outlaws" that accosted respectable Chicagoans outside White City's gates, the Spanish gypsies brought none of the moral grime of the city streets into the park. Their camp, replete with the sounds of their strange tongue and "caravan" lifestyle, served as an object of curiosity that modeled the strange sensory habits of the nomad.[46]

Two years after the opening season, White City went even further afield geographically to put Pacific Islanders on display. The "Igorrote [sic] Village" made the same claims to anthropology seen in the native villages at other world's fairs; in fact, the Philippine islanders had been featured at St. Louis's 1904 exposition. As a multisensory spectacle, the villagers registered in fairgoers' minds as the antithesis of Chicago's respectable classes. Visually, they appeared almost naked, an indication that White City had started to welcome racy attractions to boast the modest profits of its first two seasons. "Their clothing," the park's magazine announced, "will consist of just a brown coating of glossy epidermis, a smile and a G'string." The scent of coconut oil wafted from the village, as its residents often rubbed it on their shiny skin as their only form of dress. They maintained the most primitive of gustatory values. White City boasted that it had hired "genuine Dog-Eating Bontoc Igorrotes [sic]." They also were reputed to eat people, because they practiced head-hunting both as a tradition of war and as a "pastime" on their home island. The highlight of the primitive spectacle was the performance of native dances and feasting, a multisensory display of the same type of racial savagery that U.S. officials invoked in the recently ended Philippine-American War to damn its enemies as threats to white civilization.[47]

The emphasis on the senses as an index of racial savagery also informed displays of domestic racism at White City. Much like other public leisure spots in turn-of-the-century Chicago, the park remained an unwelcome place for African Americans.[48] The *Defender,* the city's main African American newspaper, may have been referring to White City when it noted that the open-to-all-races commercial district in black Chicago mocked the "narrow ideas in the treatment afforded various races" at amusement parks.[49]

White City's dunk tanks, the "African Dips," is one example of the racial ethos lamented by the *Defender.* A reporter for the *Tribune,* Oney Fred Sweet, described how he took a turn as one of the "dunkees," applying blackface to mimic the attraction's racial theme. He drew the distinctions between himself and the three African American men who sat on the dunking plank in aural terms too. Sweet listened as they sang among themselves, a "weird cotton picking, steamboat loading melody" reminiscent of Southern slaves. Writing in dialect, he then reported how the men playfully antagonized the customers who hurled baseballs at the dunking mechanism: "Yas, sah; no sah; cain't drown me!" When Sweet questioned the "foolhardy" strategy as one that compelled patrons to try harder, he reported the answer in the same dialect ("Dat's what you enlist for—to be throwed at"), a suggestion that such speech was not simply part of the show. Sweet eventually took his turn in the cold water, a bath that purportedly washed off the blackface to end the charade and anger the attraction's white manager. The reporter surrendered the seat to a black employee, one whose racial identity was also confirmed aurally in a departing remark that captured White City's racial policies, also in dialect, "We draws the color line."[50]

Vile, Vulgar, Vicious: Urban Reformers and White City

Despite Beifeld's attempts to create a respectable amusement park, moral reformers looked askance at White City. Progressive reformers generally disapproved of amusement parks, seeing them as places that preyed on the innocence of children and peddled in the unsavory. White City escaped none of the criticisms, especially after its opening seasons, when declining profits forced management to largely abandon its uplifting fare. After five years in business, the historians Perry Duis and Glen Holt point out, White City's stock had declined from its initial offering price of between twenty and fifty dollars to a meager four dollars per share.[51] The park's management, desperate to attract business, began renting out space to racy shows, losing control over the quality of the attractions and the overall ambiance. In 1909, evidencing White City's changing ethos, Chicago's Law and Order League investigated charges that some of its offerings had become, in the words of a disapproving South Side minister, "vile, vulgar and vicious."[52]

In 1911 the Vice Commission of Chicago issued a report that emphasized the league's concern that amusement parks tempted young female wage earners to sin. Echoing Beifeld's general ideas about the role of amusement in the city's civic health, the report argued that leisure had "more to do with character building than any other external influence," because the choices were so varied in quantity and quality.[53] The combination of the blandishments of consumer culture and the modest wages of young, female workers, however, often encouraged women to seek out strange men to pay their way. Doubting the innocence of young men and women spending a day together at the amusement park, the Vice Commission feared that such fraternization continued in nearby saloons. There, it charged, disreputable men took advantage of their company in back rooms or even forced women into prostitution.[54]

Undercover investigators for the Vice Commission visited multiple amusement parks in the city, finding that the gates designed to shut out the vice districts had been breached by prostitutes on a limited number of cases. Even more, reformers lamented how the park's dance halls lacked the supervision to prevent regular patrons from pushing the suggestive touching provided by rides like the Squeeze-Her. In October 1909 the *Tribune* reported on an investigation of White City's dance halls by the president of the city's Law and Order League, Arthur Farwell. He found the sight of unescorted women clad in short dresses offensive, but Farwell reserved his harshest judgment for the tactile behaviors that transgressed his notions of respectability. "Couples waltzed in the hugging position," he said, precisely the type of intimate contact that indicated moral danger.[55] He saw young men and women leave together at the end of the night as well, raising the prospect that they gratified the temptations created by the intimate touching allowed at White City.[56]

Farwell also targeted some of the theatrical spectacles at White City as affronts to the eyes and the ears of refined persons. Barkers, men who stood in front of exhibition spaces and called out advertisements for their show, raised the ire of both the league and the Chicago police. At a July 1909 news conference, Farwell joined the chief of police, as well as the managers of White City and Riverview Park on the North Side, to issue an ultimatum to barkers who used vulgar language to encourage ticket sales. The chief decried how the barkers assaulted the ears of innocent boys and "senile men," firing their imagination with promises of indecency. Farwell provided samples of what his investigators heard to argue that the aural landscape of White City differed little from sleazy haunts like the gateway to the levee on State Street. One barker, beckoning patrons to a hootchy-kootchy show, announced that one of the dancers had recently acquired a skimpy costume in the mail, one that "only cost 3 cents to send." "This is not a ladies' show," the barker reportedly cried. "We will keep this show going" until the "police back up with the wagon and take us away." The manager of White City promised to purge the offensive barkers from his park, lest they be taken away by the police and prosecuted.[57]

A committee of ministers visited White City the same month to investigate the suggestiveness of the shows themselves. Observing the "Blood Dance," they charged the park's management with allowing "one of the nastiest performances which any amusement park has ever dared produce in Chicago." The ministers echoed the complaints about the offensive cries of the barkers, but they believed the show itself merited prosecution for indecency. "A fifteen foot snake was the chief accessory of one of the most scantily clad performers," they noted.[58] The performer added a short Scottish kilt the next evening so that the show might continue without police intervention, but the ministers were not satisfied. The performance demonstrated how the indecorous sights of the South Side vice district had intruded on Beifeld's park to undermine his intention to excite the senses in only respectable and healthy ways.

The summer of 1909 eventually saw the police raid one of the racy shows at White City, the "Bare Bronze Beauties." On an evening in mid-July, as Farwell and other members of the Law and Order League waited in the audience to observe the show, an officer of Chicago's censorship squad went backstage to inspect the performers' dress. Seeing that the women intended to take the stage covered in little more than a thin layer of bronze paint and a girdle, he arrested Bertha Faulk, a twenty-five-year-old German immigrant. Faulk argued that she performed in similarly scanty attire in Europe without trouble, but the claims did little to dissuade the officer, who escorted her to the Harrison Street police station.

The manager of the concession accompanied Faulk to the police station, promising to make a test case in the name of free expression. The owners of White City, now formally charged with indecency, took no position on the merits of the case.[59]

A jury frustrated the efforts of the Law and Order League and police, taking a mere ten minutes to decide that the sight of women outfitted in girdles and bronze paint was acceptable for the Chicago stage. Five local theatrical agents testified to the moral soundness of the "Bare Bronze Beauties," though the chief of police later claimed that the verdict had much more to do with the sympathy of an all-male jury for a beautiful defendant. The arresting officer, shocked at the outcome, told the *Tribune* that the verdict "seems to throw the gate wide open for all sorts of shows."[60] The police resolved to continue their investigations of immoral spectacles at the city's amusement parks. Immediately after the Faulk case, the department announced that it planned to arrest two female impersonators at Riverview. The chief of police assured citizens that his department was doing all it could to protect Chicago's collective morality, but he thought that nothing would change until the city council defined with greater clarity what an "immoral or dangerous" stage performance looked like.[61]

White City limped on after the 1909 trial, but any claims about the pure, uplifting mission that Beifeld articulated as its founding principle failed to comport with the well-known court case. The 1910s and 1920s saw further problems for the amusement park as Chicagoans turned to an increasingly national consumer culture to fulfill their desires for fun and sensorial excitement. Consumers took to the roads in newly purchased automobiles, reveling in the sensation of speed and expanding their options for play across the city and in the regions beyond. Chicago's palatial movie palaces, outfitted with the dazzling electrical displays that signaled a refreshing break from routine, attracted a growing share of consumer dollars. Chicagoans also stayed home, turning their ears to the radio as a form of entertainment. White City died a symbolic death in 1927, when a fire burned the Jewel Tower and other attractions. The park's owners responded with promises of a new and improved White City, but their efforts came to naught. In 1933, as the Great Depression wore on Chicago's consumers, White City was placed in receivership.[62]

The 1920s, the decade when White City faded in the light of a national consumer culture, is a fitting point to end this discussion about the senses, civic health, and social distinction. In 1909 Jane Addams, the progressive reformer who found Chicago's Hull House, worried about the growing pull of commercialized leisure in a book titled *The Spirit of Youth and the City Streets.*[63] She respected the human desire for pleasure and fun. The "perpetual springs of life's renewal" were varied, she wrote, not limited to the high literature that intellectuals like Upton Sinclair privileged as noble. For workers who were tired after a hard day, children provided an example of the joys of healthy play, demonstrating the "gaiety and enthusiasm, to persuade [the adults] that living is a pleasure." Everyone benefited from a desire to "jump out of the humdrum experience of life" every now and again.[64]

The problem, as Addams saw it, was that municipal authorities failed to properly channel the desire for pleasure. Just as Chicago's industries organized work down to the smallest detail, the city needed to manage play. "At the very moment when the city has become distinctively industrial and daily labor is continually more monotonous and subdivided," she argued, municipal authorities permitted business to sell amusement as a commodity.[65] Commercial amusements often peddled the basest of passions: the desires for sex and violence. Public recreation, managed by experts at city parks, promised to stimulate the senses, strengthen the body, and impart lessons about the value of self-control and discipline that made healthy citizens.[66]

Addams was not opposed to all commercial amusements, but she thought the sensory pleasures of the saloon, dance hall, and amusement park confused "gaiety with debauchery" to encourage addiction, sex, and crime. "'Looping the Loop' amid shrieks of simulated terror," she wrote in a comment that may have referred to the multisensory thrills at White City, was "perhaps [one of] the natural reactions to a day spent in noisy factories," but the city had to provide other outlets for leisure, lest it risk the future of its youth. The remark about the wearying impact of "noisy factories" expressed the value of sensory rejuvenation, but Addams stressed the need to provide more than "mere excitement" to city dwellers. Recreation promised to build character, but not if reformers allowed commercial outlets to "incite that which should be controlled, to degrade that which should be exalted." The best forms of play involved mental and muscular exercise along with a rush to the senses.[67]

Addams emphasized generational differences when she wrote about urban leisure. "Perhaps never before," she observed, "have the pleasures of the young and mature become so definitely separated." The observation captured the changing landscape of the city itself in the 1920s, as young people embraced the retailing and entertainment districts that came to symbolize the national consumer culture. It also alluded to Addams's ideas about the senses. "We must bear in mind that the senses of youth are singularly acute," she wrote. Arguing that puberty and newly found sexual desire constituted an "awakening" of the sensory apparatus, Addams maintained that young people's "senses are helplessly wide open to the world." Such exposure left the young vulnerable to the designs of the architects of consumer culture, people who sought only to lighten the wallet, not enhance character.[68]

For Addams the commercial landscape of the city degraded the character of young people by debasing their senses. "The newly awakened senses are appealed to by all that is gaudy and sensual," she asserted in a comment that indicated how a commitment to sensory habits more akin with social distinction informed her thinking. The "flippant street music, the highly colored theatre, the trashy love stories, [and] the feathered hats," all indicated the rise of a vulgar, commercial culture that valorized sensuality over sensibility to harm the younger generation's chances of respectability and the city's civic health more generally. Quoting the philosopher and poet George Santayana, Addams continued, "We are told upon good authority that 'if the imagination is retarded, while the senses remain awake,' we will have a state of esthetic insensibility." "In other words," she averred, "the senses become sodden and cannot be lifted from the ground."[69]

Addams's emphasis on commercial culture as a force that degraded the senses indicated how the consumer marketplace sat among the factory and slum as features of the city's sensory landscape that raised concerns about civic health and social distinction. Joseph Beifeld's White City reflected the emerging connection too. The success of other turn-of-the-century amusement parks like Coney Island proved that a new generation of consumers sought the kinetic thrills that refreshed senses worn by the industrial city. Beifeld's mistake was to stress refinement and order over "vulgar exuberance." Yet Beifeld was simply ahead of his time. As White City went into receivership in 1933, the gravity of American consumer culture was already shifting from the industrial city to the suburbs. The White City of 1905 presaged a suburban sensory landscape—predictable, secure, racially homogeneous—that offered later generations a retreat from the industrial city itself.[70]

NOTES

Introduction

1. John Callan O'Laughlin, "Grime and Noise Mar Chicago Life," *Chicago Tribune,* October 4, 1909, 1.

2. Ibid.

3. I use the term "distinction" in the general fashion of the French sociologist Pierre Bourdieu, as something that refers to both aesthetic judgment and social hierarchy. On the interrelationship of "taste" and "class," see Pierre Bourdieu, *Distinction: A Social Critique of the Judgement of Taste,* trans. Richard Nice (Cambridge: Harvard University Press, 1984). For a contextualization of Bourdieu's oeuvre, see David Swartz, *Culture and Power: The Sociology of Pierre Bourdieu* (Chicago: University of Chicago Press, 1997).

4. For example, the historian John Henry Hepp provides a rich, multisensory description of a commercial street in nineteenth-century Philadelphia but then concludes that a person walking it "likely noticed few of these sights, sounds, and smells . . . they were simply background to everyday life in one of the world's largest cities." In Hepp's otherwise instructive study of middle-class culture, the dismissal of sense experience needs to be rethought in light of the emerging work on the sensory history of the city. John Henry Hepp IV, *The Middle-Class City: Transforming Space and Time in Philadelphia, 1876–1926* (Philadelphia: University of Pennsylvania Press, 2003), 22.

5. For example, the German sociologist Georg Simmel argued that metropolitan life was characterized by "the rapid telescoping of changing images, pronounced

differences within what is grasped at a single glance, and the unexpectedness of violent stimuli." Unlike residents of small towns—people accustomed to "the slower, more habitual, more smoothly flowing rhythm" of social intercourse—city dwellers faced multitudinous sights and sightings "with every crossing of the street, with the tempo and multiplicity of economic, occupational and social life," leading to interpersonal disengagement or apathy. The metropolitan personality was reserved, a tactic Simmel saw as part of an effort to insulate oneself against potentially unhealthy, nerve-wracking amounts of sensory data. Georg Simmel, "The Metropolis and Mental Life," in *The Blackwell City Reader,* ed. Gary Bridge and Sophie Watson (Oxford: Wiley-Blackwell, 2002), 11–12.

6. Alan Trachtenberg, *The Incorporation of America: Culture and Society in the Gilded Age,* 25th Anniversary ed. (New York: Hill and Wang, 2007), 103–104.

7. Like most scholarly turns, sensory studies rest on a series of classics in twentieth-century social thought, identified in David Howes, "Sensory Stirrings," in *Sense of the City: An Alternate Approach to Urbanism,* ed. Mirko Zardini (Montréal: Canadian Centre for Architecture and Lars Müller Publishers, 2005), 332–33. For a genealogy of the field's early expressions in anthropology, consult Constance Classen, "Foundations for an Anthropology of the Senses," *International Social Science Journal* 153 (September 1997): 401–12; David Howes, ed., *The Varieties of Sensory Experience: A Sourcebook on the Anthropology of the Senses* (Toronto: University of Toronto Press, 1991). The first call for work on the sensate in U.S. history appeared in George H. Roeder Jr., "Coming to Our Senses," *Journal of American History* 81 (December 1994): 1112–22. On the long, even ancient, history of formal thinking on the senses, see Anthony Synnott, "Puzzling Over the Senses: From Plato to Marx," in Howes, *Varieties of Sensory Experience,* 61–76.

8. As the cultural historian James W. Cook put it, vision is the perceptual register with "the longest and deepest historiographical paper trail." Cook notes that the scholarly emphasis on vision should not be confused with an "uncritical celebration" of sight as a wholly objective sense, or, "totalizing claims" about ocularcentrism seldom made by mainstream historians of visual culture. The value of sensory history, in this respect, is to avoid the habit of treating "vision as synecdoche for human perception." His essay also provides a helpful outline of the visual culture literature. James W. Cook, "Seeing the Visual in U.S. History," *Journal of American History* 95 (September 2008): 432, 433.

9. Howes terms the sensory hierarchy that privileges vision the "sensory model of modernity." David Howes, "Architecture of the Senses," in Zardini, *Sense of the City,* 324. The association of the eye with reason is an ancient one, found in the philosophy of Aristotle, though it became entrenched on the heels of modern developments in science and technology. Following the invention of the printing press and, later, the theories of Darwin and Freud (both of whom equated seeing with evolutionary progress), the eye became a leading index of truth, rationality,

and civilization in the West. The nonvisual senses lost cultural stature in general as touch, taste, and smell became linked with "animalistic" values like impulse, passion, and savagery.

The sensory model of modernity represents a set of cultural values, not a set of absolute distinctions about sense experience in history. Much of the initial work in sensory history corrected the sweeping claims of orality theory (or, the "Great Divide" thesis), as famously articulated by Marshall McLuhan in *The Gutenberg Galaxy: The Making of Typographic Man* (Toronto: University of Toronto Press, 1962). The "divide" refers to the break with an oral-aural emphasis in communication in the West generated by the invention of print and rising literacy, a change that, for McLuhan, indicated the arrival of the "modern" era. For a detailed critique, see Mark M. Smith, *Sensing the Past: Seeing, Hearing, Smelling, Tasting, and Touching in History* (Berkeley: University of California Press, 2007), 8–18.

10. William Cronon, *Nature's Metropolis: Chicago and the Great West* (New York: W. W. Norton, 1991), 106.

11. Howes, "Architecture of the Senses," 323.

12. See, for example, Mark M. Smith, "Producing Sense, Consuming Sense, Making Sense: Perils and Prospects for Sensory History," *Journal of Social History* 40 (Summer 2007): 841–58.

13. Howes, "Architecture of the Senses," 329.

14. Daniel E. Bender, "Sensing Labor: The Stinking Working Class after the Cultural Turn," in *Rethinking U.S. Labor History: Essays on the Working-Class Experience, 1756–2009*, ed. Donna T. Haverty-Stacke and Daniel J. Walkowitz (New York: Continuum, 2010), 250, 52.

15. Ibid., 244. On the various typologies of class as an analytical category, see Bender's "Sensing Labor" as well as Stuart M. Blumin's still instructive essay "The Hypothesis of Middle-Class Formation in Nineteenth-Century America: A Critique and Some Proposals," *American Historical Review* 90 (April 1985): 299–338.

16. Alain Corbin, "Charting the Cultural History of the Senses," in *Empire of the Senses: The Sensual Culture Reader*, ed. David Howes (Oxford: Berg, 2005), 136, 137.

17. Robert H. Wiebe, *The Search for Order, 1877–1920* (New York: Hill and Wang, 1967). Here sensory distinction works as an index within what Wiebe described as an "almost obsessive interest in 'class'" among those who worried about losing their sense of self in the city. My own use of the term "middle class" owes much to the scholarship that has extended notions of social class beyond material wealth or occupational labels, including Blumin's "Hypothesis of Middle-Class Formation" and his book *The Emergence of the Middle-Class: Social Experience in the American City, 1760–1900* (Cambridge: Cambridge University Press, 1989). In general, I use "middle classes" to refer to two broad categories of people, professionals as well as specialists in business and labor, extending what Wiebe termed the urban

middle classes' "broad areas of mutual concern" (e.g., public health) to sensory values, representation, and reform. Wiebe, *Search for Order,* quotations on 111, 128.

18. Karen Halttunen, *Confidence Men and Painted Women: A Study of Middle-Class Culture in America, 1830–1870* (New Haven, CT: Yale University Press, 1982), xv.

19. Perry R. Duis, *Challenging Chicago: Coping with Everyday Life, 1837–1920* (Urbana: University of Illinois Press, 1998), 248.

20. Theodore Dreiser, *Sister Carrie,* Modern Library Classics ed. (New York: Modern Library, 1999), chapter 1.

21. Halttunen, *Confidence Men,* 36–37.

22. John F. Kasson, *Rudeness and Civility: Manners in Nineteenth-Century America* (New York: Hill and Wang, 1990).

23. Richard L. Bushman and Claudia L. Bushman, "The Early History of Cleanliness in America," *Journal of American History* 74 (March 1988): 1228.

24. My point about dirt and manual labor as indicative of class boundaries recalls Stuart M. Blumin's 1985 recommendation to study the workplace as a changing environment—and not simply occupational labels—to clarify markers of social class in the nineteenth-century United States. Studying the sensory environment of meatpacking factories, an issue I discuss in chapter 4, offers a particularly rich way to take up Blumin's suggestion. Blumin, "Hypothesis of Middle-Class Formation," 312–13.

25. John B. Jentz and Richard Schneirov, *Chicago in the Age of Capital: Class, Politics, and Democracy during the Civil War and Reconstruction* (Urbana: University of Illinois Press, 2012), 18.

26. Mark M. Smith, *How Race Is Made: Slavery, Segregation, and the Senses* (Chapel Hill: University of North Carolina Press, 2006).

27. Corbin, "Charting the Cultural History of the Senses," 133. The idea that languages of disgust or repulsion serve a self-reflective purpose echoes Bourdieu's point about aesthetic tastes as "the practical affirmation of an inevitable difference." He explains, "It is no accident that, when they [tastes] have to be justified, they are asserted purely negatively, by the refusal of other tastes. In matters of taste, more than anywhere else, all determination is negation; and tastes are perhaps first and foremost distastes, disgust provoked by horror or visceral intolerance . . . of the tastes of others." Bourdieu, *Distinction,* 56.

28. Mark Pittenger, "A World of Difference: Constructing the 'Underclass' in Progressive America," *American Quarterly* 49 (March 1997): 29.

29. As to olfaction, the authors of *Aroma: The Cultural History of Smell* observe that odors "cannot be readily contained, they escape and cross boundaries, blending different entities into olfactory wholes," a type of fluidity "opposed to our modern, linear worldview, with its emphasis on privacy [and] discrete divisions." Constance Classen, David Howes, and Anthony Synnott, *Aroma: The Cultural History of Smell* (New York: Routledge, 1994), 4–5.

30. Dell Upton, *Another City: Urban Life and Urban Spaces in the New American Republic* (New Haven: Yale University Press, 2008), 336.

31. Hepp, *Middle-Class City*, 2.

32. The emphasis on noise control likely reflects the focus on hearing that marked the first generation of sensory history, as well as the recent writing on noise pollution in the national media. Influential works by historians of hearing include Richard Cullen Rath, *How Early America Sounded* (Ithaca, NY: Cornell University Press, 2003); Leigh Eric Schmidt, *Hearing Things: Religion, Illusion, and the American Enlightenment* (Cambridge: Harvard University Press, 2000); Mark M. Smith, *Listening to Nineteenth-Century America* (Chapel Hill: University of North Carolina Press, 2001); Emily Thompson, *The Soundscape of Modernity: Architectural Acoustics and the Culture of Listening in America, 1900–1933* (Cambridge: MIT Press, 2002). On the contemporary attention to noise in urban environments, the writer George Prochnik has penned some of the most sensitive analysis. See his article "I'm Thinking. Please. Be Quiet," *New York Times*, August 24, 2013, http://www.nytimes.com/2013/08/25/opinion/sunday/im-thinking-please-be-quiet.html, as well as his larger meditation on silence in modern life, *In Pursuit of Silence: Listening for Meaning in a World of Noise* (New York: Doubleday, 2010).

33. Peter Payer, "The Age of Noise: Early Reactions in Vienna, 1870–1914," *Journal of Urban History* 33 (July 2007): 786 (all quotations).

34. Emily Thompson, "Noise and Noise Abatement in the Modern City," in Zardini, *Sense of the City*, 192.

35. Derek Vaillant, "Peddling Noise: Contesting the Civic Soundscape of Chicago, 1890–1913," *Journal of the Illinois State Historical Society* 96 (Autumn 2003): 257–87.

36. Lilian Radovac, "The 'War on Noise': Sound and Space in La Guardia's New York," *American Quarterly* 63 (September 2011): 744.

37. Carl Smith's book on nineteenth-century urban disorder traces the strong link between Chicago's growth and the fear of social disorder in the middle-class mind. Focusing on literary representations of disorder, he argues that the tumultuous decades of the late nineteenth century "witnessed the emergence of an outlook in which reality, city, and disorder became closely related, if not interchangeable terms." Carl Smith, *Urban Disorder and the Shape of Belief: The Great Chicago Fire, the Haymarket Bomb, and the Model Town of Pullman* (Chicago: University of Chicago Press, 1995), 8. Other important works on urban disorder include Wiebe, *Search for Order*; and Paul Boyer, *Urban Masses and Moral Order in America, 1820–1920* (Cambridge: Harvard University Press, 1978).

38. Jentz and Schneirov, *Chicago in the Age of Capital*, 13–15.

39. C. Smith, *Urban Disorder and the Shape of Belief*, 5.

40. Ibid.

41. Timothy B. Spears, *Chicago Dreaming: Midwesterners and the City, 1871–1919* (Chicago: University of Chicago Press, 2005).

42. Asa Briggs, *Victorian Cities* (1963; repr., Berkeley: University of California Press, 1993), 56.

43. References to Chicago as a shock city appear in a number of recent works, including Dominic A. Pacyga's authoritative *Chicago: A Biography* (Chicago: University of Chicago Press, 2009). A recent example of the application of the term in a non-U.S. context is Howard Spodek's *Ahmedabad: Shock City of Twentieth-Century India* (Bloomington: Indiana University Press, 2011).

44. Harold L. Platt, *Shock Cities: The Environmental Transformation and Reform of Manchester and Chicago* (Chicago: University of Chicago Press, 2005), xiv.

Chapter 1. Smelling Civic Peril

1. "The Chicago River: A Second Inspection of Its Smells," *Chicago Tribune*, August 21, 1869, 4 (all quotations).

2. Scholars have been linking the two fields since the 1990s, in part as a follow-up to William Cronon's influential book *Nature's Metropolis: Chicago and the Great West* (New York: W. W. Norton, 1991). For a genealogy of works in urban-environmental history, see Kathleen A. Brosnan, "Effluence, Affluence, and the Maturing of Urban Environmental History," *Journal of Urban History* 31 (November 2004): 115–23.

3. Christine Meisner Rosen traces the varied responses of business leaders to smoke pollution in "Businessmen against Pollution in Late Nineteenth-Century Chicago," *Business History Review* 69 (Autumn 1995): 351–97.

4. David Stradling, "Dirty Work and Clean Air: Locomotive Firemen, Environmental Activists, and Stories of Conflict," *Journal of Urban History* 28 (November 2001): 48. Also relevant in terms of smoke and social class is Angela Gugliotta's "Class, Gender, and Coal Smoke," *Environmental History* 5 (April 2000): 165–93.

5. Christine Meisner Rosen, "Noisome, Noxious, and Offensive Vapors, Fumes, and Stenches in American Towns and Cities, 1840–1865," *Historical Geography* 25 (1997): 49–82.

6. Andrew Hurley, "Busby's Stink Boat and the Regulation of the Nuisance Trades, 1865–1918," in *Common Fields: An Environmental History of St. Louis*, ed. Andrew Hurley (St. Louis: Missouri Historical Society Press, 1997),145–62.

7. Ibid., 149.

8. Alain Corbin, *The Foul and the Fragrant: Odor and the French Social Imagination*, trans. Miriam L. Kochan, Roy Porter, and Christopher Prendergast (Cambridge, MA: Harvard University Press, 1986), 134–41; Connie Y. Chiang, "The Nose Knows: The Sense of Smell in American History," *Journal of American History* 95 (September 2008): 405–16.

9. David Inglis, "Sewers and Sensibilities: The Bourgeois Faecal Experience in the Nineteenth-Century City," in *The City and the Senses: Urban Culture Since 1500*, ed. Alexander Cowan and Jill Steward (Aldershot, England: Ashgate, 2007), 122.

10. *Report of the Board of Health of the City of Chicago for 1867, 1868 and 1869; and a Sanitary History of Chicago; from 1833 to 1870* (Chicago: Lakeside Publishing and Printing Company, 1871), 11–12 (hereafter *BOH* 1871).

11. Ibid., 11–12, 22, 13–14.

12. Ibid., 24, 54.

13. Ibid., 299.

14. On the antebellum transportation revolution, see Daniel Walker Howe, *What Hath God Wrought: The Transformation of America, 1815–1848* (Oxford: Oxford University Press, 2009).

15. The year 1848 also saw the organization of the board of trade; the first telegraph message sent from the city (to Detroit); and the opening of Cyrus McCormick's Reaper Works. Dominic Pacyga, *Chicago: A Biography* (Chicago: University of Chicago Press, 2009), 38.

16. The plan called for the river to receive all the sewage from the West Side; all the sewage of the North Side except from the lakefront, and approximately 50 percent of the sewage from the South Side. Louis P. Cain, "Raising and Watering a City: Ellis Sylvester Chesbrough and Chicago's First Sanitation System," *Technology and Culture* 13 (July 1972): 360.

17. Quoted in ibid., 364.

18. On the effort to raise the grade of the city's streets, see Harold M. Mayer and Richard C. Wade, *Chicago: Growth of a Metropolis* (Chicago: University of Chicago Press, 1969), 94–99.

19. Harold L. Platt, *Shock Cities: The Environmental Transformation and Reform of Manchester and Chicago* (Chicago: University of Chicago Press, 2005), 121; Louis P. Cain, *Sanitation Strategy for a Lakefront Metropolis: The Case of Chicago* (DeKalb: Northern Illinois University Press, 1978), 23–26, 35.

20. Between 1850 and 1870 the city's population grew by ten times: from just under thirty thousand to nearly three hundred thousand. Mayer and Wade, *Chicago: Growth of a Metropolis*, 54.

21. Platt, *Shock Cities*, 140; *BOH* 1871, 299.

22. Platt, *Shock Cities*, 141.

23. "The Water Question," *Chicago Tribune*, January 16, 1863, 4.

24. The Union Stockyards opened on Christmas Day, 1865. On the growing concentration of the meatpacking industry around the yards over the next decade, see Louise Carroll Wade, *Chicago's Pride: The Stockyards, Packingtown, and Environs in the Nineteenth Century* (Urbana: University of Illinois Press, 1987), part 1.

25. "The North Branch," *Chicago Tribune*, July 3, 1864, 4 (all quotations).

26. Cronon, *Nature's Metropolis*, 210.

27. "The Chicago River," *Chicago Tribune*, July 28, 1864, 4.

28. "The Stench Nuisance," *Chicago Tribune*, August 20, 1876, 4.

29. Donald Miller, *City of the Century: The Epic of Chicago and the Making of America* (New York: Simon and Schuster, 1996), 441–42. As Miller put it, "To the Protestant

press, led by . . . *The Tribune* [the Irish in Bridgeport] were 'paddies'—coarse, loud, hard-drinking, and clannish, smelling of whiskey and boiled cabbage." Greater attention to the meanings of the multiple social differences sensed in this passage—tactile ("coarse"), aural ("loud"), olfactory ("smelling of"), and gustatory ("whiskey and boiled cabbage")—is an example of how work in sensory history might expand existing narratives of social class in industrial Chicago.

30. "Stench Nuisance," 4.

31. Corbin, *Foul and the Fragrant*, 141.

32. *Second Annual Report of the Board of Public Works to the Common Council of the City of Chicago* (Chicago: Tribune Book and Job Printing Office, 1863), 38 (hereafter *BPW* 1863).

33. *First Annual Report of the Board of Public Works to the Common Council of the City of Chicago* (Chicago: S. P. Rounds, 1862), 40 (hereafter *BPW* 1862).

34. Cain, "Raising and Watering a City," 365; *BPW* 1862, 38, 41–42; *BPW* 1863, 10.

35. *BPW* 1863, 10.

36. The calls for drinking water that looked clean illustrates David Inglis's observation that nineteenth-century urban elites increasingly demanded that pollution be hidden from both their eyes and their noses. Writing about the construction of modern sewer systems, Inglis terms the contrast between those demands and the feces-ridden waters of Western European cities in the early nineteenth century a "faecal crisis," made worse by fears of disease. Inglis, "Sewers and Sensibilities," 114.

37. "Abominable Water," *Chicago Tribune*, March 12, 1862, 4 (all quotations).

38. Ibid.

39. *BPW* 1862, 38–39.

40. Charles Rosenberg's study of cholera, *The Cholera Years*, points out that studies by the English physician John Snow, first published in 1849 and demonstrated empirically after London's 1854 cholera outbreak, showed that contaminated water had spread the disease, undermining the miasma theory. Charles E. Rosenberg, *The Cholera Years: The United States in 1832, 1849, and 1866* (1962; repr., Chicago: University of Chicago Press, 1987), 6. On the rise of germ theory and disease transmission, see Nancy Tomes, *The Gospel of Germs: Men, Women, and the Microbe in American Life* (Cambridge, MA: Harvard University Press, 1998).

41. "Odors," *Chicago Times*, July 15, 1871, 2.

42. "Abominable Water," *Chicago Tribune*, March 12, 1862, 4 (all quotations).

43. Ibid.

44. Perry R. Duis, *The Saloon: Public Drinking in Chicago and Boston, 1880–1920* (Urbana: University of Illinois Press, 1983), 95–97.

45. "The Beverage We Drink," *Chicago Tribune*, February 24, 1860, 1.

46. Quoted in Rosenberg, *Cholera Years*, 148.

47. "The River Basin," *Chicago Tribune*, September 30, 1859, 1.

48. Suellen Hoy, *Chasing Dirt: The American Pursuit of Cleanliness* (Oxford: Oxford University Press, 1995), 17.

49. Rosenberg, *Cholera Years*, 5; On the United States Sanitary Commission, see Hoy, *Chasing Dirt*, chapter 2.

50. "Abominable Water," *Chicago Tribune*, March 12, 1862, 4.

51. Vincent Vinikas, *Soft Soap, Hard Sell: American Hygiene in an Age of Advertisement* (Ames: Iowa State University Press, 1992).

52. Hoy, *Chasing Dirt*, 88.

53. *BPW* 1862, 6–8; *BPW* 1863, 5–7.

54. *Eighth Annual Report of the Board of Public Works to the Common Council of the City of Chicago* (Chicago: Press of Jameson and Morse, 1869), 95–115 (hereafter *BPW* 1869); Cain, "Raising and Watering a City," 369; *Fifth Annual Report of the Board of Public Works to the Common Council of the City of Chicago* (Chicago: Jameson and Morse, Book and Job Printers, 1866), 54 (hereafter *BPW* 1866). The total cost of construction, up to the opening of the tunnel in March 1867, was $457,844, a figure about $150,000 greater than the original estimate (*BPW* 1869, 116).

55. *Seventh Annual Report of the Board of Public Works to the Common Council of the City of Chicago* (Chicago: Press of Jameson and Morse, 1869), 59 (hereafter *BPW* 1868).

56. "Our Water Supply," *Chicago Tribune*, July 17, 1867, 4 (all quotations).

57. *BPW* 1868, 4; *Tenth Annual Report of the Board of Public Works to the Common Council of the City of Chicago* (Cambridge, MA: Welch, Bigelow and Co.: 1871), 8 (hereafter *BPW* 1871); *Twelfth Annual Report of the Board of Public Works to the Common Council of the City of Chicago* (Chicago: National Printing Company, 1873), 7 (hereafter *BPW* 1873).

58. *BOH* 1871, 67–69 (quotations, 68–69).

59. "Removing Nuisances," *Chicago Tribune*, July 8, 1865, 4.

60. Ibid.

61. "Is it Fair?" *Chicago Tribune*, June 28, 1862, 4.

62. "Chicago River," *Chicago Tribune*, June 21, 1862, 2.

63. "The Chicago River: The Evil and the Remedy," *Chicago Tribune*, December 30, 1864, 2.

64. Ibid.

65. "A Pork Packer on the Chicago River," *Chicago Tribune*, December 30, 1862, 4 (all quotations, emphases in the original).

66. Platt, *Shock Cities*, 154.

67. "The Chicago River: The Packing Houses," *Chicago Tribune*, December 22, 1864, 2 (all quotations).

68. "The North Branch," *Chicago Tribune*, July 3, 1864, 4.

69. "The Water Question Again," *Chicago Tribune*, March 5, 1862, 2.

70. "Meeting of the Common Council," *Chicago Tribune*, June 24, 1862, 4.

71. Ibid.

72. "The Chicago River: A Suggestion," *Chicago Tribune,* June 26, 1862, 2.

73. "The Chicago River: The Evil and the Remedy," *Chicago Tribune,* December 18, 1864, 2.

74. "The Chicago River," *Chicago Tribune,* January 4, 1865, 4.

75. Ibid.

76. Ibid.

77. Wade, *Chicago's Pride,* 39.

78. David M. Solzman, *The Chicago River: An Illustrated Guide to the River and Its Waterways,* 2nd ed. (Chicago: University of Chicago Press, 2006), 48–49; "Steam Navigation on the Illinois Canal: The Deep Cut," *Chicago Tribune,* June 15, 1859, 2; "Canal Enlargement," *Chicago Tribune,* December 4, 1861, 2.

79. "The City Charter," *Chicago Tribune,* January 4, 1865, 4; *Fourth Annual Report of the Board of Public Works to the Common Council of the City of Chicago* (Chicago: George H. Fergus, Book and Job Printer, 1865), 140–47 (hereafter *BPW* 1865); *BPW* 1866, 18–20.

80. *BPW* 1866, 11–12; "The Canal Completed," *Chicago Tribune,* July 16, 1871, 2; *BPW* 1871, 17. The total cost, reported in 1872, was $3,300,883.71 (*BPW* 1872, 22).

81. Cain, "Sanitation Strategy," 61; Platt, *Shock Cities,* 186–87; Solzman, *Chicago River,* 50.

82. "The River," *Chicago Times,* July 16, 1871, 2; "Our Dear Gazelles," *Chicago Tribune,* July 18, 1871, 2.

Chapter 2. Sensory Overload

1. "John G. Shorthall," Chicago Fire of 1871, Personal Narratives, Chicago History Museum, Chicago, Illinois (hereafter CFN). The bulk of the witness reports utilized in this chapter (including Shorthall's) are drawn from the Chicago History Museum's "Fire Narratives" collection. A rich stockpile of personal accounts written chiefly by middle- and upper-class survivors, the narratives include personal recollections written in the days immediately after the disaster as well as ones penned months and years after the fact.

2. "Shorthall," CFN.

3. Jörg Friedrich, *The Fire: The Bombing of Germany, 1940–1945,* trans. Allison Brown (New York: Columbia University Press, 2006), 446, 447.

4. The performance scholar Lynn Sally defines spectacle as multisensory—a "total body experience"—in the context of turn-of-the-century consumer culture. I return to the issue of a multisensory consumer culture in chapter 5. Lynn Sally, "Fantasy Land and Kinesthetic Thrills: Sensorial Consumption, the Shock of Modernity, and Spectacle as Total-Body Experience at Coney Island," *Senses and Society* 1 (November 2006): 300. On disasters as creating atavistic contexts, see Mark M. Smith, *Camille, 1969: Histories of a Hurricane* (Athens: University of Georgia Press, 2011), 4, 20.

5. M. Smith, *Camille, 1969,* 20.

6. Sawislak emphasizes the classed nature of the relief and rebuilding effort, while Smith deals with the idea of the fire in the longer term, especially in literary portrayals. Karen Sawislak, *Smoldering City: Chicagoans and the Great Fire, 1871–1874* (Chicago: University of Chicago Press, 1995); Carl Smith, *Urban Disorder and the Shape of Belief: The Great Chicago Fire, the Haymarket Bomb, and the Model Town of Pullman* (Chicago: University of Chicago Press, 1995). On the fire as a literary narrative, also see Ross Miller, *The Great Chicago Fire,* Illinois Paperback ed. (Urbana: University of Illinois Press, 2000).

7. Sawislak, *Smoldering Cities,* 16.

8. Studying the experiential dimensions of the fire expands on Sawislak's argument that the disaster fomented the "shattering of urban social divisions" by foregrounding those divisions as sensed. Sawislak, *Smoldering Cities,* 40.

9. C. Smith, *Urban Disorder,* 25.

10. "Charles Elliot [Anthony]," CFN.

11. Ibid.

12. Quoted in C. Smith, *Urban Disorder,* 26.

13. Elias Colbert and Everett Chamberlin, *Chicago and the Great Conflagration* (Cincinnati: C. F. Vent, 1872), 211.

14. Ibid., 211–12.

15. H. A. Musham, "The Great Chicago Fire, October 8–10, 1871," in *Papers in Illinois History and Transactions for the Year 1940* (Springfield: Illinois State Historical Society, 1941), 84–86.

16. Ibid., 98–104; 162 (quotation).

17. "Mrs. Alfred Hebard," CFN (emphasis in original).

18. "William Gallagher," CFN.

19. Ibid.

20. Robert H. Woody, "A Description of the Chicago Fire of 1871," *Mississippi Valley Historical Review* 33 (March 1947): 614.

21. Ibid.

22. C. Smith, *Urban Disorder,* 32–33.

23. Karen Halttunen, *Confidence Men and Painted Women: A Study of Middle-Class Culture in America, 1830–1870* (New Haven, CT: Yale University Press, 1982), 36–37.

24. Paul M. Angle, ed., *The Great Chicago Fire: Described in Seven Letters by Men and Women Who Experienced Its Horrors, and Now Published in Commemoration of the Seventy-Fifth Anniversary of the Catastrophe* (Chicago: Chicago Historical Society, 1946), 36n5.

25. Ibid., 40, 43.

26. Edward P. Roe, *Barriers Burned Away* (New York: Dodd Mead and Company, 1872), 408.

27. "Emma Hambelton," CFN.

28. "Gilbert Merrill," CFN (all quotations).

29. Sawislak, *Smoldering City*, 40–42.

30. "Samuel Greeley," CFN.

31. Ibid.

32. Ibid.

33. Kathy Rannalletta, "Illinois Commentary: 'The Great Wave of Fire' at Chicago: The Reminiscences of Martin Stamm," *Journal of the Illinois State Historical Society* 70 (June 1977): 151.

34. Ibid.

35. Ibid., 159.

36. "Lavina Clark Perkins," CFN. The scene at the lakefront was depicted in the film *In Old Chicago*, directed by Henry King, 20th Century Fox Studio Classics, 1937.

37. Roe, *Barriers Burned Away*, 423–24.

38. Ibid., 424.

39. Ibid.

40. John F. Kasson, *Rudeness and Civility: Manners in Nineteenth-Century America* (New York: Hill and Wang, 1990), 129.

41. "Charles Monreau Sampson," CFN.

42. Ibid.

43. After the fire, both public and military officials testified that very little, if any, looting and criminal assault occurred during the disaster (C. Smith, *Urban Disorder*, 51–55; Kevin Rozario, "Making Progress: Disaster Narratives and the Art of Optimism in Modern America," in *The Resilient City: How Modern Cities Recover from Disaster*, ed. Lawrence J. Vale and Thomas J. Campanella (Oxford: Oxford University Press, 2005), 38.

44. "Gallagher," CFN.

45. Ibid.

46. "Mary Fales," CFN.

47. "James W. Milner," CFN.

48. "Thomas D. Foster," CFN (all quotations).

49. C. Smith, *Urban Disorder*, 22; Sawislak, *Smoldering City*, 29; Louis P. Cain, *Sanitation Strategy for a Lakefront Metropolis: The Case of Chicago* (DeKalb: Northern Illinois Press, 1978), 55–56.

50. William Cronon, *Nature's Metropolis: Chicago and the Great West* (New York: W. W. Norton, 1991), 345–46.

51. "H. W. S. Cleveland," CFN (all quotations).

52. "Charles Elliot [Anthony]," CFN.

53. "John G. Shorthall," CFN.

54. Angle, *Great Chicago Fire*, 24.

55. James W. Sheahan and George P. Upton, *The Great Conflagration: Chicago, Its Past, Present, and Future* (Philadelphia: Union Publishing Co., 1871), 245.

56. Jeffrey H. Jackson, "Envisioning Disaster in the 1910 Paris Flood," *Journal of*

Urban History 37 (March 2011): 176–207. On visualizing ruin, also see Michael S. Roth, Claire L. Lyons, and Charles Merewether, *Irresistible Decay: Ruins Reclaimed* (Los Angeles: Getty Research Institute for the History of Art and the Humanities, 1997); Rebecca Solnit, "The Ruins of Memory," in *After the Ruins, 1906 and 2006: Rephotographing the San Francisco Earthquake and Fire,* ed. Mark Klett, (Berkeley: University of California Press, 2006), 18–32; Rose Macaulay, *Pleasure of Ruins* (New York: Thames and Hudson, 1953). On sensing ruin broadly, see the cultural geographer Tim Edensor's article on present-day Manchester, England, "Sensing Ruin," *Senses and Society* 2 (July 2007): 217–32.

57. C. Smith, *Urban Disorder,* 91–94.

58. Sheahan and Upton, *Great Conflagration,* 255.

59. Ibid., 256.

60. Ibid., 257 (all quotations).

61. *Lakeside Memorial of the Burning of Chicago* (Chicago: University Publishing Company, 1872), 55, 54.

62. Ibid., 18. The Chicago Relief and Aid Society took on the responsibility for immediate aid. The agency collected a total of nearly $5,000,000 in cash and materials, sent from around the nation and the world; it disbursed $4,400,000, including slightly more than $540,000 for administrative costs. From the days immediately after the fire through the suspension of the official relief effort in 1873, the society provided aid to 39,242 families, or 156,968 persons. The agency's housing committee constructed 7,983 houses, most in the first month after the fire, and thus provided "respectable and comfortable" homes for at least 35,000 people. C. Smith, *Urban Disorder,* 66; Chicago Relief and Aid Society, *Report of the Chicago Relief and Aid Society of Disbursement of Contributions for the Sufferers of the Chicago Fire* (Cambridge, MA: Riverside Press, 1874), 149, 188. The fullest accounting of the aide effort can be found in Sawislak, *Smoldering City,* 69–120. On the rapid rebuilding, see Harold M. Mayer and Richard C. Wade, *Chicago: Growth of a Metropolis* (Chicago: University of Chicago Press, 1969), 117–24.

63. On the recovery narrative in the twentieth century, see "Commemorating the Catastrophe," Northwestern University and the Chicago Historical Society, "The Great Chicago Fire and the Web of Memory," 2011, http://www.greatchicago fire.org/commemorating-catastrophe. The Sixteen restaurant at Chicago's Trump Hotel has recently served up the recovery narrative in a gustatory sense, memorializing the fire as one course in its "culinary exploration of Chicago's birth, growth, and golden age." Roasted venison, "served tableside and pulled from the ashes," represents the fire to diners' sense of taste. "Sixteen's Culinary Exploration of Chicago," http://www.trumphotelcollection.com/press/sixteens-culinary -exploration-of-chicago.

64. Sheahan and Upton, *Great Conflagration,* 336.

65. Kevin Rozario, "Making Progress," 29, 41.

Chapter 3. To Quiet the Roar of the Mob

1. "The Dangerous Classes," *Chicago Tribune*, July 29, 1877, 4 (all quotations).

2. John B. Jentz and Richard Schneirov, *Chicago in the Age of Capital: Class, Politics and Democracy during the Civil War and Reconstruction* (Urbana: University of Illinois Press, 2012), 194, 208. Also essential on labor politics in Chicago in the second half of the nineteenth century is Schneirov's *Labor and Urban Politics: Class Conflict and the Origins of Modern Liberalism in Chicago, 1864–97* (Urbana: University of Illinois Press, 1998). See also Schneirov, "Chicago's Great Upheaval of 1877," *Chicago History* 9 (March 1980): 2–17.

On the 1877 strikes more generally see David O. Stowell, ed., *The Great Strikes of 1877* (Urbana: University of Illinois Press, 2008); Robert V. Bruce, *1877: Year of Violence* (Lanham, MD: Ivan R. Dee, 1989); and Philip S. Foner, *The Great Labor Uprising of 1877* (New York: Monad Press, 1977). David O. Stowell's *Streets, Railroads, and the Great Strike of 1877* (Chicago: University of Chicago Press, 1999) makes the unique argument that the objections to the passage of railroads through urban neighborhoods constituted a source of the strike. A recent narrative history of the year in which the strikes took place is Michael A. Bellesiles's *1877: America's Year of Living Violently* (New York: New Press, 2011).

An emphasis on the meaning of the strike beyond U.S. borders is Christopher Phelps's analysis of Robert Koehler's painting *The Strike* (1886). Phelps explores how the 1877 strikes generated discussions of labor conflict in a transatlantic context and how the interpretations of the painting shifted alongside the changing political movements of the twentieth century. Christopher Phelps, "The Strike Imagined: The Atlantic and Interpretive Voyages of Robert Koehler's Painting *The Strike*," *Journal of American History* 98 (December 2011): 670–97.

3. "The Dangerous Classes," *Chicago Tribune*, July 29, 1877, 4.

4. Ibid.

5. Ibid.

6. Eugene E. Leach, "Chaining the Tiger: The Mob Stigma and the Working Class, 1863–1894," *Labor History* 35 (Spring 1994): 187–215.

7. Ibid., 197.

8. Mark M. Smith, *Listening to Nineteenth-Century America* (Chapel Hill: University of North Carolina Press, 2001), 248.

9. Ibid., 259, 16–17.

10. On the model town, see Carl Smith, *Urban Disorder and the Shape of Belief: The Great Chicago Fire, the Haymarket Bomb, and the Model Town of Pullman* (Chicago: University of Chicago Press, 1995), 177–231; James Gilbert, *Perfect Cities: Chicago's Utopias of 1893* (Chicago: University of Chicago Press, 1991), 131–68; and Stanley Buder, *Pullman: An Experiment in Industrial Order and Community Planning* (Oxford: Oxford University Press, 1967). For a full-length study of George M. Pullman's biography, see Liston Edgington Leyendecker, *Palace Car Prince: A Biography of George Mortimer Pullman* (Boulder: University Press of Colorado, 1992).

11. On the Pullman strike in general, see Carl Smith's *Urban Disorder and the Shape of Belief*, 232–70; Richard Schneirov, Shelton Stromquist, and Nick Salvatore, eds., *The Pullman Strike and the Crisis of the 1890s: Essays on Labor and Politics* (Urbana: University of Illinois Press, 1999); and Almont Lindsey, *The Pullman Strike: The Story of a Unique Experiment and of a Great Labor Upheaval* (Chicago: University of Chicago Press, 1942). The legal aspects of the strike are covered in David Ray Papke, *The Pullman Case: The Clash of Labor and Capital in Industrial America* (Lawrence: University Press of Kansas, 1999). On the Pullman company and labor relations after 1894, see Susan Eleanor Hirsch, *After the Strike: A Century of Labor Struggle at Pullman* (Urbana: University of Illinois Press, 2003).

12. C. Smith, *Urban Disorder and the Shape of Belief*, 88–98; Christine Meisner Rosen, *The Limits of Power: Great Fires and the Process of City Growth in America* (Cambridge: Cambridge University Press, 1986), 92–176.

13. E. Leach, "Chaining the Tiger," 195–97; Troy Rondinone, "'History Repeats Itself': The Civil War and the Meaning of Labor Conflict in the Late Nineteenth Century," *American Quarterly* 59 (June 2007): 397–419.

14. Foner, *Great Labor Uprising of 1877*, 8.

15. "Riot's Rule," *Chicago Times*, July 22, 1877, 3.

16. "Chicago: The General Situation," *Chicago Times*, July 23, 1877, 3.

17. "Chicago: Feeling in the City," *Chicago Tribune*, July 21, 1877, 5.

18. "Lawless Labor," *Chicago Times*, July 23, 1877, 5.

19. "Terror's Reign: The Streets of Chicago Given Over to Howling Mobs of Thieves and Cut-Throats," *Chicago Times*, July 26, 1877, 1 (all quotations).

20. "It Is Here," *Chicago Tribune*, July 25, 1877, 3.

21. "Organize for the Common Defense," *Chicago Tribune*, July 25, 1877, 4.

22. Dominic A. Pacyga, *Chicago: A Biography* (Chicago: University of Chicago Press, 2009), 88.

23. Untitled article ["Dispatches"], *Chicago Tribune*, July 26, 1877, 4.

24. "Plain Words with the Strikers," *Chicago Tribune*, July 27, 1877, 8.

25. "A Review of the Situation," *Chicago Tribune*, July 28, 1877, 4.

26. "At the Bridge," *Chicago Tribune*, 27 July 27, 1877, 2.

27. Quoted in Foner, *Great Labor Uprising of 1877*, 154–55.

28. For example, Cheryl A. Wells, *Civil War Time: Temporality and Identity in America, 1861–1865* (Athens: University of Georgia Press, 2005), 70–89.

29. Rondinone, "'History Repeats Itself,'" 410.

30. "The Cavalry Hounds," *Chicago Tribune*, July 27, 1877, 2.

31. Pacyga, *Chicago: A Biography*, 88.

32. "Halstead Street," *Chicago Tribune*, July 28, 1877, 1.

33. "Around the Viaduct," *Chicago Tribune*, July 27, 1877, 1.

34. "Review of the Situation," 4.

35. Constance Classen, *The Deepest Sense: A Cultural History of Touch* (Urbana: University of Illinois Press, 2012), 173. Mark Smith traced the relationship between coarsened racial bodies and violent disciplinary measures in the context of

Southern slavery in *How Race Is Made: Slavery, Segregation, and the Senses* (Chapel Hill: University of North Carolina Press, 2006), 37–47.

36. "Review of the Situation," 4.

37. "A Day for Reflection," *Chicago Tribune,* July 29, 1877, 4.

38. [Duane Doty], "The Story of Pullman," 4–5, Pullman-Miller Family Papers, box 10, folder "The Story of Pullman," Chicago History Museum, Chicago, Illinois.

39. C. Smith, *Urban Disorder and the Shape of Belief,* 177–84.

40. Thomas J. Jablonsky, *Pride in the Jungle: Community and Everyday Life in Back of the Yards* (Baltimore: Johns Hopkins University Press, 1993), 45, 47, 41. The residential and ecological landscape of Back of the Yards, which I discuss in greater detail in chapter 4, is also characterized well in James R. Barrett, *Work and Community in the Jungle: Chicago's Packinghouse Workers* (Urbana: University of Illinois Press, 1987), 64–107; Dominic A. Pacyga, *Polish Immigrants and Industrial Chicago: Workers on the South Side, 1880–1912* (Columbus: Ohio State University Press, 1991), 43–81.

41. Jacob A. Riis, "The Story of a Slum, Part IV," *Chicago Tribune,* April 1, 1900, 37 (all quotations).

42. Gilbert, *Perfect Cities,* 135.

43. Mrs. Duane Doty, *The Town of Pullman: Its Growth with Brief Accounts of Its Industries* (1893; repr., Pullman, IL: Pullman Civic Organization, 1974), 19.

44. Pacyga, *Chicago: A Biography,* 122–23.

45. Buder, *Pullman,* 93.

46. Doty, *Town of Pullman,* 17–18.

47. Ibid., appendix, 33.

48. Ibid., appendix, 24.

49. Woodward quoted in Doty, *Town of Pullman,* 27–30 (all quotations).

50. Ibid.

51. Ibid., 74.

52. Clay McShane and Joel A. Tarr describe the substantial production of manure by horses in the nineteenth-century city, including its potent malodor, to make the significance of this design decision clear. McShane and Tarr, *The Horse in the City: Living Machines in the Nineteenth Century* (Baltimore: Johns Hopkins University Press, 2007), 123–25.

53. Doty, *Town of Pullman,* 104, 204.

54. Ibid., 204.

55. Quoted in Gilbert, *Perfect Cities,* 160.

56. Ibid., 151, 159–60; Buder, *Pullman,* 88; Doty, *Town of Pullman,* 32.

57. "Extracts from the Report of the Commissioners of the State Bureaus of Labor Statistics on the Industrial, Social, and Economic Conditions of Pullman, Illinois," in Doty, *Town of Pullman,* appendix, 8.

58. Ibid., 6, 11, 15.

59. Richard T. Ely, "Pullman: A Social Study," *Harper's New Monthly Magazine,* February 1885, 466, 453, 465.

60. Ibid., 456, 457, 462.

61. Upton Sinclair, *The Jungle*, ed. Christopher Phelps (Boston: Bedford/St. Martin's, 2005), 65.

62. "Extracts from the Report of the Commissioners of the State Bureaus of Labor Statistics," appendix, 6.

63. Ibid., 463, 455, 462.

64. Ibid.

65. There are reports by "spotters" in the Pullman-Miller Family Papers at the Chicago History Museum. One undated report describes a scene of workers at one of the town's parks in the context of concerns about disorder from an unnamed strike: "The lieutenant of police at Kensington called to see me. I told him that I had just come from the ball grounds and that the crowd was quiet and orderly, and I did not think it necessary to make any show of police authority (n.d., box 11, folder "Statements Pullman Company Employees," Chicago History Museum, Chicago, Illinois).

66. Ely, "Pullman," 463, 464.

67. Alan Trachtenberg, *The Incorporation of America: Culture and Society in the Gilded Age*, 25th Anniversary edition (New York: Hill and Wang, 2007), 223–25. James Gilbert adds nuance to the broad parallels historians have drawn between the World's Columbian Exposition and the Town of Pullman when he points out that the fair, unlike the town, sought to display diverse forms of cultural expression by setting the amusements of the Midway Plaisance alongside (though distinctly outside) the exhibits of the White City. I discuss the fair in greater detail, including the relationship between the White City and the Midway, in chapter 5 (Gilbert, *Perfect Cities*, 137).

68. [Duane Doty], *Story of Pullman*, 32.

69. C. Smith, *Urban Disorder and the Shape of Belief*, 233, 245.

70. Janice L. Reiff, "A Modern Lear and His Daughters: Gender in the Model Town of Pullman," in *The Pullman Strike and the Crisis of the 1890s: Essays on Labor and Politics*, ed. Richard Schneirov et al., 77. Carl Smith also discusses the charge that George Pullman undermined the "manhood" of his workers in this respect in *Urban Disorder and the Shape of Belief*, 243–44.

71. Frederic Remington, "Chicago Under the Mob," *Harper's Weekly*, July 21, 1894, 680–81 (all quotations).

72. Reiff, "Modern Lear," 79–80.

73. "They Cry for Gore: Amazons Menace the Holland Laundry Girls at Pullman," *Chicago Tribune*, July 21, 1894, 1.

74. Ibid. (all quotations).

75. Reiff, "Modern Lear."

76. Gilbert, *Perfect Cities*, 162–63, 199.

77. Buder, *Pullman*, 187.

78. U.S. Commission, *Report on the Chicago Strike of June-July 1894* (Washington, D.C.: Government Printing Office, 1895), xxvii, xxxv.

79. Ibid., xxiii.

80. Ibid., xxi–xxii.

81. William H. Carwardine, *The Pullman Strike* (Chicago: Charles H. Kerr, 1894), 25 (all quotations).

Chapter 4. A Revolutionary and a Puritan

1. On the discussions of the novel's centennial anniversary, including *The Jungle*'s contemporary relevance, see James O'Shea, "Raking the Muck," *Chicago Tribune,* May 21, 2006; Adam Cohen, "100 Years Later, the Food Industry Is Still 'The Jungle,'" *New York Times,* January 2, 2007; Karen Olsson, "Welcome to the Jungle: Does Upton Sinclair's Famous Novel Hold Up?" *Slate,* July 10, 2006, http://www .slate.com/articles/arts/books/2006/07/welcome_to_the_jungle.html (accessed May 4, 2013). For scholarly considerations in light of the centennial, see James R. Barrett, "Remembering *The Jungle,*" *Labor: Studies in Working-Class History of the Americas* 3 (Winter 2006): 7–12; and Christopher Phelps, introduction to Upton Sinclair, *The Jungle,* ed. Christopher Phelps (Boston: Bedford/St. Martin, 2005), 1–39.

The foreword to Penguin's anniversary edition, written by Eric Schlosser, also delves into echoes of *The Jungle* in contemporary meat processing. Foreword to Upton Sinclair, *The Jungle,* Penguin Classics Deluxe ed. (New York: Penguin Books, 2006), vii–xv. Schlosser's *Fast Food Nation: The Dark Side of the American Meal* (New York: Houghton Mifflin, 2001) recalls Sinclair's disturbing findings about the meatpacking industry and immigrant labor. Also instructive on current issues of food safety is the documentary "Great Books: The Jungle," DVD, Discovery Channel (Silver Spring, MD: Discovery Communications, 2005).

The centennial also saw the publication of two Sinclair biographies, which I draw from below: Anthony Arthur, *Radical Innocent: Upton Sinclair* (New York: Random House, 2006); Kevin Mattson, *Upton Sinclair and the Other American Century* (Hoboken, NJ: John Wiley and Sons, 2006). Readers should also consult Leon Harris's earlier biography, *Upton Sinclair: American Rebel* (New York: Crowell, 1975). Sinclair's autobiographical reflections are also essential: Upton Sinclair, *American Outpost: A Book of Reminiscences* (Pasadena, CA: Station A, 1932); *The Autobiography of Upton Sinclair* (New York: Harcourt, Brace and World, 1962).

2. Upton Sinclair, *The Jungle,* ed. Christopher Phelps, 164–65 (all quotations). Unless otherwise noted, all quotations from *The Jungle* are from the 2005 Bedford edition. Doubleday, Page published the first edition in February 1906.

3. Ibid., 165–68.

4. The historian Christopher Phelps notes that Sinclair's discussion of the alienation of labor as "the sensation of being a mere appendage to the machine, denied creativity and fulfillment in work" is "strikingly similar to Karl Marx's then unknown early writings" but goes on to say that the parallels are coincidental

(Phelps, introduction, 18, 36n50). Phelps's contention seems to rest on the fact that one of Marx's works, the *Economic and Philosophical Manuscripts of 1844,* was not available for American readers until at least the 1930s. It is true that the *Manuscripts* include rich references to the senses, as I discuss below. But Marx's other key works, which also deal with alienation as a sensory phenomenon, were widely known and available in the United States long before Sinclair wrote *The Jungle.* Phelps offers no clarification about Sinclair's engagement with Marx's other works, so his contention is, at best, confusing. Sinclair himself studied Marx in the spring and summer of 1904, months before he traveled to Chicago to conduct research for the novel. Phelps, introduction, 36n50.

One of Sinclair's most recent biographers also downplays the influence of Marx, arguing that Sinclair's turn to socialism "had less to do with the scientific socialism of Karl Marx and more to do with the feeling of being snubbed as a writer." Mattson, *Upton Sinclair and the Other American Century,* 44. I discuss Sinclair's engagement with Marx's key works, which I argue he enjoyed precisely because of their "scientific" bent, below. On Marxist thought in the United States, see Daniel Bell, *Marxian Socialism in the United States,* Cornell University Paperback ed. (Ithaca, NY: Cornell University Press, 1996); Jason D. Martinek, *Socialism and Print Culture in the America, 1897–1920* (London: Pickering and Chatto, 2012).

5. Arthur, *Radical Innocent,* 262.

6. Sinclair, *Jungle,* 75.

7. A thorough contextualization of *The Jungle* in terms of the Progressive movement is Christopher Phelps's introductory essay to the Bedford/St. Martin's edition. Phelps, introduction, 1–39. The story of *The Jungle* and the passage of the 1906 Pure Food and Drug Act is best told in John Braeman, "The Square Deal in Action: A Case Study in the Growth of the 'National Police Power,'" in *Change and Continuity in Twentieth-Century America,* ed. John Braeman, Robert H. Bremmer, and Everett Walters (Columbus: Ohio State University Press, 1964), 35–80; and James Harvey Young, "The Pig That Fell into the Privy: Upton Sinclair's 'The Jungle' and the Meat Inspection Amendments of 1906," *Bulletin of the History of Medicine* 59 (Winter 1985): 467–80.

8. The full quotation, from the blurb on the dust jacket of the author's first autobiography, *American Outpost,* reads: "Frankly and engagingly he traces from his strange childhood the dramatic incidents and moods that have made him a social novelist and propagandist, loving mankind, hating drink and lust—that extraordinary combination: a Revolutionary and a Puritan!" Arthur, *Radical Innocent,* 222.

9. Phelps, introduction, 7; Upton Sinclair, *American Outpost,* 10–11.

10. Sinclair, *American Outpost,* 40.

11. Ibid., 65–66.

12. Ibid., 58.

13. Ibid., 64, 108.

14. Ibid., 135 (all quotations, emphasis in original).

15. Arthur, *Radical Innocent,* 122–23.

16. Ibid., 122–23, 62; Mattson, *Upton Sinclair and the Other American Century,* 77.

17. Arthur, *Radical Innocent,* 27.

18. Ibid., 20–21.

19. Ibid.

20. Upton Sinclair, *Love's Pilgrimage: A Novel* (New York: Mitchell Kennerley, 1911), quotations on 529, 537.

21. Ibid., 535.

22. Ibid., 528.

23. Mattson, *Upton Sinclair and the Other American Century,* 45–48.

24. Jason D. Martinek, *Socialism and Print Culture in America,* especially chapter 2.

25. Karl Marx and Frederick Engels, *The Communist Manifesto,* ed. John E. Toews (Boston: Bedford/St. Martin's, 1999), 71, 79.

26. Anthony Synnott, "Puzzling Over the Senses: From Plato to Marx," in David Howes, ed., *The Varieties of Sensory Experience: A Sourcebook in the Anthropology of the Senses* (Toronto: University of Toronto Press, 1991), 74.

27. Karl Marx, "The Working Day" (excerpt from *Capital*), in *The Cry for Justice: An Anthology of the Literature of Social Protest,* ed. Upton Sinclair (Philadelphia: John C. Winston Co., 1915), 795.

28. Synnott, "Puzzling Over the Senses," 75.

29. Karl Marx, *Economic and Philosophic Manuscripts of 1844,* trans. and ed. Martin Milligan (org., 1961 by Foreign Languages Publishing House, Moscow; Mineloa, NY: Dover Publications, 2007). Christopher Phelps points out that the book was published first in the 1930s in German and then became more widely available in the 1960s in English. Phelps, introduction, 36n50.

30. Marx, *Economic and Philosophic Manuscripts,* 108 (both quotations); emphasis in original.

31. Upton Sinclair, "You Have Lost the Strike! And Now What Are You Going to Do About It?" *Appeal to Reason,* September 17, 1904, 1.

32. Ibid.

33. Upton Sinclair, "Farmers of America, Unite!" *Appeal to Reason,* October 15, 1904, 2.

34. On racism in the socialist movement, a prejudice that also included anti-Asian attitudes, see Daniel E. Bender, *American Abyss: Savagery and Civilization in the Age of Industry* (Ithaca, NY: Cornell University Press, 2009), 10, 88–89, 96–97; Martinek, *Socialism and Print Culture in America.*

35. A. M. Simons, *Packingtown* (Chicago: Charles H. Kerr and Company, 1899).

36. Quoted in Phelps, introduction, 5.

37. Phelps, introduction, 5.

38. William Cronon, *Nature's Metropolis: Chicago and the Great West* (New York:

W. W. Norton, 1991), 225–32; James R. Barrett, *Work and Community in the Jungle: Chicago's Packinghouse Workers, 1894–1922* (Urbana: University of Illinois Press, 1987) 19.

39. Barrett, *Work and Community in the Jungle*, 21.

40. Barrett, "Remembering *The Jungle*," 7–12; James R. Barrett, introduction to *The Jungle*, by Upton Sinclair (Urbana: University of Illinois Press, 1988), xiv–xvi.

41. By 1900 meatpacking had emerged as Chicago's largest manufacturing employer. Barrett, *Work and Community in the Jungle*, 18–19.

42. Barrett, *Work and Community in the Jungle*, 74.

43. Ibid., 36–37, 44.

44. Sinclair, *Jungle*, 67.

45. Thomas J. Jablonsky, *Pride in the Jungle: Community and Everyday Life in Back of the Yards Chicago* (Baltimore: Johns Hopkins University Press, 1993), 41.

46. Sinclair, *Jungle*, 68–69.

47. Jablonsky, *Pride in the Jungle*, 11.

48. Barrett, introduction, xvii; Dominic A. Pacyga, *Polish Immigrants and Industrial Chicago: Workers on the South Side, 1880–1922* (Columbus: Ohio State University Press, 1991), 60–62, 72. For example, Barrett reports that between 1894 and 1900, the population of the stockyards district was almost twice as large as Hyde Park, but that deaths from infectious disease (e.g., bronchitis, consumption) in the industrial neighborhood hit levels from double to five times that of Hyde Park. Barrett, introduction, xvii.

49. Barrett, *Work and Community in the Jungle*, 1–10, 83–87; Barrett, introduction, xxi–xxii.

50. The family's largest purchase is to lease a house, from which they are eventually evicted. The lease turns out to be a scam, introduced to the family through advertisements distributed in their neighborhood. The issue is covered in chapter 4, where Sinclair also makes cutting and perceptive remarks about the other types of false advertising of the day, including those selling the dangerous medicines that were eventually regulated by the 1906 Pure Food and Drug Act.

In *The Jungle*'s final chapter, Sinclair evinces his debt to Thorstein Veblen for his ideas about the dangers of a consumption-oriented culture. Speaking through one of the socialists that he uses to explain the basic tenants of the movement, he describes consumption as mere "competition in display," a wasteful curse on modern society. In "a society dominated by the fact of commercial competition, money is necessarily the test of prowess, and wastefulness the sole criterion of power." Sinclair, *Jungle*, 354–55. Veblen's notion of "conspicuous consumption" is outlined in his 1899 classic, *The Theory of the Leisure Class* (New York: Penguin Books, 1994).

51. David Howes, "The Material Body of the Commodity," in *Sensual Relations: Engaging the Senses in Culture and Social Theory*, ed. David Howes (Ann Arbor: University of Michigan Press, 2003), 230–34.

52. Mark Pittenger, "A World of Difference: Constructing the 'Underclass' in Progressive America," *American Quarterly* 49 (March 1997): 26–65; Catherine Cocks, *Doing the Town: The Rise of Urban Tourism in the United States, 1850–1915* (Berkeley: University of California Press, 2001).

53. Bender, *American Abyss*, 137.

54. Sinclair, *American Outpost*, 154.

55. Pittenger, "World of Difference," 42–43.

56. Antanas Kaztaukis [Ernest Poole], "From Lithuania to the Chicago Stockyards—An Autobiography," *Independent*, July 1904, 241–48.

57. Arthur, *Radical Innocent*, 47; Louise Carroll Wade, "The Problem with Classroom Use of *The Jungle*," *American Studies* 32 (Summer 1991): 83.

58. A. M. Simons, *Packingtown*.

59. Arthur, *Radical Innocent*, 47.

60. Ibid., 47–48.

61. Ibid., 48–49.

62. The articles were all published in *The Lancet* in January 1905.

63. Sinclair, *American Outpost*, 155.

64. Phelps, introduction, 9.

65. The literary criticism of *The Jungle* is too voluminous to list in its entirety. In addition to the critical introductions to *The Jungle* listed above, the best starting points are Morris Dickstein, introduction to Upton Sinclair, *The Jungle* (New York: Bantam, 1981); Alfred Kazin, *On Native Grounds: An Interpretation of Modern American Prose Literature* (New York: Doubleday, 1956); Walter Rideout, *The Radical Novel in the United States: 1900–54* (New York: Hill and Wang, 1956); Abraham Blinderman, ed., *Critics on Upton Sinclair* (Coral Gables, FL: University of Miami Press, 1975). On naturalism, see Maxwell Geismar, *Rebels and Ancestors: The American Novel, 1890–1915* (Boston: Houghton Mifflin, 1953); Richard Lehan, *Realism and Naturalism: The Novel in an Age of Transition* (Madison: University of Wisconsin Press, 2005).

66. Stephen Crane, "An Experiment in Misery," in *Great Short Works of Stephen Crane,* ed. James B. Colvert (New York: Harper and Row, 1968), 248–58; Linda H. Davis, *Badge of Courage: The Life of Stephen Crane* (Boston: Houghton Mifflin, 1998), 80–81.

67. Pittenger, "World of Difference," 39.

68. Sinclair, *Jungle,* 50.

69. The wedding scene has been of particular interest to literary critics. See especially Orm Øverland, "*The Jungle:* From Lithuanian Peasant to American Socialist," *American Literary Realism* 37 (Fall 2004): 1–23; Suk Bong Suh, "Lithuanian Wedding Traditions in Upton Sinclair's *The Jungle*," *Lituanus* (Spring 1987): 5–17.

70. Phelps, introduction, 19–20; Suk Bong Suh, "Lithuanian Wedding Traditions," 5–17.

71. Øverland, "*The Jungle:* From Lithuanian Peasant to American Socialist," 8–9.

72. Sinclair, *American Outpost*, 156.
73. Ibid.
74. Ibid.
75. Sinclair, *Jungle*, 46.
76. Ibid., 60.
77. Ibid., 44 (all quotations).
78. Ibid., 61.
79. Ibid., 95.
80. Ibid., 61.
81. Ibid., 95.
82. Ibid., 117 (all quotations).
83. Ibid., 117–18 (all quotations).
84. Ibid., 137 (all quotations).
85. Jurgis's workplace injury accurately reflected the high injury rate in meatpacking and the periodic unemployment it created. Barrett notes that in the first six months of 1910, Swift and Company reported thirty-five hundred injuries that required the attention of a doctor, a figure that obviously does not account for unreported injuries. Five years earlier the U.S. commissioner of labor found that "12 percent of all family heads noted periods of unemployment, averaging about 12.4 weeks, as a result of accidents or illness on the job." Barrett, introduction, xvi.
86. Sinclair, *Jungle*, 152–57 (all quotations).
87. Ibid., 162.
88. Ibid., 163 (all quotations).
89. Ibid., 168.
90. Ibid., 172.
91. This is the historian Louise Carroll Wade's key objection to the novel. She questions its usefulness as a tool to teach about immigrant life because Sinclair "loaded the dice" when he piled misfortune onto the Rudkus family (Wade, "Problem with Classroom Use of *The Jungle*," 97). Wade makes a good point for readers who might interpret Jurgis's many misfortunes in a literal fashion and not as a literary device used to comment on the immigrant experience more generally. Even so, as I note above, most of Jurgis's individual misfortunes are accurate reflections of the living and working conditions in the stockyards district. In addition to the high rates of pollution, disease, and workplace injuries (noted above), the infant death rate was disproportionally high. In 1909, Barrett observes, it exceeded the infant death rate of nearby Hyde Park by more than seven times. Barrett, introduction, xvii.
92. On the 1904 stockyards strike, see Barrett, *Work and Community in the Jungle*, 165–87. On black migration to Chicago in the early twentieth century, see James R. Grossman, *Land of Hope: Chicago, Black Southerners, and the Great Migration* (Chicago: University of Chicago Press, 1989); and Davarian L. Baldwin, *Chicago's New*

Negroes: Modernity, the Great Migration, and Black Urban Life (Chapel Hill: University of North Carolina Press, 2007). Rick Halpern, *Down on the Killing Floor: Black and White Workers in Chicago's Packinghouses, 1904–1954* (Urbana: University of Illinois Press, 1997), 30.

93. Sinclair, *Jungle*, 290–91. Sinclair suggests that the black strikebreakers came to Chicago under false pretenses. He writes that the recruiting agents failed to mention the ongoing strike, but the concession does little to humanize his subjects. Sinclair, *Jungle*, 292.

94. Mark M. Smith, *How Race Is Made: Slavery, Segregation, and the Senses* (Chapel Hill: University of North Carolina Press, 2006).

95. On race and notions of savagery, see Bender, *American Abyss*; Matthew Frye Jacobson, *Barbarian Virtues: The United States Encounters Foreign Peoples at Home and Abroad, 1876–1917* (New York: Hill and Wang, 2001).

96. Sinclair, *Jungle*, 295–96 (all quotations).

97. During the stockyards strike, as the labor historian Rick Halpern explains, blacks arrived as "a permanent component in the packinghouse labor force." Their role as strikebreakers in that year made "the words 'Negro' and 'scab' synonymous" in the minds of the working-class whites there. Halpern, *Down on the Killing Floor*, 38–39.

Race and labor in meatpacking is covered in Rick Halpern, *Down on the Killing Floor*; Roger Horowitz, *"Negro and White, Unite and Fight!" A Social History of Industrial Unionism in Meatpacking, 1930–1990* (Urbana: University of Illinois Press, 1997). Lizabeth Cohen's *Making a New Deal* traces the success of the Congress of Industrial Organizations (CIO) in bridging racial divides in Chicago in the 1930s. Lizabeth Cohen, *Making a New Deal: Industrial Workers in Chicago, 1919–1939*, 2nd ed. (Cambridge: Cambridge University Press, 2008).

98. Halpern, *Down on the Killing Floor*, 30.

99. Cohen, *Making a New Deal*, 12–21; Chicago Commission on Race Relations, *The Negro in Chicago: A Study of Race Relations and a Race Riot* (1922; repr., New York: Arno Press, 1968); William M. Tuttle Jr., *Race Riot: Chicago in the Red Summer of 1919* (1970; repr., Urbana: University of Illinois Press, 1996). The 1919 riot, a bloody spasm that brought the state militia to Chicago, lasted nearly two weeks. The first four days saw the worst rioting. In the end, thirty-eight people were killed; more than five hundred injured; and more than one thousand people made homeless.

100. "A Group of Novels," *Outlook*, March 31, 1906, 758.

101. Martinek, *Socialism and Print Culture*, 6.

102. Sinclair, *Jungle*, 349, 53–54, 357–58.

103. Ibid., 347–48.

104. Robert Blatchford, *Merrie England: A Plain Exposition of Socialism: What It Is and What It Is Not* (New York: Commonwealth Company, 1895); Edward Bellamy, *Looking Backward* (Boston: Houghton Mifflin, 1889).

Chapter 5. Sensory Refreshment

1. "The Story of White City," *White City Magazine* (hereafter *WCM*), February 1905, 10, Chicago History Museum, Chicago, Illinois (both quotations).

2. There is a vast literature on the 1893 world's fair. The studies that have shaped my thinking on Burnham's White City include Robert Rydell, *All the World's a Fair: Visions of Empire at American International Expositions, 1876–1916* (Chicago: University of Chicago Press, 1985), 38–71, and *Buffalo Bill in Bologna: The Americanization of the World, 1869–1922* (Chicago: University of Chicago Press, 2005), 47–73; John Kasson, *Amusing the Million: Coney Island at the Turn of the Century* (New York: Hill and Wang, 1978), 11–28; James Gilbert, *Perfect Cities: Chicago's Utopia's of 1893* (Chicago: University of Chicago Press, 1991), 75–130; William Cronon, *Nature's Metropolis: Chicago and the Great West* (New York: W. W. Norton, 1991), 341–69; and Alan Trachtenberg, *The Incorporation of America: Culture and Society in the Gilded Age* (New York: Hill and Wang, 1982), 208–34. On elite cultural uplift in Chicago, see Helen Lefkowitz Horowitz, *Culture and the City: Cultural Philanthropy in Chicago from 1880s to 1917* (Chicago: University of Chicago, 1976).

3. Kasson, *Amusing the Million*, 18.

4. The Midway Plaisance, or Midway of Pleasure, was a combination of amusement park spectacles and exotic anthropological displays designed to appeal to popular tastes. It stood apart, both thematically and physically, from Burnham's White City. The contrast between the Midway and the White City is described well in Gilbert, *Perfect Cities,* 107–21.

5. "The Necessity of White City," *WCM*, March 1905, 11.

6. "The Story of White City," *WCM*, February 1905, 12.

7. The literature on mass amusements, consumer pleasure, and urban culture is too extensive to list here. In addition to Kasson's *Amusing the Million*, germinal works include Elaine Abelson, *When Ladies Go A-Thieving: Middle-Class Shoplifters in the Victorian Department Store* (Oxford: Oxford University Press, 1989); Richard D. Butsch, *For Fun and Profit: The Transformation of Leisure into Consumption* (Philadelphia: Temple University Press, 1990); Lizabeth Cohen, *Making a New Deal: Industrial Workers in Chicago, 1919–1939,* 2nd ed. (Cambridge: Cambridge University Press, 2008); William Leach, *Land of Desire: Merchants, Power, and the Rise of a New American Culture* (New York: Vintage Books, 1993); and Roy Rosenzweig, *Eight Hours for What We Will: Workers and Leisure in an Industrial City* (Cambridge: Cambridge University Press, 1983).

Chicago featured multiple amusement parks after the turn of the century. Riverview Park, on the city's North Side, enjoyed the longest life, from 1904 to 1967. Unlike White City, Riverview has been the subject of several popular histories, including Chuck Wlodarczyk, *Riverview: Gone but Not Forgotten* (Chicago: Riverview Publications, 1977); Derek Gee and Ralph Lopez, *Laugh Your Troubles Away: The*

Complete History of Riverview Park (Livonia, MI: Sharpshooters Productions, 2000); and Dolores Haugh, *Riverview Amusement Park* (Charleston, SC: Arcadia, 2004).

8. Neil Harris, *Humbug: The Art of P. T. Barnum* (Chicago: University of Chicago Press, 1973); W. Leach, *Land of Desire*; Grace Elizabeth Hale, *Making Whiteness: The Culture of Segregation in the South, 1890–1940* (New York: Vintage Books, 1999).

9. Readers should not take the baseball reference to suggest that fans attend games—professional or otherwise—only to watch, as a trip to any Chicago stadium will attest. The point is that watching constitutes the main way to take in the game. There are also, of course, a few examples of Chicago fans literally taking to the field. The most infamous episode is the 1979 "Disco Demolition Night" at Comiskey Park, in which hundreds of attendees stormed the field after a local disc jockey exploded dozens of disco records at the midpoint of a double-header. See Gillian Frank, "Discophobia: Antigay Prejudice and the 1979 Backlash against Disco," *Journal of the History of Sexuality* 16 (May 2007): 276–306.

10. Kasson, *Amusing the Million*, 8.

11. Lynn Sally, "Fantasy Land and Kinesthetic Thrills: Sensorial Consumption, the Shock of Modernity, and Spectacle as Total-Body Experience at Coney Island," *Senses and Society* 1 (November 2006): 300.

12. I define "privacy in public" as a standard of middle-class etiquette in chapter 2. In essence, the standard called on women to avoid unwelcome stares, compliments, and especially touching, because such violations raised questions about their respectability. John F. Kasson, *Rudeness and Civility: Manners in Nineteenth-Century Urban America* (New York: Hill and Wang, 1990), 129.

13. Eric Avila, *Popular Culture in the Age of White Flight: Fear and Fantasy in Suburban Los Angeles* (Berkeley: University of California Press, 2004), 109.

14. Kasson, *Amusing the Million*, 206.

15. On the questions about the respectability of baseball raised by the infamous 1919 "Black Sox" scandal, see Robin F. Bachin, "At the Lexus of Labor and Leisure: Baseball, Nativism, and the 1919 Black Sox Scandal," *Journal of Social History* 36 (Summer 2003): 941–62.

16. Robin F. Bachin, *Building the South Side: Urban Space and Civic Culture in Chicago, 1890–1919* (Chicago: University of Chicago Press, 2004), quotations on 206, 230.

17. "Necessity of White City," 9.

18. Ibid., 9,10; "Those Who Made White City Possible," *WCM*, May 1906, 5.

19. Ava Baron and Elieen Boris, "'The Body as a Useful Category for Working-Class History," *Labor: Studies in Working-Class History of the Americas* 4 (Summer 2007): 36.

20. Jackson Lears, *No Place of Grace: Antimodernism and the Transformation of American Culture, 1880–1920* (New York: Pantheon Books, 1981), 47–58; David G. Schuster, *Neurasthenic Nation: America's Search for Health, Happiness, and Comfort, 1869–1920* (New Brunswick, NJ: Rutgers University Press, 2011).

21. Jackson Lears, "From Salvation to Self-Realization: Advertising and the Therapeutic Roots of the Consumer Culture, 1880–1930," in *The Culture of Consumption: Critical Essays in American History, 1880–1980,* ed. Richard Wightman Fox and T. J. Jackson Lears (New York: Pantheon Books, 1983), 1–38.

22. "What a Physician Says: Longevity the Result of Indulgence in Amusements," *WCM,* March 1905, 68.

23. "How the Levee Is Encroaching on State Street," *Chicago Tribune,* August 2, 1908, F4.

24. Ibid.

25. For slummers in Chicago, see Chad Heap, *Slumming: Sexual and Racial Encounters in American Nightlife, 1885–1940* (Chicago: University of Chicago Press, 2009).

26. "How the Levee Is Encroaching on State Street," F4.

27. David Nasaw, "Cities of Light, Landscapes of Pleasure," in *The Landscape of Modernity: New York City, 1900–1940,* ed. David Ward and Olivier Zunz (Baltimore: Johns Hopkins University Press, 1997), 282.

28. White City Construction Company Records (hereafter WCC), Chicago History Museum, Chicago, Illinois.

29. "Sanitary Arrangements," *WCM,* March 1905, 26.

30. "Police Force," *WCM,* Season 1907, 42.

31. "Necessity of White City," 12; "Rules of Conduct," n.d., White City, Chicago, Miscellaneous Pamphlets, Chicago History Museum, Chicago, Illinois; "Fire Department," *WCM,* Season 1907, 42.

32. Nasaw, "Cities of Light," 273–77; Jill Jones, *Empires of Light: Edison, Tesla, Westinghouse, and the Race to Electrify the World* (New York: Random House, 2003), 264–66.

33. "Large Electric Light Contract," *WCM,* February 1905, 21; "Features of White City," *WCM,* February 1905, 32; "White City by Night," *WCM,* May 1906, 36.

34. John S. Reid to Hilda M. Sweet, December 25, 1908, John S. Reid Letters, 1908–09, Chicago History Museum, Chicago, Illinois; Nasaw, "Cities of Light," 277.

35. "White City by Night," *WCM,* May 1906, 36; "White City by Day," *WCM,* May 1906, 34.

36. Constance Classen, *The Deepest Sense: A Cultural History of Touch* (Urbana: University of Illinois Press, 2012), 179.

37. Joseph Beifeld to George C. Tilyou, February 7, 1912; Falls Rivet & Machinery Company to White City, February 6, 1912; Joseph Beifeld to Ontario Beach Hotel and Amusement Co., April 13, 1912, WCC, folders 4, 5, 7. White City also borrowed visual affects from Marshall Field's department store. In one case, for instance, Beifeld offered to purchase the holiday window decorations from Marshall Field. The decorations, in this case, had already been sold to another buyer.

Joseph Beifeld to Marshall Field & Company, January 5, 1912, WCC. On the tactile merchandising at department stores, see Classen, *Deepest Sense,* 191–98.

38. "Crowds at the Gardens," *Chicago Tribune,* May 28, 1905, 6.

39. "Bumps," *WCM,* March 1905, 29.

40. "Shooting the Chutes," *WCM,* Season 1907, 39.

41. "What a Physician Says," *WCM,* 68.

42. "Chicago Fire," *WCM,* May 1906, 11, 10.

43. "The Spectacular Fire Show," *WCM,* May 1906, 21.

44. John S. Reid to Hilda M. Sweet, December 25, 1908.

45. "Features of White City," February 1905, 32.

46. "Camp of Gypsies," *WCM,* March 1905, 15 (all quotations).

47. "Igorrote Village," *WCM,* Season 1907, 17; Paul A. Kramer, "Race Making and Colonial Violence in the U.S. Empire: The Philippine-American War as Race War," *Diplomatic History* 30 (April 2006): 169–210.

48. Bachin, *Building the South Side,* 247–50, 254–64. The rise of a separate black commercial district is covered in Bachin, *Building the South Side,* chapter 6; Lizabeth Cohen, *Making a New Deal,* 147–58.

49. Quoted in Bachin, *Building the South Side,* 247.

50. Oney Fred Sweet, "Hunting New Thrills as an Understudy at the Amusement Parks," *Chicago Tribune,* July 25, 1915, B14.

51. Perry R. Duis and Glen H. Holt, "Bright Lights, Hard Times of White City II," *Chicago Magazine,* August 1978, 176.

52. Duis and Holt, "Bright Lights, Hard Times"; Bachin, *Building the South Side,* 207.

53. Vice Commission of Chicago, *The Social Evil in Chicago: A Study of Existing Conditions* (1911; repr., New York: Arno Press, 1970), 246.

54. Ibid., 246, 213.

55. "Steward's Order Throttles Levee," *Chicago Tribune,* October 11, 1909, 1.

56. Vice Commission of Chicago, *The Social Evil in Chicago,* 163; "Steward's Order Throttles Levee," 1.

57. "Police Warning to Park Barkers," *Chicago Tribune,* July 8, 1909, 5.

58. "Pastors Want Park Purged," *Chicago Tribune,* July 17, 1909, 3 (both quotations).

59. "Arrest Bare Bronze Beauties," *Chicago Tribune,* July 13, 1909, 3.

60. "Paint and Girdle Enough for Stage," *Chicago Tribune,* July 20, 1909, 3

61. The language "immoral or dangerous" is from the city ordinance regulating amusement parks. Vice Commission of Chicago, *Social Evil,* appendix 20, 328. The campaign against White City reflected a broader crackdown on Chicago's notorious reputation for vice. After the Vice Commission's 1911 report, police raided the worst offenders in the South Side levee, ending the semi-official policy of segregating vice in a red-light district.

62. Duis and Holt, "Bright Lights, Hard Times," 178.

63. Jane Addams, *The Spirit of Youth and the City Streets* (New York: Macmillan, 1909).

64. Ibid., 3–4, 63.

65. Ibid., 4–5.

66. On playgrounds in the Progressive Era, see Paul Boyer, *Urban Masses and Moral Order in America, 1820–1920* (Cambridge, MA: Harvard University Press, 1978), 233–55.

67. Ibid., 7, 69, 19.

68. Ibid., 13, 25, 26.

69. Ibid., 27. George Santayana, *The Sense of Beauty: Outlines of an Aesthetic Theory* (New York: Charles Scribner's Sons, 1896), 56.

70. The idea of the commercial landscape of the suburbs as secure, homogenous, and predictable is described in Avila, *Popular Culture in the Age of White Flight*; Adam Mack, "The Senses in the Marketplace: Commercial Aesthetics for a Suburban Age," in *A Cultural History of the Senses in the Modern Age,* ed. David Howes (Oxford: Berg, forthcoming).

BIBLIOGRAPHY

Primary Sources

ARCHIVAL SOURCES

Chicago History Museum (formerly the Chicago Historical Society):
  Annie McClure Hitchcock Collection
  Chicago Fire of 1871, Personal Narratives
  Emily C. Pullman Papers, 1830–1913
  Frances L. Roberts Letters
  George M. Pullman Papers, 1845–1957
  Grant-Pullman Letters, 1871
  John S. Reid Letters, 1908–1909
  Pullman-Miller Family Papers
  White City Construction Company Records
  The White City Magazine and Souvenir Program, 1906–1907, 1912–1914
  White City, Chicago, Miscellaneous Pamphlets

GOVERNMENT DOCUMENTS

Annual Report of the Board of Public Works to the Common Council of the City of Chicago, 1862–1869, 1871–1874.

The Chicago Commission on Race Relations. *The Negro in Chicago: A Study of Race Relations and a Race Riot.* 1922. Reprint, New York: Arno Press, 1968.

Report of the Board of Health of the City of Chicago for 1867, 1868, and 1869; and a Sanitary History of Chicago; from 1833 to 1870. Chicago: Lakeside Publishing and Printing Company, 1871.

Report of the Board of Health of the City of Chicago for the Years 1870, 1871, 1872, and 1873. Chicago: Bulletin Printing Company, 1874.

U.S. Congress. House. *Conditions in Chicago Stock Yards*. 59th Cong., 1st sess., 1906. Doc. 873.

U.S. Strike Commission. *Report on the Chicago Strike of June–July 1894*. Washington, DC: Government Printing Office, 1895.

The Vice Commission of Chicago. *The Social Evil in Chicago: A Study of Existing Conditions*. 1911. New York: Arno Press, 1970.

NEWSPAPERS AND MAGAZINES

Appeal to Reason
Chicago Times
Chicago Tribune
Harper's New Monthly Magazine
Harper's Weekly
The Independent
The Lancet
Outlook

PUBLISHED MATERIALS, BOOKS, AND PAMPHLETS

Addams, Jane. *The Spirit of Youth and the City Streets*. New York: Macmillan, 1909.

Blatchford, Robert. *Merrie England: A Plain Exposition of Socialism: What It Is and What It Is Not*. New York: Commonwealth Company, 1895.

Carwardine, William H. *The Pullman Strike*. Chicago: Charles H. Kerr, 1894.

Chicago Relief and Aid Society. *Report of the Chicago Relief and Aid Society of Disbursement of Contributions for the Sufferers of the Chicago Fire*. Cambridge, MA: Riverside Press, 1874.

Colbert, Elias, and Everett Chamberlin. *Chicago and the Great Conflagration*. Cincinnati: C. F. Vent, 1872.

Crane, Stephen. "An Experiment in Misery." In *Great Short Works of Stephen Crane*, edited by James O. Colvert, 248–58. New York: Harper and Row, 1968.

Doty, Mrs. Duane. *The Town of Pullman: Its Growth with Brief Accounts of Its Industries*. 1893. Reprint, Pullman, IL: Pullman Civic Organization, 1974.

Dreiser, Theodore. *Sister Carrie*. New York: Modern Library, 1999.

Kipling, Rudyard. *American Notes*. London: Standard Book Company, 1930.

Lakeside Memorial of the Burning of Chicago. Chicago: University Publishing Company, 1872.

Marx, Karl. "The Working Day" (excerpt from *Capital*). In *The Cry for Justice: An Anthology of the Literature of Social Protest*, edited by Upton Sinclair, 795–96. Philadelphia: John C. Winston Co., 1915.

———. *Economic and Philosophic Manuscripts of 1844*. Translated and edited by Martin Milligan. Mineola, NY: Dover Publications, 2007.

Marx, Karl, and Frederick Engels. *The Communist Manifesto.* Edited by John E. Toews. Boston: Bedford/St. Martin's, 1999.

Roe, Edward P. *Barriers Burned Away.* New York: Dodd Mead and Company, 1872.

Santayana, George. *The Sense of Beauty: Outlines of an Aesthetic Theory.* New York: Charles Scribner's Sons, 1896.

Sheahan, James W., and George P. Upton. *The Great Conflagration: Chicago, Its Past, Present, and Future.* Philadelphia: Union Publishing Co., 1871.

Simmel, Georg. "The Metropolis and Mental Life." In *The Blackwell City Reader,* edited by Gary Bridge and Sophie Watson, 11–19. Oxford: Wiley-Blackwell, 2002.

Simons, A. M. *Packingtown.* Chicago: Charles H. Kerr and Company, 1899.

Sinclair, Upton. *American Outpost: A Book of Reminiscences.* Pasadena, CA: Station A, 1932.

———. *The Autobiography of Upton Sinclair.* New York: Harcourt, Brace and World, 1962.

———. *The Jungle.* Edited by Christopher Phelps. Boston: Bedford/St. Martin's, 2005.

———. *Love's Pilgrimage: A Novel.* New York: Mitchell Kennerley, 1911.

Secondary Sources

Abelson, Elaine. *When Ladies Go A-Thieving: Middle-Class Shoplifters in the Victorian Department Store.* Oxford: Oxford University Press, 1989.

Angle, Paul M., ed. *The Great Chicago Fire: Described in Seven Letters by Men and Women Who Experienced Its Horrors, and Now Published in Commemoration of the Seventy-fifth Anniversary of the Catastrophe.* Chicago: Chicago Historical Society, 1946.

Arthur, Anthony. *Radical Innocent: Upton Sinclair.* New York: Random House, 2006.

Avila, Eric. *Popular Culture in the Age of White Flight: Fear and Fantasy in Suburban Los Angeles.* Berkeley: University of California Press, 2004.

Bachin, Robin, F. "At the Lexus of Labor and Leisure: Baseball, Nativism, and the 1919 Black Sox Scandal." *Journal of Social History* 36 (Summer 2003): 941–62.

———. *Building the South Side: Urban Space and Civic Culture in Chicago, 1890–1919.* Chicago: University of Chicago Press, 2004.

Baldwin, Davarian L. *Chicago's New Negroes: Modernity, The Great Migration, and Black Urban Life.* Chapel Hill: University of North Carolina Press, 2007.

Barnes, David S. *The Great Stink of Paris and the Nineteenth-Century Struggle against Filth and Germs.* Baltimore: Johns Hopkins University Press, 2006.

Baron, Ava, and Eileen Boris. "'The Body as a Useful Category for Working-Class History." *Labor: Studies in Working-Class History of the Americas* 4 (Summer 2007): 23–43.

Barrett, James R. Introduction to *The Jungle,* by Upton Sinclair. Urbana: University of Illinois Press, 1988.

———. "Remembering *The Jungle.*" *Labor: Studies in Working-Class History of the Americas* 3 (Winter 2006): 7–12.

———. *Work and Community in the Jungle: Chicago's Packinghouse Workers, 1894–1922.* Urbana: University of Illinois Press, 1987.

Bederman, Gail. *Manliness and Civilization: A Cultural History of Gender and Race in the United States, 1880–1917.* Chicago: University of Chicago Press, 1995.

Bell, Daniel, ed. *Marxian Socialism in the United States,* Cornell University Paperback ed. Ithaca, NY: Cornell University Press, 1996.

Bellamy, Edward. *Looking Backward.* Boston: Houghton Mifflin, 1889.

Bellesiles, Michael A. *1877: America's Year of Living Violently.* New York: New Press, 2011.

Bender, Daniel E. *American Abyss: Savagery and Civilization in the Age of Industry.* Ithaca, NY: Cornell University Press, 2009.

———. "Sensing Labor: The Stinking Working Class after the Cultural Turn." In *Rethinking U.S. Labor History: Essays on the Working-Class Experience, 1756–2009,* edited by Donna T. Haverty-Stacke and Daniel J. Walkowitz, 243–65. New York: Continuum, 2010.

———. *Sweated Work, Weak Bodies: Anti-Sweatshop Campaigns and Languages of Labor.* New Brunswick, NJ: Rutgers University Press, 2004.

Bledstein, Burton J., and Robert D. Johnston. *The Middling Sorts: Explorations in the History of the American Middle Class.* New York: Routledge, 2001.

Blinderman, Abraham, ed. *Critics on Upton Sinclair.* Coral Gables, FL: University of Miami Press, 1975.

Blumin, Stuart M. *The Emergence of the Middle Class: Social Experience in the American City, 1760–1900.* Cambridge: Cambridge University Press, 1989.

———. "The Hypothesis of Middle-Class Formation in Nineteenth-Century America: A Critique and Some Proposals." *American Historical Review* 90 (April 1985): 299–338.

Bourdieu, Pierre. *Distinction: A Social Critique of the Judgement of Taste.* Translated by Richard Nice. Cambridge, MA: Harvard University Press, 1984.

Boyer, Paul. *Urban Masses and Moral Order in America, 1820–1920.* Cambridge, MA: Harvard University Press, 1978.

Braeman, John. "The Square Deal in Action: A Case Study in the Growth of the 'National Police Power.'" In *Change and Continuity in Twentieth Century America,* edited by John Braeman, Robert H. Bremmer, and Everett Walters, 35–80. Columbus: Ohio State University Press, 1964.

Briggs, Asa. *Victorian Cities.* 1963. Reprint, Berkeley: University of California Press, 1993.

Brosnan, Kathleen A. "Effluence, Affluence, and the Maturing of Urban Environmental History." *Journal of Urban History* 31 (November 2004): 115–23.

Bruce, Robert V. *1877: Year of Violence.* Lanham, MD: Ivan R. Dee, 1989.

Buder, Stanley. *Pullman: An Experiment in Industrial Order and Community Planning, 1880–1930.* Oxford: Oxford University Press, 1967.

Bushman, Richard L. *The Refinement of America: Persons, Houses, Cities.* New York: Alfred A. Knopf, 1992.

Bushman, Richard L., and Claudia L. Bushman. "The Early History of Cleanliness in America." *Journal of American History* 74 (March 1988): 1213–38.

Butsch, Richard D. *For Fun and Profit: The Transformation of Leisure into Consumption.* Philadelphia: Temple University Press, 1990.

Cain, Louis P. "Raising and Watering a City: Ellis Sylvester Chesbrough and Chicago's First Sanitation System." *Technology and Culture* 13 (July 1972): 353–72.

———. *Sanitation Strategy for a Lakefront Metropolis: The Case of Chicago.* DeKalb: Northern Illinois Press, 1978.

Chiang, Connie Y. "The Nose Knows: The Sense of Smell in American History." *Journal of American History* 95 (September 2008): 405–16.

———. *Shaping the Shoreline: Tourism and Fisheries on the Monterey Coast.* Seattle: University of Washington Press, 2008.

Classen, Constance. *The Deepest Sense: A Cultural History of Touch.* Urbana: University of Illinois Press, 2012.

———. "Foundations for an Anthropology of the Senses." *International Social Sciences Journal* 153 (September 1997): 401–12.

Classen, Constance, David Howes, and Anthony Synnott. *Aroma: The Cultural History of Smell.* New York: Routledge, 1994.

Cocks, Catherine. *Doing the Town: The Rise of Urban Tourism in the United States: 1850–1915.* Berkeley: University of California Press, 2001.

Cohen, Adam. "100 Years Later, the Food Industry Is Still 'The Jungle.'" *New York Times*, January 2, 2007.

Cohen, Lizabeth. *Making a New Deal: Industrial Workers in Chicago, 1919–1939.* 2nd ed. Cambridge: Cambridge University Press, 2008.

"Commemorating the Catastrophe." Northwestern University and the Chicago Historical Society. "The Great Chicago Fire and the Web of Memory," 2011. http://www.greatchicagofire.org/commemorating-catastrophe.

Cook, James W. "Seeing the Visual in U.S. History." *Journal of American History* 95 (September 2008): 432–41.

Corbin, Alain. *The Foul and the Fragrant: Odor and the French Social Imagination.* Translated by Miriam L. Kochan, Roy Porter, and Christopher Prendergast. Cambridge, MA: Harvard University Press, 1986.

Cott, Nancy F. *The Bonds of Womanhood: "Women's Sphere" in New England, 1780–1835.* 2nd ed. New Haven, CT: Yale University Press, 1997.

Cowan, Alexander, and Jill Steward, eds. *The City and the Senses: Urban Culture since 1500.* Aldershot, England: Ashgate, 2007.

Cronon, William. *Nature's Metropolis: Chicago and the Great West.* New York: W. W. Norton, 1991.

Davis, Linda H. *Badge of Courage: The Life of Stephen Crane.* Boston: Houghton Mifflin, 1998.

Diaconu, Mădălina, Eva Heuberger, Ruth Mateus-Berr, and Marcel Vosicky. *Senses and the City: An Interdisciplinary Approach to Urban Sensescapes.* Berlin: Lit Verlag, 2011.

Dickstein, Morris. Introduction to *The Jungle,* by Upton Sinclair. New York: Bantam Books, 1981.

Duis, Perry R. *Challenging Chicago: Coping with Everyday Life, 1837–1920.* Urbana: University of Illinois Press, 1998.

———. *The Saloon: Public Drinking in Chicago and Boston, 1880–1920.* Urbana: University of Illinois Press, 1983.

Duis, Perry R., and Glen H. Holt. "Bright Lights, Hard Times of White City II." *Chicago Magazine,* August 1978, 176–79.

Edensor, Tim. "Sensing the Ruin." *Senses and Society* 2 (July 2007): 217–32.

Edwards, Elizabeth, and Kaushik Bhaumik, eds. *Visual Sense: A Cultural Reader.* Oxford: Berg, 2008.

Ferguson, Priscilla Parkhurst. "The Senses of Taste." *American Historical Review* 116 (April 2011): 371–84.

Foner, Philip S. *The Great Labor Uprising of 1877.* New York: Monad Press, 1977.

Frank, Gillian. "Discophobia: Antigay Prejudice and the 1979 Backlash against Disco." *Journal of the History of Sexuality* 16 (May 2007): 276–306.

Friedrich, Jörg. *The Fire: The Bombing of Germany, 1940–1945.* Translated by Allison Brown. New York: Columbia University Press, 2006.

Gee, Derek, and Ralph Lopez. *Laugh Your Troubles Away: The Complete History of Riverview Park.* Livonia, MI: Sharpshooters Productions, 2000.

Geismar, Maxwell. *Rebels and Ancestors: The American Novel, 1890–1915.* Boston: Houghton Mifflin, 1953.

Gilbert, James. *Perfect Cities: Chicago's Utopia's of 1893.* Chicago: University of Chicago Press, 1991.

Goldsmith, Mike. *Discord: The Story of Noise.* Oxford: Oxford University Press, 2012.

Gottesman, Ronald. Introduction to the Penguin Classics Deluxe edition of *The Jungle,* by Upton Sinclair. New York: Penguin Books, 2006.

"Great Books: The Jungle." DVD. Discovery Channel. Silver Spring, MD: Discovery Communications, 2005.

Grossman, James R. *Land of Hope: Chicago, Black Southerners, and the Great Migration.* Chicago: University of Chicago Press, 1989.

Gugliotta, Angela. "Class, Gender, and Coal Smoke: Gender Ideology and Environmental Injustice in Pittsburgh, 1868–1914." *Environmental History* 5 (April 2000): 165–93.

Hale, Grace Elizabeth. *Making Whiteness: The Culture of Segregation in the South, 1890–1940.* New York: Vintage Books, 1999.

Halpern, Rick. *Down on the Killing Floor: Black and White Workers in Chicago's Packinghouses, 1904–54.* Urbana: University of Illinois Press, 1997.

Halttunen, Karen. *Confidence Man and Painted Women: A Study of Middle-Class Culture in America, 1830–1870.* New Haven, CT: Yale University Press, 1982.

Harris, Leon. *Upton Sinclair: American Rebel.* New York: Crowell, 1975.

Harris, Neil. *Humbug: The Art of P. T. Barnum.* Chicago: University of Chicago Press, 1973.

Haugh, Dolores. *Riverview Amusement Park*. Charleston, SC: Arcadia, 2004.

Heap, Chad. *Slumming: Sexual and Racial Encounters in American Nightlife, 1885–1940*. Chicago: University of Chicago Press, 2009.

Hepp, John Henry, IV. *The Middle-Class City: Transforming Space and Time in Philadelphia, 1876–1926*. Philadelphia: University of Pennsylvania Press, 2003.

Herz, Rachel. *The Scent of Desire: Discovering Our Enigmatic Sense of Smell*. New York: William Morrow, 2007.

———. *That's Disgusting: Unraveling the Mysteries of Repulsion*. New York: W. W. Norton and Company, 2012.

Hirsch, Susan Eleanor. *After the Strike: A Century of Labor Struggle at Pullman*. Urbana: University of Illinois Press, 2003.

Hoffer, Peter Charles. *Sensory Worlds in Early America*. Baltimore: Johns Hopkins University Press, 2003.

Horowitz, Helen Lefkowitz. *Culture and the City: Cultural Philanthropy in Chicago from the 1880s to 1917*. Chicago: University of Chicago, 1976.

Horowitz, Roger. *"Negro and White, Unite and Fight!": A Social History of Industrial Unionism in Meatpacking, 1930–90*. Urbana: University of Illinois Press, 1997.

Howe, Daniel Walker. *What Hath God Wrought: The Transformation of America, 1815–1848*. Oxford: Oxford University Press, 2009.

Howes, David. "Can These Dry Bones Live? An Anthropological Approach to the History of the Senses." *Journal of American History* 95 (September 2008): 442–51.

———, ed. *Empire of the Senses: The Sensual Culture Reader*. Oxford: Berg, 2005.

———. "The Material Body of the Commodity." In *Sensual Relations: Engaging the Senses in Culture and Social Theory*, edited by David Howes, 204–48. Ann Arbor: University of Michigan Press, 2003.

———, ed. *The Varieties of Sensory Experience: A Sourcebook in the Anthropology of the Senses*. Toronto: University of Toronto Press, 1991.

Hoy, Suellen. *Chasing Dirt: The American Pursuit of Cleanliness*. Oxford: Oxford University Press, 1995.

Hurley, Andrew. "Busby's Stink Boat and the Regulation of the Nuisance Trades, 1865–1918." In *Common Fields: An Environmental History of St. Louis*, edited by Andrew Hurley, 145–62. St. Louis: Missouri Historical Society Press, 1997.

Inglis, David. "Sewers and Sensibilities: The Bourgeois Faecal Experience in the Nineteenth-Century City." In *The City and the Senses: Urban Culture since 1500*, edited by Alexander Cowan and Jill Steward, 105–30. Aldershot, England: Ashgate, 2007.

Jablonsky, Thomas J. *Pride in the Jungle: Community and Everyday Life in Back of the Yards*. Baltimore: Johns Hopkins University Press, 1993.

Jacobson, Matthew Frye. *Barbarian Virtues: The United States Encounters Foreign People at Home and Abroad, 1876–1917*. New York: Hill and Wang, 2001.

Jackson, Jeffrey H. "Envisioning Disaster in the 1910 Paris Flood." *Journal of Urban History* 37 (March 2011): 176–207.

Jay, Martin. *Downcast Eyes: The Denigration of Vision in Twentieth-Century French Thought*. Berkeley: University of California Press, 1993.

Jentz, John B., and Richard Schneirov. *Chicago in the Age of Capital: Class, Politics, and Democracy during the Civil War and Reconstruction.* Urbana: University of Illinois Press, 2012.

Jones, Jill. *Empires of Light: Edison, Tesla, Westinghouse, and the Race to Electrify the World.* New York: Random House, 2003.

Junger, Richard. *Becoming the Second City: Chicago's Mass Media, 1833–1898.* Urbana: University of Illinois Press, 2010.

Kasson, John F. *Amusing the Million: Coney Island at the Turn of the Century.* New York: Hill and Wang, 1978.

———. *Rudeness and Civility: Manners in Nineteenth-Century America.* New York: Hill and Wang, 1990.

Kazin, Alfred. *On Native Grounds: An Interpretation of Modern American Prose Literature.* New York: Doubleday, 1956.

Kramer, Paul A. "Race Making and Colonial Violence in the U.S. Empire: The Philippine-American War as Race War." *Diplomatic History* 30 (April 2006): 169–210.

Leach, Eugene E. "Chaining the Tiger: The Mob Stigma and the Working Class, 1863–1894." *Labor History* 35 (Spring 1994): 187–215.

Leach, William. *Land of Desire: Merchants, Power, and the Rise of a New American Culture.* New York: Vintage Books, 1993.

Lears, Jackson. "From Salvation to Self-Realization: Advertising and the Therapeutic Roots of the Consumer Culture, 1880–1930." In *The Culture of Consumption: Critical Essays in American History, 1880–1980,* edited by Richard Wightman Fox and T. J. Jackson Lears, 1–38. New York: Pantheon Books, 1983.

———. *No Place of Grace: Antimodernism and the Transformation of American Culture, 1880–1920.* New York: Pantheon Books, 1981.

———. *Rebirth of a Nation: The Making of Modern America, 1877–1920.* New York: HarperCollins, 2009.

Lehan, Richard. *Realism and Naturalism: The Novel in an Age of Transition.* Madison: University of Wisconsin Press, 2005.

Leyendecker, Liston Edgington. *Palace Car Prince: A Biography of George Mortimer Pullman.* Boulder: University Press of Colorado, 1992.

Lindsey, Almont. *The Pullman Strike: The Story of a Unique Experiment and of a Great Labor Upheaval.* Chicago: University of Chicago Press, 1942.

Macaulay, Rose. *Pleasure of Ruins.* New York: Thames and Hudson, 1953.

Mack, Adam. "The Senses in the Marketplace: Commercial Aesthetics for a Suburban Age." In *A Cultural History of the Senses in the Modern Age,* edited by David Howes. Oxford: Berg, forthcoming.

Martinek, Jason D. *Socialism and Print Culture in America, 1897–1920.* London: Pickering and Chatto, 2012.

Massard-Guilbaud, Geneviève, Harold L. Platt, and Dieter Schott, eds. *Cities and Catastrophes: Coping with Emergency in European History.* Frankfurt, Germany: Peter Lang, 2002.

Mattson, Kevin. *Upton Sinclair and the Other American Century*. Hoboken, NJ: John Wiley and Sons, 2006.

Mayer, Harold M., and Richard C. Wade. *Chicago: Growth of a Metropolis*. Chicago: University of Chicago Press, 1969.

McLuhan, Marshall. *The Gutenberg Galaxy: The Making of Typographic Man*. Toronto: University of Toronto Press, 1962.

McShane, Clay, and Joel A. Tarr. *The Horse in the City: Living Machines in the Nineteenth Century*. Baltimore: Johns Hopkins University Press, 2007.

Melosi, Martin V. *The Sanitary City: Urban Infrastructure in America from Colonial Times to the Present*. Baltimore: Johns Hopkins University Press, 2000.

Miller, Donald L. *City of the Century: The Epic of Chicago and the Making of America*. New York: Simon and Schuster, 1996.

Miller, Ross. *The Great Chicago Fire*. Illinois Paperback ed. Urbana: University of Illinois Press, 2000.

Musham, H. A. "The Great Chicago Fire, October 8–10, 1971." In *Papers in Illinois History and Transactions for the Year 1940*. Springfield: Illinois State Historical Society, 1941.

Nasaw, David. "Cities of Light, Landscapes of Pleasure." In *Landscape of Modernity: New York City, 1900–1940*, edited by David Ward and Olivier Zunz, 273–86. Baltimore: Johns Hopkins University Press, 1992.

Noon, Mark. "'It ain't your color, it's your scabbing': Literary Depictions of African American Strikebreakers." *African American Review* 38 (Autumn 2004): 429–39.

Olsson, Karen. "Welcome to the Jungle: Does Upton Sinclair's Famous Novel Hold Up?" *Slate*. July 10, 2006. http://www.slate.com/articles/arts/books/2006/07/welcome_to_the_jungle.html.

Øverland, Orm. "*The Jungle*: From Lithuanian Peasant to American Socialist." *American Literary Realism* 37 (Fall 2004): 1–23.

Pacyga, Dominic A. *Chicago: A Biography*. Chicago: University of Chicago Press, 2009.

———. *Polish Immigrants and Industrial Chicago: Workers on the South Side, 1880–1922*. Chicago: University of Chicago Press, 1991.

Papke, David Ray. *The Pullman Case: The Clash of Labor and Capital in Industrial America*. Lawrence: University Press of Kansas, 1999.

Payer, Peter. "The Age of Noise: Early Reactions in Vienna, 1870–1914." *Journal of Urban History* 33 (July 2007): 773–93.

Phelps, Christopher. Introduction to Upton Sinclair, *The Jungle*, edited by Christopher Phelps, 1–39. Boston: Bedford/St. Martin, 2005.

———. "The Strike Imagined: The Atlantic and Interpretive Voyages of Robert Koehler's Painting *The Strike*." *Journal of American History* 98 (December 2011): 670–97.

Pittenger, Mark. "A World of Difference: Constructing the 'Underclass' in Progressive America." *American Quarterly* 49 (March 1997): 26–65.

Platt, Harold L. *Shock Cities: The Environmental Transformation and Reform of Manchester and Chicago.* Chicago: University of Chicago Press, 2005.

Prochnik, George. "I'm Thinking. Please. Be Quiet." *New York Times.* August 24, 2013. http://www.nytimes.com/2013/08/25/opinion/sunday/im-thinking -please-be-quiet.html.

———. *In Pursuit of Silence: Listening for Meaning in a World of Noise.* New York: Doubleday, 2010.

Radovac, Lilian. "The 'War on Noise': Sound and Space in La Guardia's New York." *American Quarterly* 63 (September 2011): 733–60.

Rannalletta, Kathy. "Illinois Commentary: 'The Great Wave of Fire' at Chicago: The Reminiscences of Martin Stamm." *Journal of the Illinois State Historical Society* 70 (June 1977): 242–329.

Rath, Richard Cullen. *How Early America Sounded.* Ithaca, NY: Cornell University Press, 2003.

Reiff, Janice L. "A Modern Lear and His Daughters: Gender in the Model Town of Pullman." In *The Pullman Strike and the Crisis of the 1890s: Essays on Labor and Politics,* edited by Richard Schneirov et al., 65–86. Urbana: University of Illinois Press, 1999.

Rideout, Walter. *The Radical Novel in the United States: 1900–1954.* New York: Hill and Wang, 1966.

Roeder, George H., Jr. "Coming to Our Senses." *Journal of American History* 81 (December 1994): 1112–22.

Rondinone, Troy. "'History Repeats Itself': The Civil War and the Meaning of Labor Conflict in the Late Nineteenth Century." *American Quarterly* 59 (June 2007): 397–419.

Rosen, Christine Meisner. "Businessmen against Pollution in Late Nineteenth-Century Chicago." *Business History Review* 69 (August 1995): 351–97.

———. "Differing Perceptions of the Value of Pollution Abatement across Time and Place: Balancing Doctrine in Pollution Nuisance Law, 1840–1906." *Law and History Review* 11 (Summer 1993): 303–81.

———. "Knowing Industrial Pollution: Nuisance Law and the Power of Tradition in a Time of Rapid Economic Change, 1840–1864." *Environmental History* 8 (October 2003): 565–97.

———. *The Limits of Power: Great Fires and the Process of City Growth in America.* Cambridge: Cambridge University Press, 1986.

———. "Noisome, Noxious, and Offensive Vapors, Fumes, and Stenches in American Towns and Cities, 1840–1865." *Historical Geography* 25 (1997): 49–82.

———. "The Role of Pollution Regulation and Litigation in the Development of the U.S. Meatpacking Industry." *Enterprise & Society* 8 (June 2007): 297–347.

Rosenberg, Charles E. *The Cholera Years: The United States in 1832, 1849, and 1866.* 1962. Reprint, Chicago: University of Chicago Press, 1987.

Rosenfeld, Sophia. "On Being Heard: A Case for Paying Attention to the Historical Ear. *American Historical Review* 116 (April 2011): 316–34.

Rosenzweig, Roy. *Eight Hours for What We Will: Workers and Leisure in an Industrial City.* Cambridge: Cambridge University Press, 1983.

Roth, Michael S., Claire L. Lyons, and Charles Merewether. *Irresistible Decay: Ruins Reclaimed.* Los Angeles: Getty Research Institute for the History of Art and the Humanities, 1997.

Rozario, Kevin. "Making Progress: Disaster Narratives and the Art of Optimism in Modern America." In *The Resilient City: How Modern Cities Recover from Disaster,* edited by Lawrence J. Vale and Thomas J. Campanella, 27–54. Oxford: Oxford University Press, 2005.

Rydell, Robert W. *All the World's a Fair: Visions of American Empire at American International Expositions, 1876–1916.* Chicago: University of Chicago Press, 1985.

———. *Buffalo Bill in Bologna: The Americanization of the World, 1869–1922.* Chicago: University of Chicago Press, 2005.

Sally, Lynn. "Fantasy Land and Kinesthetic Thrills: Sensorial Consumption, the Shock of Modernity, and Spectacle as Total-Body Experience at Coney Island." *Senses and Society* 1 (November 2006): 293–309.

Sawislak, Karen. *Smoldering City: Chicagoans and the Great Fire, 1871–1874.* Chicago: University of Chicago Press, 1995.

Schivelbusch, Wolfgang. *The Railway Journey: The Industrialization of Time and Space in the 19th Century.* Berkeley: University of California Press, 1986.

Schlosser, Eric. *Fast Food Nation: The Dark Side of the American Meal.* New York: Houghton Mifflin, 2001.

———. Foreword to *The Jungle* by Upton Sinclair, Penguin Classics Deluxe edition. New York: Penguin Books, 2006.

Schmidt, Leigh Eric. *Hearing Things: Religion, Illusion, and the American Enlightenment.* Cambridge: Harvard University Press, 2000.

Schneirov, Richard. "Chicago's Great Upheaval of 1877." *Chicago History* 9 (March 1980): 2–17.

———. *Labor and Urban Politics: Class Conflict and the Origins of Modern Liberalism in Chicago, 1864–97.* Urbana: University of Illinois Press, 1998.

Schneirov, Richard, Shelton Stromquist, and Nick Salvatore, eds. *The Pullman Strike and the Crisis of the 1890s: Essays on Labor and Politics.* Urbana: University of Illinois Press, 1999.

Schuster, David G. *Neurasthenic Nation: America's Search for Health, Happiness, and Comfort, 1869–1920.* New Brunswick, NJ: Rutgers University Press, 2011.

Sennett, Richard. *Families against the City: Middle-Class Homes of Industrial Chicago.* Cambridge: Harvard University Press, 1984.

———. *Flesh and Stone: The Body and the City in Western Civilization.* New York: W. W. Norton, 1994.

"Sixteen's Culinary Exploration of Chicago." Trump Hotel Collection. http://www.trumphotelcollection.com/press/sixteens-culinary-exploration-of-chicago.

Slayton, Robert. *Back of the Yards: The Making of Local Democracy.* Chicago: University of Chicago Press, 1986.

Smith, Carl S. *Chicago and the American Literary Imagination, 1880–1920.* Chicago: University of Chicago Press, 1984.

———. *Urban Disorder and the Shape of Belief: The Great Chicago Fire, the Haymarket Bomb, and the Model Town of Pullman.* Chicago: University of Chicago Press, 1995.

Smith, Mark M. *Camille, 1969: Histories of a Hurricane.* Athens: University of Georgia Press, 2011.

———. *How Race Is Made: Slavery, Segregation, and the Senses.* Chapel Hill: University of North Carolina Press, 2006.

———. *Listening to Nineteenth-Century America.* Chapel Hill: University of North Carolina Press, 2001.

———. "Producing Sense, Consuming Sense, Making Sense: Perils and Prospects for Sensory History." *Journal of Social History* 40 (Summer 2007): 841–58.

———. *Sensing the Past: Seeing, Hearing, Smelling, Tasting, and Touching in History.* Berkeley: University of California Press, 2007.

Solnit, Rebecca. "The Ruins of Memory." In *After the Ruins, 1906 and 2006: Rephotographing the San Francisco Earthquake and Fire,* edited by Mark Klett, 18–32. Berkeley: University of California Press, 2006.

Solzman, David M. *The Chicago River: An Illustrated Guide to the River and Its Waterways.* 2nd ed. Chicago: University of Chicago Press, 2006.

Spears, Timothy B. *Chicago Dreaming: Midwesterners and the City, 1871–1919.* Chicago: University of Chicago Press, 2005.

Spodek, Howard. *Ahmedabad: Shock City of Twentieth-Century India.* Bloomington: Indiana University Press, 2011.

Stowell, David O., ed. *The Great Strikes of 1877.* Urbana: University of Illinois Press, 2008.

———. *Streets, Railroads, and the Great Strike of 1877.* Chicago: University of Chicago Press, 1999.

Stradling, David. "Dirty Work and Clean Air: Locomotive Firemen, Environmental Activists, and Stories of Conflict." *Journal of Urban History* 28 (November 2001): 35–54.

Suh, Suk Bong. "Lithuanian Wedding Traditions in Upton Sinclair's *The Jungle.*" *Lituanus* (Spring 1987): 5–17.

Swartz, David. *Culture and Power: The Sociology of Pierre Bourdieu.* Chicago: University of Chicago Press, 1997.

Synnott, Anthony. "Puzzling Over the Senses: From Plato to Marx." In *The Varieties of Sensory Experience: A Sourcebook in the Anthropology of the Senses,* edited by David Howes, 61–76. Toronto: University of Toronto Press, 1991.

Thompson, Emily. *The Soundscape of Modernity: Architectural Acoustics and the Culture of Listening in America.* Cambridge: MIT Press, 2002.

Tomes, Nancy. *The Gospel of Germs: Men, Women, and the Microbe in American Life.* Cambridge, MA: Harvard University Press, 1998.

Trachtenberg, Alan. *The Incorporation of America: Culture and Society in the Gilded Age.* 25th Anniversary ed. New York: Hill and Wang, 2007.

Tuttle, William M. Jr. *Race Riot: Chicago in the Red Summer of 1919.* 1970. Reprint, Urbana: University of Illinois Press, 1996.

Upton, Dell. *Another City: Urban Life and Urban Spaces in the New American Republic.* New Haven: Yale University Press, 2008.

Urry, John. "City Life and the Senses." In *The New Blackwell Companion to the City,* edited by Gary Bridge and Sophie Watson, 347–56. Oxford: Wiley-Blackwell, 2011.

Vaillant, Derek. "Peddling Noise: Contesting the Civic Soundscape of Chicago, 1890–1913." *Journal of the Illinois State Historical Society* 96 (Autumn 2003): 257–87.

Vale, Lawrence J., and Thomas J. Campanella, eds. *The Resilient City: How Modern Cities Recover from Disasters.* New York: Oxford University Press, 2005.

Veblen, Thorstein. *The Theory of the Leisure Class.* 1899. Reprint, New York: Penguin Books, 1994.

Vinikas, Vincent. *Soft Soap, Hard Sell: American Hygiene in an Age of Advertisement.* Ames: Iowa State University Press, 1992.

Wade, Louise Carroll. *Chicago's Pride: The Stockyards, Packingtown, and Environs in the Nineteenth Century.* Urbana: University of Illinois Press, 1987.

———. "The Problem with Classroom Use of *The Jungle.*" *American Studies* 32 (Summer 1991): 79–101.

Wells, Cheryl A. *Civil War Time: Temporality and Identity in America, 1861–1865.* Athens: University of Georgia Press, 2005.

Wiebe, Robert H. *The Search for Order, 1877–1920.* New York: Hill and Wang, 1967.

Wlodarczyk, Chuck. *Riverview: Gone but Not Forgotten.* Chicago: Riverview Publications, 1977.

Woody, Robert H. "A Description of the Chicago Fire of 1871." *Mississippi Valley Historical Review* 33 (March 1947): 607–16.

Young, James Harvey. "The Pig That Fell into the Privy: Upton Sinclair's 'The Jungle' and the Meat Inspection Amendments of 1906." *Bulletin of the History of Medicine* 59 (Winter 1985): 467–80.

Zardini, Mirko, ed. *Sense of the City: An Alternative Approach to Urbanism.* Montréal: Canadian Centre for Architecture and Lars Müller Publishers, 2005.

Zunz, Olivier. *Making America Corporate, 1870–1920.* Chicago: University of Chicago Press, 1990.

INDEX

15–20, 47, 120n36; as shock city, 8–9; street vendors of, 7; Vice Commission, 108. *See also* commerce and industry
Chicago and the Great Conflagration, 38
"Chicago by Moonlight," 48–49
Chicago City Hydraulic Company, 20
Chicago Fire of 1871, 33–36, 36–46, 122n1; city alarm system and, 38–39; compared to the Civil War, 40–41; damage due to, 46–50, 124n43; people displaced by, 41–45; sensory overload and, 37–38; social classes and, 41–44; White City exhibit, 105–6
Chicago Relief and Aid Society, 38, 41, 125n62
Chicago River, the, 3, 11–15; blood color of, 27–28; dead animals dumped in, 15–16; drinking water pollution and, 20–25, 26; efforts to clean up, 16, 24–25, 30–31; infection disease spread and, 25–26; meat packing industry and, 17, 19, 27–28; public concern about, 27–30; used as sewer, 15–20
Chicago Times, 22
cholera, 15, 16
Cincinnati, Ohio, 17, 23
civic health, 8
Civil War, the: Chicago Fire compared to, 40–41; railroad strike of 1877 compared to, 57–58
Classen, Constance, 104
Cleveland, Grover, 69
Cleveland, H. W. S., 47
Colbert, Elias, 38
Comiskey, Charles, 98
Comiskey Park, 98–99
commerce and industry: Great Fire effects on, 48–50; Marx on, 72; meatpacking, 17, 19, 27–28, 80–82,

87–89, 135n85; public concern over odors due to, 27–30; sounds of, 53. *See also Jungle, The*
communism, 51, 76
Communist Manifesto, The, 76, 77
Coney Island, 97–98, 103–4, 112
Cook, James W., 114n8
Corbin, Alain, 4, 14
Crane, Stephen, 82
Croffut, W. A., 49
Cronon, William, 3
Currier and Ives, 40

Debs, Eugene V., 78, 79, 92
Defender, 107
Dexter, Wirt, 30
distilleries, 18
Dreiser, Theodore, 4
drinking water, 20–25, 26, 120n36
Duis, Perry, 108

Economic and Philosophical Manuscripts of 1844, 78
Ellis, Thomas Harding, 40–41
Ely, Richard T., 64–66
"Experiment in Misery, An," 82

Fales, Mary, 46
"Farmers of America, Unite!" 78–79
Farwell, Arthur, 108–9
Faulk, Bertha, 109–10
fish in city water, 21–22
Fletcher, Horace, 75, 93
Ford, Henry, 80
Foster, Thomas D., 46
Friedrich, Jörg, 35
Fuller, Meta, 74–75

Gallagher, William, 40, 45–46
Gilbert, James, 60
Great Depression, 7, 110
Great Fire. *See* Chicago Fire of 1871

ADAM MACK is assistant professor of History
in the Department of Liberal Arts at the
School of the Art Institute of Chicago.

The University of Illinois Press
is a founding member of the
Association of American University Presses.

_____

Composed in 10/13 ITC New Baskerville
with Trade Gothic Condensed display
by Jim Proefrock
at the University of Illinois Press
Manufactured by Sheridan Books, Inc.

University of Illinois Press
1325 South Oak Street
Champaign, IL 618200-6903
www.press.uillinois.edu